Russia and the Austrian State Treaty

Russia and the Austrian State Treaty

A Case Study of Soviet Policy in Europe

by Sven Allard

The Pennsylvania State University Press
University Park and London

Standard Book Number 271–00083–X
Library of Congress Catalogue Card 68–8176
Copyright © 1970 by Sven Allard
Printed in the United States of America

Foreword

A few years ago, a former American Ambassador to Austria asked me if I had read Sven Allard's book *Diplomat in Wien* (the German translation of the original Swedish edition). Since I had not, he arranged for a long-distance meeting with the author, who had been Sweden's Ambassador to Austria during the crucial period in the fifties when the East-West confrontation on the Austrian State Treaty was uppermost in the minds of the diplomatic corps in Vienna. Subsequently, an interesting and pleasant correspondence developed. Ambassador Allard sent me a copy of his book, which was not available in the United States. I read it with fascination and admiration and found it to be the work of a man who combines the talents of a highly skilled diplomat with the knowledge and analytical powers of a consummate scholar. It occurred to me immediately that the book should be published in as many languages as possible, especially in English.

In 1966, while vacationing in Scandinavia, I had the pleasure of meeting Ambassador Allard and spending some hours with him and Mrs. Allard at their beautiful estate in southern Sweden. We discussed the problem of a translation, and upon my return to the United States I undertook to interest a publisher in the book.

Allard's work fulfills a double function: it reveals the behind-the-scenes maneuvering that eventually led to Austria's freedom, and it does so within the frame of reference of the Soviet political system. It is one of the few books I have read in which a writer-diplomat never forgets that Soviet foreign policy differs from that of a traditional state, in that it is not only a national but also a Communist foreign policy.

Prior to his Vienna assignment, Ambassador Allard was

accredited for five years to four different Communist countries: from the beginning of 1949 until the middle of 1951 to Hungary, Rumania, and Bulgaria; from then to March 1954 to Hungary and Czechoslovakia. During these years he learned the hard way how Communist parties and governments work and came to recognize the essential premises of Soviet foreign policy and its dualistic character. Allard recalls that the *Great Soviet Encyclopedia* emphasizes the fundamental differences between a "socialist" foreign policy and that vis-à-vis non-Communist countries; the principles of international relations which are implemented by the Party in matters of foreign policy are an organic part of the Party programs, strategy, and tactics. Communist tactics do not necessarily reject compromise but conceive it as a means to further the Kremlin's goals in Europe and elsewhere in the world. While it is true that, due to the advent of polycentric communism and the Sino-Soviet conflict, relations between the Moscow center and the former satellites have changed to some extent—an extent which should not be exaggerated—Allard's analysis of Soviet foreign policy is basically as valid today as it was when he wrote the book. As a result, his examination of the crucial months of negotiations preceding the Austrian State Treaty, which finally led to that country's independence and status as a neutral power, is one of the clearest exposés of Soviet political behavior in existence. I fully agree with the author when he concludes that few negotiations have been so valuable for throwing light on Soviet foreign policy, contributing as they do to understanding the strategic and tactical goals of world communism, or explaining the "balancing of national and revolutionary interests."

No less interesting is Allard's story of the tortuous negotiations that led toward the treaty. As a representative of a neutral country he had friendly connections with diplomats from the East and West and was particularly close to Bruno Kreisky, then the State Secretary of the Austrian Foreign Ministry. The cool detachment which distinguishes the ambassador's narrative is rare in contemporary political literature. If the author has any bias, it is sympathy for the aspirations of the Austrian people to be free and independent. And yet, even on this issue, his analysis of how this goal was finally achieved remains objective. It is an intriguing "inside" story by a man who watched developments behind the scenes —developments in which he was personally involved because of his contacts with leading officials of the Austrian Government and because of his many discussions with Soviet and Western representatives. In shedding new light on East-West diplomatic maneuvering, he provides extremely useful material for students of modern history.

It is my hope that this sophisticated case study of Soviet political behavior will find the acclaim it deserves. Its clear organization and lucid style make it easy reading for the interested layman and a pleasure for students of international affairs. Allard is not only a diplomat but also a warm-hearted humanitarian. I can think of only one other man whose historical works and memoirs display an equal amount of political erudition and literary talent—George Kennan. But I prefer Allard's interpretation.

KURT L. LONDON

Institute for Sino-Soviet Studies
The George Washington University

Contents

Vienna, July 29, 1964

Dear Friend,

First of all I want to thank you for giving me the opportunity to read the manuscript of your book.

Not only did it recall so many things that we two experienced together, but also the conclusions to which you come are extremely interesting. You will understand that I cannot agree with you in all your opinions and that I see and saw many things differently, but that is part of the nature of our profession. From what you have written, it is apparent how frequently we met and took counsel together during your long stay in Vienna. I want to assure you that I have no objection to your presenting the conversations between us with such openness. As you know, I have always been an opponent of so-called secret diplomacy and consider it important that people in a democracy should be able to picture foreign relations for themselves. And they can only do that if the facts are not hidden from them. Still less can I object that those facts which have come to your knowledge have been revealed in your memoirs.

I would also like to take the opportunity to thank you in this way for what you accomplished for the relations between our two countries during your activity in Austria, especially for your valuable role as mediator in difficult situations.

Assuring you of my sincere friendship, I remain

Your

BRUNO KREISKY

1

Departure From Prague . . .

At the end of 1953 I received the news of my approaching transfer to Vienna from the position of minister in Prague and Budapest. At that time I had been behind the Iron Curtain for five years without interruption. During that time I was accredited in four of the so-called people's democracies. To be sure, I had interesting tasks and many exciting experiences and could also acquire valuable experience, but, nevertheless, these years had been very exacting and tiring. One who has not experienced it himself can scarcely imagine the constant psychological pressure involved in a long stay behind the Iron Curtain at the beginning of the fifties. So I received the news of my approaching transfer not only with pleasure but with great relief.

Even more, I felt very gratified because my further diplomatic activity was to be moved to Austria. True, I had never before held a diplomatic post in Austria, but for a long time I had had the opportunity to observe Austrian affairs and to make myself familiar with them. Even before the Second World War and in the first years after its outbreak, which I had spent in the Balkans, I had visited Austria regularly once or twice a year. With constant interest I followed the political development of this country, both before it had lost its independence in 1938 and when it had won it back again in 1945, after the collapse of the Third Reich. Still, my interest in Austria cannot be explained merely by the political significance which this country has because of its geographical situation; this interest is based also on the sympathy which I felt —and continue to feel—for the people, who are just as happy, easygoing, and charming, as they are industrious and clever.

Although almost ten years had passed since the end of the Second World War, the four victorious great powers still occupied Austria. They had, it is true, begun negotiations among themselves concerning the restoration of full independence to the country, according to the obligations which they had assumed by the so-called Moscow Declaration of 1943, but these negotiations had been as good as at a complete standstill for several years. Meanwhile, at the end of 1953 the Western powers and the Soviet Union had agreed to take up the Austrian question again at a conference which was to take place in the second half of January 1954 in Berlin.

Since Stalin had died in March 1953 and the new men in the Kremlin had introduced a "new policy," as they wished people to believe, the Austrians now waited full of suspense for fulfillment of the hope that the change of regime in Moscow had awakened. In leading political circles the Berlin Conference was naturally considered a test of the sincerity of the aims which the new men in the Kremlin had embraced, according to their own declarations. Especially in Vienna, everyone asked himself, not without apprehension, whether this conference would end successfully or without result, just as other negotiations over the Austrian question had ended. This was the situation at the time I was to take over my new post.

Although my transfer had already been agreed upon at the end of 1953, it was postponed from month to month for different reasons which I will not deal with here. Meanwhile, the Berlin Conference ended with the same negative outcome as had earlier discussions of the great powers concerning the question of the restoration of Austrian independence. The hopes widely cherished in Austria, that finally, after a long and oppressive occupation, the hour of freedom would strike, had been dashed again.

The immediate cause of the wishful thinking, which had spread throughout Austria and other countries, had been the change of regime in Moscow. It had, however, brought about no fundamental change in the attitude of the Soviet Union toward important foreign-policy questions. The occupation of Austria was apparently going to last indefinitely. From one day to the next, the relative optimism of the people changed suddenly to the most dismal pessimism. Not the smallest ray of sunshine was to be seen on the horizon, and on several short visits to Vienna before my move I could perceive the general depression.

At the beginning of March 1954 I was supposed to take my leave, first from Prague and then from Budapest. The transfer of a Western diplomat from a Communist country is not at all as easy as one might imagine. It requires exhaustive preparations of various kinds. Especially tedious are the transactions with the authorities about minor questions which would never come up at all in "capitalist" countries; and if they did, they would speedily be taken care of without unnecessary complications. It is probably generally known that mistrust of the "capitalist" world is very pronounced in Communist states. It is part of the system, the result of conscious and intensive propaganda through the press, radio, schools, study circles, and so forth. This mistrust is aimed, above all, at Western diplomats whose freedom of movement and activity is extremely limited by countless rigid regulations. Ambitious, bureaucratic officials use these regulations in order to demonstrate their loyalty to the regime. They indulge in senseless, even childlish, vexations which embitter still more the existence, already dismal in itself, of Western diplomats in these countries. During the period which my experience spans, such harassment was aimed primarily at the Americans, English, and French. But diplomats of "neutral" countries could also get into difficulties.

At the time of my departure from Prague, one of the many regulations of this type in principle prohibited foreign diplomats from taking their private possessions with them. Actually, permission was granted as a rule; still, it had to be given for each object. As a result, before his departure, the authorities required of each diplomat, regardless of his rank, a complete list of his personal possessions, and sometimes the assurance, with receipts, that none of them had been bought in Czechoslovakia. Not only furniture—especially antiques—silver, and household items were to be precisely entered on these lists, but also coats, suits, shoes, underwear, and so forth. And this could be required although the shoes and clothes, for example, made in the country were of such poor quality and so highly priced that no one would even think of purchasing them in Czechoslovakia if he had the opportunity to shop in Western Europe. In some cases, which can be considered exceptions it is true, the authorities had even required—as my colleagues liked to tell—special lists of the books which were included with the things being moved; not only the number of volumes was to be given, but also the names of the authors and the complete titles. Occasionally the authorities had tried to confiscate or prevent the export of literary or scholarly works which were considered dangerous from the viewpoint of the regime. Since my own library contained a considerable collection of this type of literature, I looked forward with some misgivings to the examination of many works which, in my opinion, were purely of a scholarly nature but which would be considered by the Communist regime as forbidden literature. An inhabitant of the country would have expected a long term in prison if they had been found in his possession.

My apprehension was soon dispelled, however, when, on a visit to Sweden, I advised Foreign Minister Undén about the unusual customs prevailing in Prague. He was upset and shocked to learn that the authorities in the "people's democracies" considered themselves justified in censoring the libraries of foreign diplomats, as the demand for the presentation of lists of books unmistakably showed. He allowed me to make several trips to Vienna before my move so that I might personally carry out those works which would be likely to cause special offense on closer examination. According to an old custom, which the Communist states respect perhaps even more than the West, the hand luggage of an envoy is never to be examined or checked. Thus, I could await the time of my departure from Prague with greater complacency.

It came nearer and nearer. The farewell visits to members of the government, to higher officials in the foreign ministry, and to colleagues in the diplomatic corps were essentially completed. Then an incident occurred which may seem a tri-

fle but must be considered as especially characteristic of conditions in the countries behind the Iron Curtain.

As with most consumer goods in the "people's democracies," there was in Prague at this time a great shortage of
packing material. I had, therefore, attempted to get permission for an Austrian forwarding agency to take over the
transport of my household goods to Vienna. It was taken for
granted, naturally, that the company could send its own
packers, moving vans, and packing material to Prague. The
plan looked good on paper, but it presupposed not only an
import license for the packing material but also entry permits for the four Austrian packers. And, as far as was known,
an entry permit had never been granted to foreigners for a
purpose which was, according to the interpretation of the
"people's democracies," so unnecessary, even dangerous, as
packing the household goods of a foreign diplomat.

Now what was really objectionable about such a request?
First, the Austrian packers, who according to Communist interpretation belonged to the working class, would be able to
get a look, however superficial, at the political and social conditions of workers in one of the countries behind the Iron
Curtain which were then isolated by an extremely strict visa
control. Second—and this was probably the most serious obstacle—a contract given to an Austrian firm would reveal to
foreigners the serious lack of consumer goods which prevailed in Czechoslovakia—or, more correctly stated, confirm
it. This shortage was so severe that a special permit was necessary even for purchasing the nails necessary for packing.
Not even foreign legations could get such nails without first
making a written request to the Czechoslovak Foreign Ministry.

When, in spite of advice to the contrary from several
sources, I decided to request entry permits for the four
Austrian packers, I realized that the Czech security police,
who would have to approve the request, would be moved
only by an important reason to agree to this presumptuous
desire. I expected a negative answer, especially since a formal
refusal could be based upon the fact that the Swedish Legation was not authorized to support requests for visas by

Austrian citizens. And, indeed, one day passed after another without any word from the foreign ministry through which the request had been made. Every time an official from the legation called the passport office of the ministry to find out how the matter had progressed, he received the same stereotyped answer: The "proper authorities" had not yet had an opportunity to make a decision on the request. It was not the first time I had received such an answer. In the four Communist states in which I had been active, it was customary, when a transaction was to be delayed or a camouflaged refusal was to be given, to state that the "proper authorities" had not yet made a decision or that an answer had not yet arrived. The reply which the legation received did not inspire any great hope for a favorable outcome.

Meanwhile, a happy chance played a trump card into my hand, and the matter suddenly took a new and unforeseen turn. After a few more days had passed without any definite word from the Czechs, my own passport official reported that the foreign ministry had asked for a visa for the Czech soccer team which was to play in Sweden the next week. When the application paper was laid before me and I had thoroughly examined it, I soon became convinced that at least four of the supposed members of the squad had little or nothing to do with soccer. There was no doubt that they belonged to the security police and had the job of watching over the players during the visit to Sweden and preventing them from staying there.

For anyone who knew a little about conditions behind the Iron Curtain, it was further clear that the players, even if they got their visas, would be allowed to leave Czechoslovakia only in company with their four keepers or at least some of them. The legation already had a general authorization which empowered me to give entry visas to all the members of the soccer team. There was, however, no obligation toward those who were not really players and certainly none at all if they had made false applications and wanted to visit Sweden for purposes other than the officially given one. On the other hand, since their mission was apparently only to watch over their own fellow citizens and had nothing to do with intelligence work, I could act freely with regard to the security police.

Under these circumstances I decided to make use of the situation in order to acquire in an indirect way the entry permit for the four Austrian packers. I would use the same tactics the Czechs themselves used. Therefore, I gave directions to call up the passport office in the Czech Foreign Ministry immediately and tell them that the visas had been granted to the members of the soccer team with the exception of the four, who were to be mentioned by name. Regarding these four (the guards), for the present we would limit ourselves to stating that the "proper Swedish authorities" had not yet made a decision.

The surprise and dismay which this answer called forth on the other end of the telephone line showed clearly that I had been right in my suspicions. Doubtless the four requests whose answer we had delayed were the most important in the eyes of the security police. Still, for obvious reasons, neither the foreign ministry nor the security police could even indirectly admit this. At the same time the police had to do everything in their power to avoid a delay in the granting of visas to the four keepers.

I therefore waited eagerly and with interest for the Czechs to play their next card. In order to expedite this and at the same time hint discreetly at a certain connection between the requests for the Austrian packers and those for the Czech guards, I gave instructions to inquire again when the visas for the four packers might be expected. I entertained a slight hope that the Czech security police might have already revised their attitude. I was wrong, however. The same answer was given: The "proper Czech authorities" had still not yet investigated. Thus, a few more days passed with queries and stereotyped answers on both sides.

After deliberating on how the obstinately negative attitude of the Czech officials might be explained, I came to the conclusion that they were not certain whether I understood the game. Perhaps they mistrusted my willingness to follow the rules. If they took the first step themselves and granted the visas to the four Austrian packers, they still had no guaranty that they would receive the compensation which they considered justified. How could these fears be overcome? In what way could I give a convincing guaranty, since neither of the parties concerned could show their hands? After I had considered all angles again, I decided to show my readiness for a solution which would be satisfactory to both sides and to do so in such a way that it would not be misunderstood by the Czechs. My colleague who had arranged the visas received instructions to call up the passport office of the Czech Foreign Ministry and to report that the "proper authorities" in Sweden had now made a decision about *one* of the four requests and had granted it.

This answer obviously dispelled every doubt on the part of the Czechs and was received, as had been intended, as confirmation that I was prepared for a tacit deal. The reaction followed almost immediately. Hardly an hour later the Czech passport office called to report that "now an answer had arrived from the proper Czech authorities." All four Austrian requests for entry permits had been allowed. My tactics had convinced the Czechs that I would keep my part in our silent agreement. Nevertheless, I allowed an hour to pass in order to avoid a formal connection between the two transactions and then gave the order to inform the Czech passport office that now we, too, had received word from the "proper Swedish authorities." Visas had also been granted for the other three Czechs. Without expressed arrangement and without one word about compensation having been exchanged, a satisfactory solution for both parties had thus been reached. After the difficulties which had appeared insurmountable in the beginning were set aside in such a way, and the desired packers, vans, and material had arrived, the packing up in Prague could begin.

But now a new complication followed: Would we receive permission to take out all our household furnishings? This matter, however, resolved itself more easily than I had dared hope. Because of our stays in other capital cities of the "people's democracies" and because of previous transfers, my wife was not without the appropriate experience which now proved useful.

When the customs officials, who had to be present at the packing, entered our house in order to examine the list which had been prepared, there awaited them in the front hall, a table which groaned under a load of food especially favored by the Czechs and which aroused memories of the abundance of times past. This was even more true of the real Pilsener beer which at that time was unobtainable for the average citizen of the country—and perhaps still is. Pilsener beer of prewar quality was reserved only for higher Party functionaries and foreign diplomats and was, therefore, valued that much more by those who seldom or never had the opportunity to enjoy it.

But the greatest impression was made with a bottle of Swedish *akvavit* which, as on many earlier occasions, seemed to possess the ability to accomplish wonders. The reading of the lists and the inspection of the crates began in an expectant atmosphere; hopes for rewarding pauses in the monotonous work and half-forgotten memories of the pleasures of a vanished day made their mark on the company. Their enjoyment of an interlude in a "capitalist" environment was soon clearly recognizable. It obviously confirmed the unflagging warnings of the Communist press concerning the devastating influence which contact with the "capitalist world" is bound to have on the moral resistance of an orthodox Party member.

The pauses became more and more frequent and lasted longer each time. At the same time, the interest in their work on the part of the representatives of the supervising authorities relaxed noticeably. It was not difficult to see that their original firm determination to count carefully every shirt and sock had slackened more and more with each glass of liqueur. The work lasted for two days in an atmosphere of increasing good will and understanding. When the second day drew toward its close, when the last plate had been cleaned, and when the last drop had been drunk with sadness from the last bottle of *akvavit,* the customs officials apparently considered their task ended. My library, which had been reserved for the last, escaped all examination. The lists were stamped as good as unread. Then orders were given to nail up the crates and load them onto the waiting moving vans. The last obstacle in the way of our departure was removed. Everything had gone better than we had dared hope. When news arrived that the shipment had crossed the border without hindrance, my wife and I could set out for Budapest in order to pay the farewell visits which diplomatic protocol prescribes.

Before I turn to a description of my last visit in Hungary, I would like to tell about an interesting little interlude that took place a few weeks before my departure from Prague. As is well known, the security police carefully watch all diplomats in Communist capitals, whether they represent great powers or small countries, N.A.T.O. members or neutral states. The supervision is carried out often—though not always—with such discretion that the foreign diplomat is firmly convinced that possibly other less careful and clear-sighted colleagues have been watched over or spied on in some way, but never himself—otherwise he would naturally have noticed it immediately. I want to tell about one of these typical cases now.

At one of the farewell dinners to which my wife and I had been invited before our departure, one of the servants, showing clear signs of dismay, whispered something to the host toward the end of the meal. The latter was obviously alarmed, arose with some excuse, and disappeared. Shortly afterwards he came back and reported that the heating system was broken. It was to be feared that in the course of about an hour the entire house would be completely cold. The question was whether there was a possibility of repairing the damage before that.

One of the guests, the military attaché of an important Western power, knew right away what to do. He said he was acquainted with an extremely clever plumber whom he, as well as one of his predecessors, had constantly engaged in similar situations. Not only did he work quickly and carefully, but, in contrast to others in his trade, he was always on hand when a pressing repair had to be made. Since he had been engaged again and again for years, he was considered almost a friend of the house. Even when he had ever so much to do, it was always possible for him to come.

"Somebody must call up my plumber," said the military attaché. "Greet him from me and say that the situation demands haste." He pulled his notebook out of his pocket, leafed around in it, and added, "I have the telephone number here. Now we only have to find someone who speaks German and Czech to explain what has happened. My plumber knows only Czech."

None of us knew Czech. Then it suddenly occurred to me that the chauffeur of one of my officials, who was also present, knew both languages. In the legation we had known for a long time that he was in the service of the Czech security police. We had even taken special precautions. But even so, there was naturally no hesitation about making use of his linguistic ability for a telephone conversation with the plumber. The chauffeur was summoned and told what to do. I followed him to the telephone in the front hall and gave him the piece of paper on which the military attaché had jotted down the number of the plumber. The chauffeur glanced at the paper. His facial expression froze and showed surprise and dismay. He gave me a look at the same time questioning and disturbed but made no motion to dial the number. Now it was my turn to be surprised. Since at first I believed he had not rightly understood, I repeated what had happened and asked him again to make the call. Again nothing happened. Finally I became annoyed and said in a determined tone of voice, "Why don't you telephone? I can't stand here forever."

A long pause followed. Then the chauffeur stammered, "But, but that is the number of the security police."

He knew the number only too well. It was the number which he himself had obviously called whenever he contacted the police for one reason or another to report about us. Now he had divulged his secret. The credulity of the military attaché and his predecessor had been revealed in an unexpected and harsh way. I don't know how they had gotten the number of this clever and obliging "plumber"; still, no one had bothered to find out who he was. No one had ever had any idea of the true connection or suspected that the plumber had received his training not only in the trade which he ostensibly carried on but also in very different spheres.

It was only natural that the obliging man was always on hand when he was needed. The care and speed with which he carried out his jobs were meant to establish his reputation as a clever worker so that he would gradually become indispensable. In this way his employers were certain that he would always have access to the home of the military attaché. That is one of my last memories of Prague—a closing illustration that seems to me especially typical.

2

. . . and Budapest

During the many years which I spent in the "people's democracies," I always looked forward to visits in Budapest with a certain pleasure and expectation. When compared with Prague, Sofia, and especially Bucharest, it offered a pleasant change. Although Hungary is a Communist country—and it can scarcely be affirmed that it treats its citizens with greater consideration and more kindness than other states behind the Iron Curtain—the agreeable usages which have for centuries distinguished the co-existence of the Magyar population with foreigners had been maintained under the present regime. Even at a time when bad manners in Communist circles were at their height, and governments and officials in the "people's democracies" competed with one another to show their Stalinist convictions by playing trivial and senseless tricks on Western diplomats, the Hungarians, aside from a few, tried very hard to act correctly, and had always gone as far as possible in their courtesy toward representatives of the "capitalist" states.

It even happened that when higher Party functionaries heard of a proposed trip of mine to Austria or another country in Western Europe, they offered, on their own, to inform the Hungarian border officials and to seek the quickest possible completion of the wearisome formalities of departure. Upon my return to Budapest they always inquired about the journey and whether I had had difficulties at the border. They wanted to be sure that their instructions had had the desired effect. Whenever I could confirm that, they were obviously and sincerely gratified. Consequently, in Budapest the activities of foreign diplomats were somewhat freer and more natural than in the other lands that I had gotten to know behind the Iron Curtain. And when I paid my farewell visit to the foreign ministry during my last two weeks in Budapest, I was invited to visit Hungary frequently even after my departure. This invitation was genuinely meant. The information that I would receive a visa for an unlimited number of trips in and out in the next six months proved it. At that time a Communist state could scarcely have been more obliging to a Western diplomat.

I paid my two last visits to Imre Nagy, who was prime minister at the time, and to the first secretary of the Party, Matyas Rakosi. A little more than two years later, during the Hungarian uprising, the first would play a role as meaningful as it was tragic. The second had been forced about a year before my visit to share his power, which had previously been almost unlimited, with Nagy. Between the two, therefore, hidden enmity and rivalry prevailed.

As was the case with Stalin in the U.S.S.R., Rakosi in Hungary had been in recent years the chairman of the council of ministers and general secretary (later "first secretary") of the Party. In exercising his power he had been limited only by the dependence of his country and Party on the powerful individuals in the Kremlin. In many areas, however, this dependence was so strong that, like the other East European states controlled by Moscow, Hungary had to adapt to every sweeping organizational change caused by the frequent variations in the balance of power in Moscow after Stalin's death. When the struggle for power broke among Stalin's successors, for example, and Malenkov, who for a short time had been premier as well as first secretary of the Party, was forced to resign his Party function, the Party leaders in the East European states found it necessary to follow his example.

Still, the adaptation was completed only slowly. In Czechoslovakia, where the post of general secretary had been combined with that of president and not, as in the other satellites, with that of prime minister, the separation was already accomplished by the spring of 1953. The chief reason for this was that Gottwald, who had occupied both offices, died only a few weeks after Stalin. In Poland, Rumania, and Bulgaria, on the other hand, the posts of first secretary and prime minister were not divided until early 1954, or about a year later than in Moscow. According to Rakosi's indirect intimations to me, the main reason for this delay was to avoid an obvious demonstration of the dependence of the "people's democracies" on the Soviet Party leadership.

In June 1953 the new division of power took place in Hungary. Only a few weeks before, Rakosi had believed himself more firmly in the saddle than ever. While in the Soviet Union the first careful steps toward the abandonment of a "personality cult" had already been taken, he was still celebrating triumphs in Hungary. During a visit to Budapest in May 1953 for the purpose of getting personal impressions concerning the current election campaign, I was astonished that Rakosi continued to be treated in newspaper articles as well as in public remarks of various Party leaders, as if he were almost a god.

The homage paid to the "great leader," to the "wise father of the Hungarian people," at a large mass meeting on the Parliament Square on May 10, 1953, at which I was present as a spectator, may have broken all previous records. The main speaker was Rakosi himself. Since I do not know Hungarian, I could only guess at what he said. The brief comments of German-speaking people in my vicinity, and the organized applause which interrupted his performance again and again, helped me in this. What I could understand astonished me; and when I read the complete text of the speech the next day in English translation, I was amazed.

As far as I can remember now, after more than ten years, Rakosi maintained among other things that Hungary had made noticeably greater economic progress in recent years than ever before in its long history. The collective system had conclusively proved its superiority over individual farming and in the future would demonstrate even more impressive development; besides this, the new five-year plan, which was to begin in 1955, would ensure that Hungary would equal or surpass the most progressive capitalist countries in all economic areas. The other speakers chimed in with songs of praise for the accomplishments of the Party and sought also to convince their listeners that this progress could be attributed mainly to the "wise" leadership of Rakosi.

Only a month after this mass demonstration of his "personality cult," Rakosi was unexpectedly called to Moscow. From the notes of Imre Nagy and his friends, we now know that the Soviet Party Presidium informed Rakosi that serious mistakes had been made under his leadership. They had shaken the social order of the "people's democracy" and had brought his country to the verge of disaster. Changes must be made immediately to avoid disturbances which could endanger the Communist regime in Hungary.

These gloomy prophecies, which turned out to be true more than three years later, must be considered in connection with the workers' riots and strikes which had taken place at the beginning of May in Pilsen, Mährisch-Ostrau, and other large industrial cities in Czechoslovakia, and had also broken out in Berlin shortly before Rakosi's Moscow trip. It was hardly surprising that the Soviet Party Presidium was extremely concerned about these events. In view of popular hostility toward the regime in Hungary, it was feared that the situation there could take a similar turn.

Not only the mood of the people, but also the economic condition of Hungary gave Moscow reason for worry. Mikoyan reproached Rakosi for an excessive expansion of the Hungarian iron and steel industry (probably in full accord with earlier Soviet instructions). This policy was especially foolish, since Hungary had little iron ore or coal. Mikoyan also blamed Rakosi for forcing the peasants into collective farms and thus wrecking a thriving Hungarian agriculture. And, indeed, while driving through the country in the summer and fall of 1953, one could see how the previously well-tended fields had deteriorated. The lack of interest of the peasants in collective agriculture had resulted in the neglect or delay of the fall sowing in spite of favorable weather. At the end of November, in many places the fall plowing had not yet begun. Only in a few fields could it be established from the sprouting green that the sowing had taken place on time.

The cattle farms were in an even worse situation, if possible. Since slaughtering had been greater than normal because of a shortage of feed, the meat supply was ample for a time. Still, if one had spent several years in the country, as I had done, and during that time had made many auto trips to or from Czechoslovakia, Rumania, Yugoslavia, and Austria, one could soon see for oneself how the cattle herds on the Hungarian *puszta* had become noticeably smaller from year to year. This decline was the result not only of ruthless slaughtering but also of increased cattle exports. Hungary had great need of foreign exchange for the purchase of capital goods. Therefore, the regime exported products which could be sold in Western Europe without difficulty. This was especially true of live animals which were exported to Switzerland in large quantities.

The agricultural situation in Hungary was thus completely different from what Rakosi had maintained in his election speech. And he himself bore much of the responsibility for the failure, as the Soviet Party Presidium maintained. That was not the only reproach, however. According to Moscow, Rakosi had also permitted and encouraged a cult around his person. Further, he had transgressed against "socialist legality" and had had innocent people arrested and executed, established concentration camps, and other similar things.

This could scarcely have been news to the rulers in the Kremlin, since they had complete and accurate information about conditions in Hungary during the entire occupation. But why this sudden and unexpected change in attitude toward Stalin's favorite, his "faithful disciple" Rakosi? I have already mentioned the severe anxiety, even panic, which the events in Pilsen and Berlin as well as the reports about developments threatening in Hungary had evoked in the rulers in the Kremlin. Indeed, the new Soviet leadership had already instituted a program aimed at easing tension. On the Soviet domestic front it displayed itself, among other things, in a moderate shift of investment from heavy to light industry and in writing off peasant debts, higher prices for obligatory deliveries of food to the state, lower taxes, and other relief for the purpose of encouraging greater agricultural production. Further, political prisoners who had been imprisoned or executed on account of disregard for "socialist legality" were freed or rehabilitated.

These and similar measures known as the "new course" had not yet been instituted in Hungary. In the face of the serious political and economic situation, however, the Soviet Party Presidium had decided to begin them without delay. Since Rakosi personified the old Stalinist line, he was considered completely unfit to carry out such reforms. Furthermore, it contradicted the new principle of "collective leadership" established after Stalin's death when the same person occupied the office of prime minister and first secretary of the Party. Therefore, it was decided to undertake the separation at this time and remove Rakosi from the office of prime minister.

Even without inside information, it is not difficult to see that a new Hungarian prime minister under the existing circumstances would need certain qualifications: He should be a reliable and convinced Communist. He should have a long residence in the Soviet Union but, nevertheless, enjoy some popularity with the people of his own country. He should, furthermore, according to the popular interpretation, not be connected with that reign of terror which had made Rakosi's regime so hated in the country. The man who best met these qualifications was Imre Nagy. He had also, in his time, divided up the large estates but could not be held responsible for the collective system which was introduced later. The division of power between Nagy and Rakosi, which was decided on as a result of this deliberation in Moscow, led to a bitter struggle between the two which the masters in the Kremlin watched with interest and perhaps also with satisfaction.

When I came to Budapest at the beginning of March 1954 in order to pay my farewell visits, I had only a very slight knowledge of the background of the rivalry between Rakosi and Nagy. I knew that after his inauguration Nagy had made a long speech in which he disclosed in detail his basic policies. Apparently they differed from those of Rakosi but agreed completely with the "new course" introduced in the Soviet Union since Stalin's death. One could also conclude that the "new line" was to be instituted in Hungary on express orders from Moscow. That Rakosi retained the leadership of the Party secretariat showed, nevertheless, that he had by no means lost his influence. This impression was further strengthened by a speech which he gave at the beginning of July 1953 in Budapest. Though ostensibly embracing the "new course," Rakosi stressed at the same time that the earlier line of the Party for the establishment of socialism in Hungary would continue unchanged. This declaration contained a clear but indirect warning to the people concerning hasty conclusions. In spite of the remarks of the new prime minister, everything would basically remain as before. I thought to myself that a Party secretary who so unequivocally repudiated his prime minister must be certain of strong support in Moscow. As can be seen from Nagy's memoirs, which have since been published, and from other evidence which became known after the Hungarian uprising, this interpretation was, nevertheless, not entirely correct.

When he delivered his pronouncement, meant as a personal declaration of war on Nagy, Rakosi evidently believed he had the support of some members of the Soviet Presidium. And the outcome of the struggle which had thus begun between the two rivals, indeed, depended on which of them ultimately secured stronger support in Moscow. This internal battle in the Hungarian Party leadership, which eventually led to the downfall of Nagy, had neared its peak as I arrived in Budapest for my farewell visits.

I had previously met Nagy only fleetingly and had never had an opportunity for a longer conversation with him. He received me in the Parliament building, which is universally admired because of its beautiful site on the Danube, and which had been the pride of the old Hungarians. Nagy was a small, thick-set, corpulent man with a dark complexion, a long black mustache, and pronounced Magyar features. He struck one as reserved and considerate, and made a completely sympathetic impression. Our conversation was by no means noteworthy. It concerned primarily the "new course," the substance of which the prime minister explained to me. He defended energetically and thoroughly the policy for which he had been appointed. He appeared to be not only personally convinced of its rightness but also to be conscious of the strong opposition which the planned measures would meet on all sides. Two years later, after the Hungarian uprising, Nagy met a tragic fate. After Budapest had been occupied again by Soviet troops, he sought asylum in the Yugoslav Embassy but was surrendered. A few years later he was brought to trial and executed.

Several days after the meeting with Nagy I made my visit to Rakosi, whom I had known for several years. I had seen him last at a Swedish-Hungarian soccer game at which I had been placed in a seat of honor along with the members of the Politburo of the Hungarian Party, who had appeared in surprising numbers. Shortly before the beginning of the game, the men seated near me got up suddenly and greeted someone with extraordinary respect. When I turned around, I saw that the greeting was for Rakosi, who had recently resigned as prime minister. He was looking for a seat. The person next to me, Farkas, a friend of Rakosi at that time, motioned eagerly and tried to make him understand that he might sit down in the first row. Rakosi declined this invitation with an ironic smile and instead sat in the most remote spot. He wanted to make it quite clear that he had renounced the "personality cult" which had brought him such extreme criticism. His self-confidence and the ironic and satisfied smile with which he received the respectful attention of his Party friends showed, nevertheless, that he still considered himself the most powerful man in Hungary.

According to protocol a farewell visit to Rakosi was scarcely necessary, since he had given up the formal leadership of the government. But when I communicated my request, I received the immediate answer that Rakosi would receive me. The visit was set for eight o'clock on the morning of the same day I wanted to leave Budapest. It was to take place in the Party secretariat building where Rakosi had his office.

The Party secretariat was housed not far from the Parlia-

ment building where I had already been received some days
before by Nagy. When I approached Rakosi's well guarded
office building, I noticed from far off a strong police complement on the streets. The Party secretariat was lodged in an
ugly building that was impressive only in its size. Steps and
halls teemed with police in uniform and plain clothes. Since
my arrival was expected and I was received at the entrance
by a young official from Rakosi's secretariat, I could proceed
directly up the steps to the second floor where Rakosi's offices
were.

After an excursion through a long row of shabby as well as
tastelessly furnished rooms, I reached the antechamber of the
powerful Party secretary. Another employee announced my
arrival and came back with the information that I would be
received immediately. I stepped into a large, long room
which reminded me vaguely of pictures I had seen a long
time before of the offices of Mussolini and other dictators.
My special attention, however, was not aroused by the size of
the room but by three large photographs on one wall. One of
them showed Stalin, not yet "unmasked" and to whom the
Hungarian Communist Party still paid dutiful homage. The
other photograph was of Malenkov, and the third was of my
host. The interesting thing about the pictures was their arrangement. The picture of Rakosi hung about an inch lower
and between the other two which, on the other hand, were
almost to the millimeter at exactly the same height. This pe-
culiar placement had a political meaning. In a way that
could not be misunderstood by anyone familiar with Communist custom, Rakosi was emphasizing his own insignifi-
cance and subordinate position in comparison to Stalin as
well as Malenkov. In this way he stressed at the same time
the leading role of the Soviet Union and the Soviet Party
within the Communist camp. If the three photographs had
been hung at the same level, that could have been interpreted to mean that the Hungarian Party considered itself as
important as the Soviet Party and claimed the same rank.

After a quick glance of inspection at the three pictures, I
discovered at a large desk in the corner of the room a small,
thick-set, obese man who was just getting up and coming to

meet me. His bald head looked as if it were carefully polished every morning. His round countenance, large mouth, and wide lips appeared at first to point to a Mongolian origin, but this impression was deceptive. His eyes were lively and intelligent. Rakosi came toward me with a rolling gait on his short, slightly bowed legs. When he stretched out his hand in greeting, he twisted his grotesque face into something like a smile which caused his physiognomy to appear even more repulsive.

In contrast to other Communist leaders whom I had met, Rakosi was extraordinarily good at languages. As I had discovered previously, he spoke fluent German, English, and French—he probably knew other languages also, in any case Russian—and liked to show off his ability. In the course of a conversation he was accustomed to change often from one language to another, in the hope that the person with whom he was talking would not know the language well. Once when I complimented him on his linguistic ability, to my surprise he gave his previous "diplomatic activity" as the origin of it. Later, when I tried to determine whether this statement was true, I found out that before World War I Rakosi was supposed to have served as an office worker in an Austro-Hungarian consulate, in Great Britain if I remember correctly.

"So, as I hear it, you want to go to Vienna," Rakosi began the conversation, which was carried on primarily in German this time. "But I really do not know," he continued, "whether I should congratulate you or commiserate with you. On closer thought," he added with a malicious smile, "I believe rather that I have reason to express my sincere condolences."

"Why is that?" I asked, a little surprised.

Rakosi answered, "Because you have been accredited in Hungary now for almost five years, and here you were a witness with your own eyes to the unheard of progress which the country has made since the feudal social order was overthrown and a popular democracy was instituted. If you judge the situation objectively, you will certainly have to admit that the standard of living of the population has risen, and their well-being is now greater than ever before in Hungary's long history.

"In other words, you are now leaving a country in which the working class, in full knowledge of its high standard of living, and in the hope of raising it even more, participates with joy and enthusiasm in the establishment of Socialism.

"In Austria, on the other hand, according to what I have heard from all sides, the situation is quite different. There you will find a people who live in extreme poverty; you will see employees and workers who scarcely have daily bread for their families. You will be going into a capital city which was severely afflicted by the devastation of the war and still lies almost in ruins. And in contrast to Budapest, hardly anything has been done to hasten reconstruction. Therefore, I am of the opinion," he added, still smiling slightly, "that I must rather pity you than congratulate you."

I had often wondered at how freely Rakosi ignored the truth. But never before had he distorted facts so impudently. It was especially surprising since he certainly knew that I visited Vienna frequently and was in a position to make comparisons with conditions in Budapest. The only explanation is that microphones were installed in Rakosi's office, with or without his consent. This could have been done on his own initiative. He could thus prove, if necessary, that in his conversations with foreign diplomats or other visitors he had always spoken in complete agreement with the general political guidelines set up in Moscow.

Still, I did not want to accept his statements without contradiction. After he had finished his monologue, I answered that the standard of living in Hungary—even though higher than in other Communist countries which I had visited—still could not be compared even approximately to that of Austria. In Vienna, through which I had come on my way to Budapest, one could certainly still see many ruins, but reconstruction of the city was considerably farther advanced than in Budapest.

Rakosi's face darkened. "I don't believe a word of what you have just said," he answered. "The accounts which I have gotten from dependable sources are incompatible with the description which you now give about conditions in Vienna."

"But I was there scarcely two weeks ago," I replied, "and I have visited the city many times since 1949."

"Nevertheless, I trust my own information more," Rakosi retorted.

"If you don't believe my account," I challenged, "you certainly have the chance to investigate personally."

"How is that?" Rakosi asked with some curiosity.

"Go to Austria yourself," I suggested, "and satisfy yourself about conditions there. In just four hours by car you'll be in Vienna."

"Yes," Rakosi answered. "I would like to visit Vienna once more. But," he added sadly, "I have no hope of ever being allowed to see that once so beautiful city again. Even if I had time to travel there, the Austrians would never give me an entry visa."

"The Austrians?" I cried out in feigned surprise. "You must mean the Russians, even though you speak of Austrians. It is complete news to me," I added ironically, "that you stand in such disfavor in Moscow and therefore can't even count on getting Russian permission for a trip to Vienna."

Unknowingly I had touched a sore spot.

"What has that got to do with my position in Moscow?" Rakosi asked in a slightly irritated tone.

"I thought you knew," I answered. "If a high ranking Party member of one of the people's democracies wants to go to Austria, he need never bother about an Austrian entry visa. He knows that the Soviet guards will let him cross the border without one. While I have waited at the Austrian customs for passport inspection, I have often seen how it happens. The Soviet guard who has been warned ahead of time gives a military salute and hurries to open the gate without examining either the passport or the visa, even for a moment. After a delay of only a few seconds, a high Communist Party functionary can continue on to Vienna. The Austrian police and customs officials have to put up with this disregard for the sovereignty of their state. Consequently," I concluded, "if you are convinced that you would never get permission to enter Austria, I can only draw the conclusion that the Russians, for one reason or another unknown to me, do not consider your presence there as desirable. Therefore, I assume that you are no longer held in such favor in Moscow as is generally believed." Rakosi answered only with a smile.

The conversation then turned to the Hungarian Party congress which was to convene in Budapest the next month. "I had never realized that diplomats from capitalist countries were interested in our congresses," said Rakosi with an ironical smile.

"Naturally we are interested," I replied. "The Party determines policy and the congress adopts the general line implementing policy. This is one of the things on which we are expected to report." And when I asked, not unintentionally, how long the congress would last, I received an answer which reflected the position of Hungary at the time.

"Our Party," Rakosi answered, "can naturally not be so presumptuous as to imagine that the questions which our congress will deal with are anywhere near as important as those problems handled by a Soviet congress. It would be ridiculous, therefore, if our Party congress should take up as much time as a Soviet congress. Since, on the one hand, a Soviet congress generally lasts two weeks, but, on the other hand, for purely technical reasons no congress can be concluded in less than three or four days, you can thus conclude that the Hungarian Party congress will last between four and fourteen days—let's say about a week."

So ended my last conversation with the Hungarian Party secretary who was so powerful in his time. One of the most hated men in Hungary, he fled to the Soviet Union during the uprising of 1956.

On March 17 at nine o'clock in the morning, I left Rakosi's headquarters and continued the trip to Vienna in company with my wife who had come to pick me up. After a three-hour ride we reached the Hungarian border station. Our passports were checked with admirable speed. Obviously the police officers had been told beforehand of our arrival. Part of the unavoidable ritual was the examination of the trunk of the car by which the police convince themselves that the traveler has not hidden a fugitive there to smuggle him out of Hungary. I submitted to this procedure, which seemed so absurd, since it was at that time the only control which a diplomat had to undergo.

Sometimes the existence of the Iron Curtain is energetically denied by Swedes as well as other foreign travelers: "We have been in Hungary as well as in Czechoslovakia," they say, "but have never gone through any Iron Curtain." One need only go by car or on foot, however, to the border between Austria and Czechoslovakia or Hungary to convince oneself that the Iron Curtain is anything but a legend. To begin with, double rows of tangled barbed wire extend from north to south along these borders. Mines are placed between them in order to make any attempt at flight more difficult or impossible. Directly next to the barbed wire extends a strip of plowed and harrowed land about a hundred yards wide on which tracks of anyone attempting flight would be clearly discernible. Beyond this strip one can see with the naked eye several rows of trip wire which are stretched about a foot and a half above the ground. A touch releases mines or rocket flares that illuminate the entire neighborhood for a few short moments with their harsh light. Farther away, watchtowers, fifty to one hundred feet high, are set up along the border at regular intervals. They are manned day and night. With a set of binoculars from the Austrian side one can watch the sentinel who sits up in the tower observing the area through his binoculars. The towers are also useful as bases for scouting patrols which regularly comb their assigned section of the border.

In places—especially along the Czech border—the barbed wire as well as the watchtowers in recent years have been set back so far that they can no longer be seen with the naked eye from Austrian territory. The reason for this may have been the interest of numerous tourists who come to the Austrian side of the border in order to look at the hermetic barricade between the East and the West. That is what Churchill was thinking of when he used the expression "Iron Curtain" in his famous Fulton speech.

After the Hungarian customs and passport formalities, we

resumed our trip to Vienna. Between the Austrian and the Hungarian customs, the road runs parallel to the border for several miles. On the Hungarian side is a desolate no man's land. Except for a few dilapidated houses, little or nothing can be detected of the cultivation which once existed. The border area remains a wasteland in order to facilitate, for the border troops, the prevention of escapes.

Upon our arrival in Austria, we were struck by the numerous idle Soviet soldiers standing around the customs station in long, poorly fitting overcoats and fur hats.

Austria was divided into four zones, of which the most easterly—the Soviet zone—extended along the Hungarian border and separated the British zone from Hungary by a narrow strip. Otherwise, the eastern zone was bounded essentially by Semmering on the south and the Enns River in the vicinity of Linz on the west.

After our arrival in Nickelsdorf, I went to the customs to present our passports. Stationed there were three Austrian customs and police officers as well as a Soviet corporal, an obviously Mongolian type. He was one of the smallest persons I have ever seen. His head with its high fur hat scarcely reached up to the bayonet on his rifle. With his coat, which was far too long, and his fur winter cap, he looked indescribably comical as he solemnly called upon the Austrian officials, to whom I had given the passports, to hand them over to him. Thereupon he sat down at a desk in one corner of the room and began to leaf through the passports. Then the little soldier sat there motionless for a long time with the passports in front of him. Finally he got up and rooted around for a long time in his pants pocket, out of which he then pulled a notebook and the stump of a pencil which was so small that he had difficulty holding it between his thumb and index finger. He scribbled spasmodically in his notebook with the pencil while at the same time leafing through the passports. Finally I lost all patience, went to see what he was doing, and discovered that he was making senseless marks, up and down, back and forth. When he thought he had convinced us of his writing ability, he got up slowly and handed over the passports with a dignified gesture. "Khorosho!"

(good) he added ceremoniously. Now we could continue the trip to Vienna.

One of the Austrian officials who accompanied me to the car confirmed that the little Mongol could neither read nor write. But he was jealous of his dignity and wanted least of all to admit his ignorance in front of foreign "capitalists." For that reason he had withdrawn to his desk to act out the little scene with the pencil and notebook.

3

Arrival in Vienna

The Vienna which I now entered was anything but a sick and dying city of ruins as Rakosi had maintained. Reconstruction had progressed at a swift pace. Of course one still saw one or two gaping holes in the long rows of houses. But these holes were being quickly filled up one after the other. If not already convinced of it, one must certainly be persuaded that the Austrians were a hard-working people driven by the firm intention to build up again in the shortest possible time what the war had destroyed.

Later, however, when I had the opportunity to travel throughout the country, it struck me that restoration in the Soviet zone showed less progress than in the other occupation zones. This was not difficult to explain. It was linked primarily with the fact that requisitioning of dwellings in the three zones held by the Western powers had almost ceased, but such encroachment by the occupation authorities in the Soviet zone was still customary. Few owners were willing to risk their limited savings for rebuilding their houses as long as seizure was still possible.

This was especially noticeable in the health resort of Baden, so elegant before the war, where the Soviet headquarters were located. The appearance of this city was bleaker than that of any other city in Austria that I visited in the first year of my stay. Aside from the numerous buildings in which the Soviet military staff was billeted and which for that reason were in a fairly respectable condition, one could scarcely see a single house on which even the slightest attempt at improvement had been undertaken.

Vienna was the seat of the Austrian Federal Government. According to agreement, the four victorious powers jointly occupied the city which lay in the Soviet zone. According to the same agreement it had been divided into five different sectors; one of these, the so-called international sector, included the inner city with the Kärntnerstrasse as the center and was under joint military rule. This cooperation, which lasted throughout the occupation, was given visible expression through regular patrols of four military policemen in an open auto—one representative from each occupation army.

Besides this international sector, Vienna was divided into British, American, French, and Russian sectors. As with the zones into which the whole country was split, these sectors were placed under high commissioners appointed by the occupying powers. In the beginning, military officers, who simultaneously commanded the occupation forces of their countries, had officiated as such. Later they were replaced by civilian officials who were at the same time accredited as ambassadors to the Austrian government. In this way Austria was recognized as a sovereign state even though not all the rights and powers connected with independence had been restored.

When I arrived in Vienna, the four high commissioners consequently exercised a double function. On one hand, they were the representatives of their countries with the Austrian government and in this role equal in principle to other foreign ambassadors. On the other hand, they were members of the Allied Council which still exercised supreme authority in certain matters. In this respect the council and its members could be considered an administrative authority superior to the Austrian government. Although the powers of the government had been broadened in recent years, significant limitations were still in force.

In spite of the division of Vienna into five different sectors, Austrians as well as foreigners could move about freely in the whole city. The border between the different sectors was marked only by signs. Thus, anyone could leave one of the Western sectors at his own risk and venture into the Soviet sector. Although there were no checkpoints on the sector borders, I was, nevertheless, advised to take my passport with me when I went on extended walks. Still, I cannot remember ever showing it or anyone requesting that I identify myself. It cannot be denied, however, that not only Austrians but also foreigners felt safer in the Western sectors. Many Austrians confided that they never entered the Soviet zone without dread. Newspaper accounts about people who had disappeared from the Soviet zone under mysterious and never explained circumstances added substantially to this fear. Cases of this sort had become infrequent, however, and were exceptions by 1954. On the whole, quiet and order prevailed in Vienna. Most of the inhabitants of the city could carry on their work and go about their daily activities without concern about personal safety.

In contrast to the East European states I had left, shortages of consumer goods had been overcome. Rationing was a thing of the past. But in many levels of the population, extreme poverty still prevailed. The earnings of industrial workers and employees were low. The people one met on the street had on worn-out, patched clothes that obviously were left over from happier years. Anyone who came from Sweden or Switzerland was astonished at the small amount of traffic. Only a few private cars were to be seen but, in contrast, that many more military vehicles of various kinds. These conditions changed quickly, however, when the occupation ended and Austria won back its complete independence. The Vienna which I saw at the end of 1955, shortly after the withdrawal of the last occupation forces, scarcely seemed to be the same city which I had found upon my arrival in March 1954.

Since I naturally came into contact with the leading personalities in the government and in the Allied Council, I will begin by sketching briefly the organization and functions of these agencies. Since 1945, when the Communists had also participated briefly, the government had been made up of a coalition between the two largest parties, the People's Party and the Social Democrats. Their predecessors in the days of the First Republic had fought each other bitterly, not only in Parliament but also in the streets. After 1938, however, several of the leaders of both parties had found themselves in the same Nazi concentration camps and had concluded on the basis of harsh experience that continued division would cause disastrous results for the country.

Violent verbal clashes often took place, and both parties attacked each other fiercely before each new parliamentary election, but the coalition remained intact and almost developed into a permanent institution in the political life of Austria. It was finally dissolved only after the 1965 electoral victory of the People's Party. According to an unwritten and strictly observed law, the coalition party with the most parliamentary seats was entitled to name the head of the government, the federal chancellor. According to the same unwritten law, the vice-chancellor belonged to the other coalition party. Whenever serious differences of opinion occurred, decisions were reached as a rule not by the government but within a so-called coalition committee of a few leading members of both parties. Even though members of this committee, which was not based upon the constitution, generally belonged to the government, this was not always the case.

The strong man and recognized leader of the People's Party at the time of my arrival in Vienna was the engineer Julius Raab. Since the end of the war he had exercised considerable influence behind the scenes but had assumed leadership of the government only after the election of 1953. Raab had begun his political career in the days of the First Republic and at that time belonged to the private army, the so-called *Heimwehr,* led by Prince Starhemberg. Later he held the post of minister of commerce in the last government of Schuschnigg. After the war, along with some similarly disposed friends, he founded the present People's Party, a successor to the Christian Social Party which had primarily represented Catholic interests in Austria at the time of the First Republic. In contrast to its predecessor, however, the People's Party has broadened its program and now includes the great majority of adherents of all the earlier non-Socialist parties in Austria.

Raab was a taciturn and reserved man, but he had far greater authority in his party than any of his successors. If, after listening to different opinions put forward in the course of a discussion, he made known his interpretation, that generally meant that a decision had been made against which no protest could be raised. In the area of domestic affairs, Chancellor Raab will certainly be considered one of the great men in the recent history of Austria, even more so because after his retirement the People's Party suffered from a noticeable lack of personalities of his type.

In questions of foreign policy, on the other hand, he lacked the experience and knowledge which were the basis for his success in domestic affairs. Among other things he showed a disquieting inclination toward illusions regarding Soviet intentions and motives. This weakness, which he shared with many other European statesmen, might explain the apparent esteem with which he was regarded by Soviet authorities, especially in his last years as head of the government. This lack of knowledge in foreign affairs, however, was largely offset by a surprisingly trustworthy instinct. Anyone who closely followed Raab's activities in the area of foreign policy, often had the impression that he intuitively made the right decision without wholly understanding why. One thing is sure: He was a great Austrian patriot, a man who fought with conviction for an independent Austria and constantly believed that his country would endure as an autonomous state.

My first official visit in Vienna would be not to the chancellor but to the foreign minister to whom, according to old diplomatic custom, I had to deliver a copy of the letter accrediting me as Royal Swedish Minister to the Austrian President. The foreign minister was then the engineer Leopold Figl, who had been Raab's predecessor as chancellor from 1945 to 1953. In the first years after the war, he had upheld Austrian interests vis-à-vis the occupation forces with great energy and courage under difficult circumstances, and few Austrian politicians enjoyed such great popularity in the country. With his open, natural, and unaffected friendliness, he is a typical representative of that temperament which is so characteristic of Austrians and has contributed in such a high degree to acquiring friends and admirers for his people in all countries. On March 17 I paid a visit to the foreign minister.

Two days later I delivered my credentials to the Austrian President with the customary formality.

In the first twenty years after the war, Austrians seemed to have an instinctive interest in maintaining a balance between the two coalition parties. Although the People's Party has gained the largest number of seats in all elections to Parliament and thus selects the chancellor, the Social Democrats have won every presidential election. The head of the government and the president thus always belonged to different parties. Since the authority of the president extends substantially beyond the sphere of the representatives, a sensible balance has been maintained and has contributed to preventing a misuse of power by one party.

At the time of my arrival, General Theodor Körner was president. He was then over eighty years old. General Körner had served in the Austro-Hungarian Army in World War I and was considered one of its most talented general-staff officers. In the last years of the war he distinguished himself as chief of staff on the Isonzo front, an important sector on which twelve bloody battles were fought. After the conclusion of peace, Körner went into politics and joined the Social Democrats. In 1945 he was appointed mayor of Vienna and in 1951 was elected President of the Republic.

Körner was a stately man with a fine, distinguished expression, white hair, and a white beard. I have seen few heads of state who projected such natural dignity and at the same time were so simple and unaffected. He detested formal occasions and tried to simplify them as much as possible. This he did when I handed him my credentials in the splendid rooms of Maria Theresia in the former imperial palace. I had already been informed that no speeches were to be exchanged; after Körner had greeted me and I had introduced my colleagues, he sat down with me on a sofa and in the course of a half hour informed me about the political situation.

The following day I began the other traditional visits prescribed by protocol: to members of the government, high officials in the foreign ministry, the mayor of the city of Vienna, and the heads of the other diplomatic missions. But with that the official formalities were not yet finished as would have been the case in other countries. The Allied Council considered itself for the time being as the sovereign power in the country and required that each envoy accredited to the Austrian government must be received by the council at one of its regular sessions. These meetings took place, if I remember correctly, every fourteen days. Each of the four high commissioners occupied the chair in turn.

Of these, the American, Llewellyn E. Thompson, was without doubt the most important, for one thing because of his great intelligence, his universally recognized and respected diplomatic ability, and, for another, because of the leading position which his country occupies in the Western world. During the last war Thompson served in the American Embassy in Moscow. He speaks fluent Russian and is an expert on Soviet affairs. After the end of the war he was entrusted with several important missions, all of which he settled with equal skill. One only has to mention the negotiations concerning Trieste. That the final solution satisfied all parties concerned may have been largely due to Thompson. At the ambassadors' and foreign ministers' conferences in Vienna concerning the restoration of Austrian independence, Thompson also played an important role. His most recent assignment has been as U.S. Ambassador to Moscow, his second tour as head of this important mission. Tommy, as his friends call him, and I soon became close and firm friends. With him I could discuss important political questions without reservation.

The Soviet High Commissioner, Ivan I. Ilyichev, belonged to the so-called Political Administration of the Soviet Army. During his term of office in Vienna, he was supposed to have had the rank of lieutenant general. He was a reserved, intractable man and maintained that he knew no other language than Russian. In any event he never carried on a conversation without an interpreter, which increased the difficulty of communicating with him a great deal. (The Austrian government invited the former ambassadors of the occupation powers to Vienna in May 1965 to mark the tenth anniversary of the signing of the State Treaty. I was also invited and was pleasantly surprised to discover that Comrade

Ilyichev had acquired a fairly good knowledge of German.)
The French High Commissioner, M. Jean Payart, was a little, fat, pompous gentleman with a carefully tended black beard. Since he often seemed to consider himself the French Governor of Austria, he acquired little popularity. He constantly emphasized that he cared little for ambassadorial concerns in their true sense and devoted most of his time to the far more important questions which came under his authority as high commissioner. In contrast to his colleagues on the Allied Council who, as far as I remember, handled affairs in their embassies, the French representative had set up a special office for business connected with his position as high commissioner. He generally stayed there when not in the Tirol or Vorarlberg. One almost got the impression that he considered these provinces, which made up the French zone, a bit like his own feudal fief.

Still, the French Ambassador was without doubt an intelligent diplomat who had long experience with the Soviet Union where he had been stationed before World War II. According to his account, he had composed the majority of the political reports which his chief, Ambassador Coulondre, had sent to the Quai d'Orsay from Moscow in 1936–38. In these reports Coulondre proceeded, as can be inferred from his memoirs, on the assumption that Stalin had long given up the idea of spreading communism and was only pursuing a national "Russian" goal. He believed, therefore, that the Soviet Union was essentially continuing the foreign policy of the tsars. Among other things, this false assumption led to the negotiations which France and Great Britain carried on with the Soviet Union shortly before the conclusion of the Hitler-Stalin pact in August 1939. The two Western governments hoped an agreement with the Soviet Union would prevent a German attack on Poland and with it the outbreak of a new world war. But Stalin had always preferred an agreement with Germany, and the Anglo-French approaches provided exactly the threat he needed to force Hitler to conclude it.

In the few but interesting conversations which I had with him, the French Ambassador admitted openly and honestly,

without ignoble regard for his prestige, that he had misjudged Soviet foreign policy before the war. That contributed not a little to my regard for him and his work.
The British High Commissioner, Geoffrey Wallinger, was
a distinguished man, tall and blond. During the years of his
stay in Vienna, he was a favorite in all circles. I had previously gotten to know him as a good and dependable friend.
The first time we met was in the late autumn of 1944 in
Chungking, the wartime capital of China, where he served as
counselor of embassy with the rank of minister and was the
first to give me an honest and realistic judgment of Chiang
Kai-shek's corrupt regime. I met Wallinger again in 1949 in
Budapest, where for a number of years we were both accredited at the same time as ministers, and finally for the
third time upon my transfer to Vienna.

The Allied Council's requirement that foreign ambassadors make an official visit before taking up their offices was
an unfortunate reminder that Austria did not yet possess full
sovereignty. This ceremony injured the feelings of many
Austrians, and the Austrian protocol chief wanted to find out
if an attempt to eliminate the audience would meet with
strong opposition from the council. After presenting my credentials to the president, I was urged to neither announce
my arrival to the Allied Council nor request an audience.
Any lack of a reaction to this would have provided a valuable precedent for Austria. Since the Western powers—with
the United States at the fore—had already begun to loosen
up the occupation regime for political reasons, it was considered possible that they might receive a step of this kind with
satisfaction. Although I personally would gladly have done
this service to show my sympathy and understanding for the
difficult situation of Austria, I did not consider it the business of a representative of Sweden to create a precedent, especially one likely to cause dissension among the occupation
powers. Thus, unfortunately, I had to refuse this proposal
and ask to be received by the Allied Council. This occurred at
its next meeting, at which the Soviet High Commissioner
presided.

The ceremony was simpler than anticipated and lasted

scarcely more than a quarter of an hour. It had been explained to me that it would consist of a short speech by the newly arrived ambassador and a short reply by the chairman. I also received ahead of time exact instructions as to how my speech should be formulated. After informing the council that I had presented my credentials to the Austrian President, I should—apparently the most important point—request the assistance and support of the council in my activity as minister in Austria. The chairman would thereupon assure me that I would always be able to count on this. After I had stood and listened to this comforting assurance, I was led around the oversized council table and introduced to the four high commissioners and their deputies, most of whom I knew already. With that the solemn and rather absurd ceremony was over. The formalities prescribed by protocol were fulfilled, and I could finally begin my real work.

But first, one fact which will perhaps surprise those who are unfamiliar with Austrian affairs. When I arrived in Vienna, Austria had no independent foreign ministry. To be sure an Office for Foreign Affairs was organized essentially along the same lines as corresponding offices in other countries, but it was merely a section of the chancellor's office and under his immediate control. Consequently, the chancellor was not only the head of the government but also the supreme and exclusive director of Austrian foreign policy. Nevertheless, Figl was acting as foreign minister in the coalition government at the time of my arrival in Vienna. He was section head of the Austrian Foreign Office under the chancellor and also a member of the government as minister without portfolio. Figl was unofficially called foreign minister and in practice exercised essentially the functions of one. Since, however, his "ministry" was merely a section of the chancellor's office, the latter found it easier to impose his will than would otherwise have been the case. This was especially true when the chancellor and foreign minister belonged to the same party.

This unique arrangement lasted until the change of government in 1959 when an independent foreign ministry was created only to be abolished again after the victory of the

People's Party in 1965. But the influence of the chancellor on foreign policy had already been limited to a certain extent in 1953 by an agreement between the two coalition parties: The office of state secretary in the foreign office was created and occupied by Bruno Kreisky, a representative of the Social Democrats.

The constitutional position of state secretaries in Austria is different from that of similar officials in most countries. They are not senior civil-servants as, for example, permanent undersecretaries in Britain, but belong to the government. They are entitled to take part in cabinet meetings but not to a vote. According to an unwritten law observed by all the coalition governments, state secretaries could not belong to the same party as their minister. Also, though in practice it was occasionally managed otherwise, the minister was supposed to consult with his state secretary. For his part, the state secretary was supposed to follow the work in his ministry closely and inform his own party leadership as well as party friends inside the government.

The influence which a state secretary actually exercised depended, above all, on his personal authority within and outside his own party and, further, on his knowledge of the work of his ministry, his cleverness, and similar factors. As far as Kreisky was concerned, I was soon able to establish that his influence behind the scenes on Austrian foreign policy was significant and increased from year to year. Too, when he took over the post of state secretary, a special understanding—apart from the coalition agreement—had been reached between the Social Democrats and the People's Party that decisions on important foreign policy questions should be made only after consultation between the chancellor and the foreign minister on the one hand and the vice-chancellor and state secretary on the other.

In the years 1954–55, so eventful for the future of Austria, four members of the government were responsible for foreign policy. We have already met the chancellor and the foreign minister; Adolf Schärf, the vice-chancellor at the time, and State Secretary Bruno Kreisky were the other two. The former began his career as a lawyer. In his youth he joined the

Social Democrats and for many years acted as secretary in their faction in Parliament. When the party arose again after the defeat of Germany in 1945, he made a substantial contribution to its organization and took his place in the government as one of its representatives. Shortly afterwards he became head of the party. From then until his election as President of the Republic in 1957, after Körner's death, he belonged to all governments. His good judgment, composed appearance, moderation, and unquestionable personal integrity quickly created for him a strong position which he maintained as head of state. As a result, he was elected to the highest office of the Republic for the second time in 1963.

I got to know Bruno Kreisky in 1953. We met for the first time in Stockholm, as far as I can remember in the "Great Society," a men's club, where we had a long and interesting political conversation. He was at that time scarcely over forty and already had a varied career behind him. It was good preparation for his rapid promotion after the end of the war up to his present influential position as leader of the Socialist Party. In the thirties, Kreisky already stood out as a leader of the youth groups of the Social Democrats. That brought him severe persecution, first from the Schuschnigg government and later, after the *Anschluss* with Germany, from the Nazis. Arrested because of his political activity in Austria, he fled to Sweden after his release in 1938. He spent twelve years there and learned Swedish, both spoken and written. Few foreigners with whom I have come into contact have such a thorough knowledge of our language. We always carried on our countless conversations in Swedish.

Before and during the war, Kreisky was active in the Swedish co-operative movement. When Austria again acquired limited independence and received permission to renew certain diplomatic connections, he was named secretary of the Austrian Legation in Stockholm. He remained there till the end of 1950 and was then called back to the foreign ministry. When Körner was elected president shortly thereafter, he made Kreisky deputy chief of his secretariat with primary responsibility in foreign affairs. In this capacity he undoubtedly influenced appreciably the speeches in which Körner as head of state emphasized how important a neutral policy was for Austria.

My many long conversations with Bruno Kreisky in the course of eleven years demonstrated that, in contrast to many earlier Austrian leaders, he always had a clear and logical comprehension, thought out to its last detail, of the foreign policy which Austria must pursue in order to maintain its independence, look after its vital interests, and strengthen its international position. Kreisky's long stay in Sweden had greatly influenced his development and marked his way of thinking. His positive attitude toward neutrality and his conviction that an alliance-free policy was the only possibility for a country in the geographical position of Austria undoubtedly had their origin in his experiences and observations in Sweden. There he had become convinced that it is possible for a small country to enjoy general respect if it carries on a free and independent policy toward all groups of great powers. Consequently, in contrast to Austrian politicians between the two world wars, he never considered Austria a "second German state," as the expression ran at the time. He believed his country should follow an exclusively Austrian policy and not proceed axiomatically from the position that its interests always coincided with those of Germany.

He was, of course, not the only one who advocated this position. It was shared by many, but not all, Austrian politicians who had acquired a place of leadership after World War II. It meant much for Austria that its foreign policy was directed during the two eventful and decisive years before the signing of the State Treaty by such individuals as Raab, Figl, and Schärf who considered an independent Austrian foreign policy a necessity. They considered themselves more Austrians than "Europeans," to use a modern and ambiguous slogan.

In spite of great differences between the two coalition parties on domestic questions, in the field of foreign policy, general accord prevailed. Unanimity was easily achieved, since there was really only one question of importance at the time: How could Austria win back its complete independence or, in other words, how could the occupation forces be induced to leave the country? Clearly from a legal point of view this presupposed the conclusion of a state treaty between the four occupation powers and Austria.

What, then, did the State Treaty mean and why was that expression chosen to designate the agreement which would end the occupation and regulate the relations between Austria and the four victorious powers? After the collapse of Germany, the government in Vienna maintained that the so-called *Anschluss* had been simply a German annexation. Austria had not existed—so it was argued—as an independent state during World War II. Therefore, it could neither be considered a belligerent during the war nor a defeated state after the war. Consequently, the agreement which was to end the new, the allied occupation could not be called a peace treaty.

Whatever interpretation one might have of this question, one had to recognize that a treaty was necessary in order to decide the multitude of questions connected with the reestablishment of Austrian independence. To those belonged the demands of Yugoslavia, supported in the beginning by the Soviet Union, for a large part of Carinthia, the Soviet demand for so-called German property as reparation for war damages, the joint demand of the allied powers for limitations on rearmament, the surrender of war criminals, and other such matters. Gradually it was accepted that the agreement settling these and similar questions should be called a "State Treaty." It was to be concluded between Austria on the one side and the four occupation powers on the other. Other former belligerent states who wanted to look after their interests were to have the right to adhere to the treaty later.

When I arrived in Vienna in March 1954, the situation appeared darker than ever before. But little more than a year later it had changed completely. The Soviet Union, which had long tried to delay the conclusion of the State Treaty and, above all, had opposed the withdrawal of its occupation troops, showed unexpected interest in bringing about an agreement in the immediate future. Few events in the post-

World War II era have produced so many myths, so much unreal speculation, as this apparently inexplicable change of attitude. Conclusion of the Austrian State Treaty contributed much to a misunderstanding of the nature and goals of Soviet policy and led to many unfounded hopes that it was to be revised. Fourteen years have passed since the State Treaty took effect, and not a few of those misinterpretations still circulate. It seems, therefore, that the time has come to examine and analyze more closely the factors on which a restoration of Austrian sovereignty depended. And the developments which led to this event are especially suited for illuminating the general aims of Soviet policies. This investigation rests partly on my own experiences and observations in the years 1954–55, and the conclusions I could draw from them, and partly on other evidence that I could evaluate but may not cite.

My description of causes and events will naturally need correction on many points if the records should ever be opened and previously unknown material made public. Still, on the basis of present knowledge it can be assumed that the favorable course of the negotiations which were initiated in the spring of 1955 and concluded with the signing of the State Treaty must be attributed more to the important change of the strategy and tactics of the Soviet Union in the field of foreign policy which took place at the same time than to influence by official or private persons or to their personal ability to convince the Soviet rulers that it was in their own interest to get rid of the Austrian question. Seldom have I heard from so many and such surprising quarters the assertion that if the Soviet Union was easier to come to terms with in the last phase of negotiations, the main reason lay in the personal connection of one or another politician, diplomat, or scientist with the leading men in Moscow or in some special ability to charm them, to instill trust in them, or to win their good will. Such myths may fulfill a purpose in the political propaganda of the day, but for historical purposes they are worthless.

What had happened was that the Communist world movement led by Moscow had, in order to facilitate its further expansion, embarked on a new course in the area of foreign affairs which gradually assumed a definite form in the years 1954–55. As we shall see later, this was the most important reason for the seemingly inexplicable volte-face in the spring of 1955 and the sudden readiness of the Soviet Union to restore the independence of Austria. Western statesmen and diplomats had no opportunity to influence this development. In order to explain the connection, one must, however, analyze not only the nature and aims of Soviet foreign policy but also survey its development from the end of World War II to Khrushchev's assumption of power. Only thus can we understand the new course. In so doing, the first question which should be asked is: Does the Soviet Union carry on a foreign policy at all in the usual sense of the term?

4

Does the Soviet Union
Have a Foreign Policy?

When, to Lenin's own surprise, the Bolsheviks seized power in Russia in 1917, their leaders were divided on many issues but united on one point, that the revolution could not survive for long in an underdeveloped, predominantly agricultural country like Russia if similar upheavals did not take place in neighboring, industrially developed countries with strong working-class movements, above all in Germany. Lenin believed that neighboring capitalist states would not tolerate the existence of an isolated Communist country for any length of time. In order to withstand a military attack, Soviet Russia needed the support of other Communist states, strong both militarily and economically. World imperialism, Lenin stressed, cannot live side by side with a successful revolution. A struggle for life or death is unavoidable. It must end sooner or later with the complete victory of one side or the other.

Lenin thought the October Revolution, like a burning spark, would ignite similar revolutions throughout Europe. The October Revolution would only be the first of a series of revolutions in Europe and later in the rest of the world which would organize the working classes under Communist leadership. This hope proved premature, and even Lenin realized before his end that the revolution would proceed at a slower tempo than he had at first imagined; at the end of World War I, however, the Bolsheviks considered the prospects for the further spread of revolution in Europe overwhelmingly favorable. And events appeared to corroborate this interpretation to a certain extent. After the fall of the Central Powers, revolutionary movements led by Communists made some progress in several countries, especially Germany and Hungary. But the situation soon changed. After greater or lesser successes in the first phase from 1918 to 1920, these revolutionary movements failed without exception.

Several years later, however, a new "revolutionary situation" arose in Germany as a result of the Ruhr crisis and the rampant inflation which it precipitated. Still, in the beginning, opinion in the Politburo appeared to be divided. While some members eagerly advocated intervention if necessary to ensure the success of the expected revolution, others opposed any attempt to seize power. Probably they wanted to avoid entangling the Soviet Union in operations which, on account of military and economic weakness, could lead to the fall of the first and only Communist state. But when the "revolutionary situation" in Germany became more acute in the fall of 1923 and the prospects for success appeared favorable, the Politburo agreed to let the development run its course and give active support.

The attempt came to nothing, however. The revolution was obviously premature and was suppressed so quickly and effectively that the question of Soviet support never actually had to be decided. The rulers in the Kremlin lost faith in the prospects for armed uprisings in Europe in the near future. As public remarks revealed, they reluctantly admitted that the revolutionary tidal wave had passed its peak and was in the process of ebbing slowly but surely. According to Communist terminology, capitalism in Europe had succeeded in establishing a "temporary stability." And when Chiang Kai-shek turned on and almost destroyed the Chinese Communists in 1927, Stalin apparently perceived that the basis for Communist successes in Europe or in Asia would not exist for a long time. During the world economic crisis which broke out in 1929, he could, it is true, have reckoned anew with the possibility of an imminent revolution in Germany, to judge by the memoirs of Margarete Buber-Neumann, a former German Communist, but after 1930 even this hope appears to have been abandoned.

This development led to a thorough examination of the future policies of the Soviet Communist Party. On the one hand, Lenin's hopes for a series of Communist revolutions in Europe had not been realized. Contrary to all expectations, the workers had not only rejected attempts at revolutionary upheaval but had joined the Social Democrats in increasing numbers. On the other hand, events had also disproved the thesis that the revolution in Russia was doomed to certain failure if communism did not succeed in a highly industrialized state. Impressed as much by this as by the serious defeats of 1923 in Germany and 1927 in China, Stalin recognized the necessity of correcting the tactics of the Party and formulated his doctrine of "socialism in one country" which was to be so significant for future Communist policy.

One cannot go into the divergence of views between Trotsky and Stalin concerning this fundamental question in this brief summary. I only want to emphasize that the thesis of the "development of socialism in a single country," contrary to the idea in middle-class circles of the time, in no way meant the renunciation by Stalin of the gradual spread of communism according to Lenin's plan. The triumph of the revolution was only postponed. As Stalin himself stressed in his *Problems of Leninism,* the victory of communism in one country could by no means be considered an end in itself or a final goal. It was rather an indispensable prerequisite for the later victory of the revolution in other lands. The doctrine of "socialism in one country" was, therefore, essentially an ideological paraphrase of Stalin's plan for industrializing the Soviet Union. As its main task, this plan would outline the necessary economic and military foundations needed to take up again, at the right time, the spread of communism, which is inevitable according to Lenin's theory. The vast economic possibilities of Russia were to be completely utilized; a great Communist power could then lead the fight for world revolution much more effectively than the backward, agrarian Russia of 1917.

This was the deeper meaning of Stalin's policy, and he did not try to keep it a secret in his writings. Since, however, very few leading statesmen in a Europe controlled by the middle class had read these publications or had taken them seriously between the wars, Stalin's thesis of "socialism in one country" was misinterpreted as evidence that the revolutionary plans of Lenin had been abandoned. Immediately before and after World War II, the foreign policies of Great Britain and France were based at least partly on this misconception, and it dominated the foreign policy of Roosevelt to an even greater extent. But at the end of World War II, the Soviet Union disappointed the expectations of the Anglo-Saxon powers for close and trusting cooperation and, to their painful surprise, ruthlessly installed Communist regimes in the countries occupied by the Red Army.

The doctrine of "socialism in one country" aimed primarily at changing the Soviet Union into a base for the future extension of the revolution to other countries. Logically viewed, this thesis had the corollary that strengthening the political, economic, and military power of the Soviet Union should be the common goal of all Communist parties; for the prospects of the success of the revolution in other countries rose in proportion to the realization of this goal. Conversely, if the international situation of the Soviet Union should be weakened, the hope for revolutionary upheavals would necessarily sink accordingly.

In the eyes of all "true" Communist parties, the doctrine of "socialism in one country" gradually led to the complete equating of world revolutionary aims with Russian national interests. This in turn contributed to establishing even more firmly in the West the fateful misunderstanding of Soviet goals, above all, the fanciful notion that the Soviet Union, while retaining its Communist façade, was slowly evolving into a traditional state. It was generally assumed in the last phase of the war and the immediate postwar years that Stalin had returned to the imperialist policies which Russia had followed under the tsars. A vast difference exists, however, between the imperialism of the tsars and Soviet imperialism. The former sought moderate territorial expansion in Europe and Asia. Its objects were limited and, as it were, local. Communist imperialism, on the contrary, is ideological and international in its innermost nature. Its objectives are unlimited and global. Its goal is, therefore, not territorial expansion in itself; rather it wants to force on all other countries its own ideology as well as the social order which was introduced in Russia after 1917.

If this is still the case, the explanation should be sought less in fanatic devotion of the leaders to the Communist ideology than in the realization that the organization of society which has been developed in the Soviet Union through the course of the years is the most efficient instrument not only for the maintenance of the power of the party in each country in which it has been established but also for the future expansion of the Communist movement in the world.

If, as frequently happens today, one asks whether Soviet policy follows world-revolutionary or national goals, the answer is that posing this question is, in itself, false and unrealistic. Both goals coincide. As Stalin rightly assumed, the continued spread of communism presupposes that the political, economic, and military power of the Soviet Union is not only maintained but strengthened. Without the overwhelming strength which a great power has at its disposal, the revolutionary movement would quickly disintegrate and with it hope for the world revolution. This is true for Europe and probably for most non-European countries, too. "Without the Soviet Union," Mao Tse Tung said at the congress of the Communist parties in Moscow in 1957, "we would all have been conquered by other countries" (*Neues Deutschland,* November 30, 1957). In a way he was right. Therefore, one can consider the Soviet state the necessary economic and military base for the Communist world movement. It is an indispensable prerequisite for realizing the final goals of this movement, that is, establishing a world Communist social order after the pattern of the Soviet Union.

At the same time, however, the U.S.S.R. has its established borders and special problems just as other countries. But even when it must assert its national demands, it does so not so much in the interest of the Russian state but rather in the common interest of all Communist parties. Russian national goals, in other words, are important insofar as they advance the world revolutionary movement. At least one goal of this movement, preservation of the Soviet regime, possesses unquestionable precedence over the interests of the Russian state in case a difference should arise between them. This does not mean that every revolutionary movement should be supported indiscriminately at the expense of Russian national interests. Rewards and risks are constantly being weighed against each other. This is especially the case when Soviet power or the survival of the regime could be endangered by rash or premature measures in support of revolutionary attempts. In this type of situation, Soviet national interests have often taken precedence over the revolutionary plans of other Communist parties. How to weigh national interests against revolutionary interests is strictly a question of tactical judgment. As the current Russian-Chinese conflict shows, opinions differ greatly on just this question and can lead to serious "contradictions" within the world Communist movement.

A few concrete examples may clearly illustrate all this: Although a revolutionary tidal wave seemed to be flowing over Germany in 1923, several members of the Politburo considered the prospects for a successful revolution too slight to justify Soviet support and the risk of military engagement which in turn could lead to the fall of the Soviet regime. Only when prospects appeared much more favorable was it agreed that certain preparations should be made in order to intervene militarily if necessary. Even though Germany was thought to be decisive for the victory of the revolution in Europe, the risk to the Bolshevik regime was carefully weighed. Similarly, as Hitler prepared for an attack on the Soviet Union in the spring of 1941, Stalin would doubtlessly have made great concessions at the cost of the Russian state in order to avoid a war with Germany which could endanger his own power.

Often, however, world revolutionary objectives seem to coincide with Russian national interests. It appears obvious that the Soviet state, with regard for its own position of power, should desire a politically and militarily weak Germany. And, indeed, the Soviet Union has attempted to prevent the establishment of a West German state, the rearmament of the Federal Republic of Germany, and the reunification of Germany.

The leaders in the Kremlin have a much more valid reason for this policy, however, when they consider the situation from the perspective of the world Communist movement. Viewed from this position, the Soviet occupation of East Germany preserves a necessary base for a future Communist regime over the whole of Germany. Even if the plans for this suffered a temporary postponement after the entry of West Germany into N.A.T.O. and at the moment exist only as a long-distance goal, Soviet consent to the reunification of Germany on a democratic basis, that is, with free elections, would mean abandoning an established Communist regime. A territory which was politically, militarily, and economically already absorbed into the socialist camp would receive permission to leave this camp. The Soviet Union would not have advanced its strategic goal—communizing Germany and thereby Europe—in this way, but would rather have contributed to the retreat of communism. Only a militarily weak Soviet state or one divided and torn by internal strife could be expected to make such a drastic concession.

On the other hand, if the Soviet Union were following a national Russian policy, German reunification on a democratic basis would not be so unpalatable. Indeed, it might be to the ultimate advantage of Russia: Just as Italy inevitably became a member of anti-Austrian combinations before World War I, so must West Germany remain anti-Russian as long as its *irredenta* is maintained as such by Soviet bayonets. The prerequisite for reunification would be a compromise which took into consideration legitimate Russian security or power interests, whatever one wants to call them. But when a state sets its main goal as Communist expansion over all of Europe, then it cannot consider such a settlement. The Western powers finally realized this in the fifties when the Soviet Union categorically rejected their proposals concerning reunification. In my opinion, they had mistakenly assumed that Soviet opposition to the reunification of Germany by means of free elections—that is, to the surrender of the Soviet zone —was dictated primarily by concern for the security of the

U.S.S.R. To be sure, Communist tactics by no means fundamentally refuse compromise, rather the contrary, but only when such compromises advance the strategic or tactical objective of those in command. The Western powers could not make such a compromise in the German question for obvious reasons.

In considering the foreign policy of the Soviet Union, one must further distinguish carefully between the attitude toward capitalist states and Communist states. The latter, as members of the same bloc, assume a special position as their relations to one another are controlled formally and actually on a Party basis. Even though now and then Soviet ambassadors are presumably used as mediators, important affairs of this kind are arranged by the secretariat of the central committee which has a department for relations with other Communist states—that is, with "ruling" parties—and one for relations with Communist parties in capitalist lands, the "non-ruling" parties.

The Soviet-Chinese conflict has been arbitrated mainly on a Party level. And the conflict between Stalin and Tito in 1948 was never considered an argument between the U.S.S.R. and Yugoslavia. As Djilas stressed in a tract published shortly after the conflict became known, it concerned, above all, the relations between the Soviet and the Yugoslav parties. After Stalin's death when negotiations began for the purpose of bringing about a settlement, these took place within the Party leadership, though from the beginning the intention was to conceal this circumstance from the Western powers.

At a reception for Khrushchev and Bulganin at the airport in Belgrade in May 1955, Tito showed obvious annoyance at a speech which Khrushchev made there. The reason for this was not, however, as many Western diplomats and journalists assumed, Khrushchev's attempt to blame the already executed Beria, which Tito would have considered a completely ridiculous effort to relieve the Soviet state and Party leadership of responsibility for the break. Actually, Khrushchev spoke of Beria "along with others," by which he meant, above all, Stalin and Molotov, a fact Tito undoubtedly understood.

According to a reliable Yugoslav source, what irritated Tito was not so much that these three were designated as the chief offenders, probably with complete justification, but that Khrushchev, by an indiscreet remark in his speech, had prematurely revealed the intention to carry on the approaching negotiations on a party level. They would necessarily assume a completely different and more important character than if they were merely a normalizing of the external relations between states. Tito, however, had little cause for worry; the significance of this remark seems to have escaped most Western observers. That the negotiations were carried on at the Party level and that the Soviet Party had assumed the initiative was later acknowledged by Khrushchev himself in a speech in Sofia on June 3, 1958.

Further discussion of the relations between "socialist" parties and states in which state organizations are only an executive organ of the Party would be beyond the scope of this book. The nature of these relations stands out most clearly if one thinks of them as "internal relations" of the "socialist camp." This is still essentially true in the case of the conflict between the Soviet Union and China which Mrs. Margareta Buber-Neumann has pertinently characterized as "a global struggle between two Communist fractions" (ein Fraktionskampf im Weltmasstab). When the expression "foreign policy of the Soviet Union" is used in everyday conversation, the policy of that country toward capitalist states is usually meant. One forgets—perhaps rightly—the dealings between the Soviet Union and other Communist parties and states.

How should the relations of the Soviet Union with capitalist states be viewed? The answer can be summed up briefly as follows: As masters of the Soviet state, the rulers in the Kremlin also formulated the policies of the Communist world movement—at least until the break with China. It is therefore misleading to designate the relations of the Soviet Union with capitalist states as foreign relations in the usual sense. Though they may be ever so meaningful, they are nevertheless only one aspect of the strategy and tactics of the world Communist movement and must constantly be attuned to it. It is, therefore, scarcely correct to speak of a foreign policy of the U.S.S.R. in the true sense. What has usually been designated as such is really the foreign policy of the "socialist camp" under the leadership of the Soviet Union. But even if this leadership is no longer undisputed, all Communist countries—China as well as the Soviet Union—pursue the same long-range goal. Their objective is still unlimited: to introduce by peaceful or violent means the Communist ideology in the whole world and to establish, with a few local variations, the social and economic order which has developed in the Soviet Union. Disputes between Communist countries, on the other hand, although sometimes harsh and spiteful, are mostly about strategic or tactical problems, the most appropriate and efficient means of achieving the common goal. In the case of China and the Soviet Union, however, the question is not only which tactics are the most appropriate in the present stage of the development of the Communist movement but also under whose leadership the expansion of the movement shall be carried out.

This special character of Soviet foreign policy has always been strongly emphasized in official Communist sources. Thus, the *Great Soviet Encyclopedia* says, among other things, that "the October Revolution created a new type of state—the socialist Soviet state—and by so doing laid the foundation for a foreign policy which differs fundamentally from that of all other countries" whether of the past or the present. "The foreign policy of the Soviet Union," the author continues, "is a socialist foreign policy. The principles which the Party follows in questions of foreign policy form an organic part of the program of the Party, its strategy and tactics."

This definition is still valid. In an important article of August 8, 1965, *Pravda* summed up the characteristic features of Soviet foreign policy in more or less the same way. The aim and direction of this policy is determined, *Pravda* stressed, by the socialist character of the social order, by the leading position of the Communist Party, by the fidelity of the Party to the principles of Marxism-Leninism, and finally by the proletarian internationalism. The functions of the Soviet state in the foreign policy field as well as all concrete actions it undertakes in the world policy, the newspaper concluded, are permeated by these principles. Finally, in a speech of August 23, 1966, Kosygin pointed out that the foreign policy of the Soviet Union associates its national with its international interests.

But if the relations of the Soviet Union with the capitalist states, as earlier mentioned, are mainly one aspect of the strategy and tactics of the world Communist movement, there is every reason to ask what then can be understood by strategy and tactics? Stalin made a sharper distinction than Lenin between these two concepts. According to Stalin's explanation, strategy should determine the general direction and the essential purpose of an attack on the capitalist social order at a certain stage of development. At each revolutionary stage strategy is determined once and for all. It is quite different in the case of tactics. These must be flexible and depend upon a constant review of the relative strength of Communist and non-Communist states. Also, they should take advantage of any tendency towards weakening or relaxation within the capitalist bloc.

As Stalin expressed it, tactics should conform to the "flood or ebbtide" of the revolutionary movement, that is, they should be modified according to the increasing or diminishing strength of this movement. What he meant is that tactics must be examined over and over again and, for longer or shorter periods, be modified according to changes in the "revolutionary situation." Bold tactics may prove useful in certain situations, in particular, if the resistance of the capitalist countries is weak, and more cautious tactics in other situations when the resistance is expected to be stronger. Thus, Soviet foreign policy has alternately displayed a tendency toward aggressiveness and an apparent relaxation of tensions, a seeming willingness to work together with capitalist states. The change from aggressiveness to *détente* has usually followed a realization that the former could no longer lead to the desired results or that the Soviet Union for one reason or another needed a respite in order to consolidate its position or prepare for new offensive action. When an aggressive policy has exhausted its possibilities, the primary importance has been transferred from aggressiveness to *détente*. Only when one analyzes Soviet foreign policy from this standpoint can one grasp the real meaning of many unexpected actions and understand the surprising and sudden fluctuations in long- or short-range tactics. The much spoken of "enigmas" of Soviet foreign policy stem from changing judgments of the general political situation by the rulers in Moscow. These enigmas are the expressions of and arise as a result of the constant reappraisals in the Kremlin of the balance of forces between the two camps. It is, therefore, hardly surprising that the repercussions on Soviet foreign policy of these reappraisals should seem enigmatic to those who believe that this policy is conditioned only by the safeguarding of the interest of the Russian state.

At this point, we must recall that the Soviet Union, while safeguarding its national interests, still pursues its permanent, unaltered revolutionary goals.

As a consequence, when phases characterized by a more or less pronounced tendency toward relaxation have followed fundamentally aggressive phases, these *détentes* have never, neither under Stalin nor later, developed into a Soviet readiness to give up political or military positions necessary for the future expansion of the Communist movement. The one seeming exception, the Soviet agreement to release Austria, was based on the assumption that in the long run it would strengthen the world Communist movement. The easing of tension has, therefore, never—as often believed in the West —aimed at the removal of real differences between the Soviet Union and capitalist states. Instead it can be characterized as an attempt to improve relations with capitalist states, for a shorter or a longer time, without significant material sacrifice with a view to weakening the opposition to Soviet demands or gaining time for a necessary consolidation at home or abroad. The immediate aim of the policy of relaxation, more seeming than actual, has mainly been to influence Western public opinion in the directions desired by the Kremlin. When properly guided, public opinion abroad, so it is assumed in Moscow, will make leading statesmen in capitalist countries more inclined toward Soviet solutions.

Since these relaxations of a tactical nature have frequently led to surprisingly favorable results and have occasionally succeeded almost completely, it is no wonder that the Soviet regime has used this ploy over and over. There have almost always been influential circles and individuals in the West who did not understand the real aims. Rather, they have considered these changes "something new," "a change of position of Soviet foreign policy, long awaited but sooner or later inevitable," or, finally, the result "of a gradually unavoidable reexamination of doctrines which are impractical in actual use."

What is the meaning of strategy and tactics in modern times? According to Marxist-Leninist interpretation, the end of World War II ushered in a new strategic era—the world revolutionary—which will end with the victory of the revolution in the whole world. As a result of the war, a Communist social and economic order as well as ideology was forced upon Eastern Europe and later, in 1949 by a victorious civil war, upon China. In this way new Communist states have emerged. "Socialism" has, thus, extended itself from a single state to a number of states, a "socialist camp" has been formed and the former "capitalist encirclement" has been conclusively broken even though this was not officially admitted until the beginning of 1955 in Molotov's speech of February 8. The formation of the "socialist camp," the rise of the Soviet Union as a Communist world-power, and the simultaneous disintegration of the colonial system created in the opinion of the rulers in the Kremlin more favorable conditions for the spread of communism over the whole world. A more pronounced offensive policy, compared with prewar times, could now be initiated. However, as this policy had to be carried out mainly by "peaceful" means, a still greater importance was attached to strategy and tactics in the coming struggle for the expansion of the Communist movement. This development influenced, at the same time, the meaning of strategy and tactics.

If we ask how these two concepts should be defined and what functions they have to fulfill in the present time, a work of official character, *The Foundations of Marxism-Len-*

inism (Moscow, 1959, 1962), provides a certain guidance. From this work, which with some justification could be called the Bible of contemporary communism, it is clear that the meaning of strategy and tactics can now be explained in the most simple way if we assume that strategy deals with long-range planning and tactics with short-range planning.

From what has now been said, it follows logically that the achievement of one or several tactical objectives constitutes by itself a necessary prerequisite for the attainment of a long-range strategic goal sometime in the future. In other words, the main task of political actions of a tactical nature undertaken by the rulers in the Kremlin is to create, step by step, more favorable conditions for the gradual realization of their long-range strategic objectives. If strategy indicates the general goal, tactics could, consequently, also be defined as the means utilized to achieve this goal. This rule applies to the foreign policy of the "socialist camp" as well as to the internal planning for the conquest of power within each country.

With this explanation the meaning and practical application of strategy and tactics in modern Communist foreign policy is, however, far from exhausted. First of all, I want to stress that the distinction between goals and means is not only of theoretical signification. My experience from a long and close observation of how Soviet foreign policy works has time and again confirmed that the rulers in the Kremlin attach a particular and real importance to this distinction in their practical policy, whereas Western politicians and diplomats, on the other hand, are too often inclined to confuse these two concepts.

Now it is evident that the attainment of a strategic goal in a near or distant future can as a rule only be carried out in successive stages of shorter or longer duration. As a consequence, each stage or even each important political action in a long chain of development has, so to speak, its own strategic goal whose attainment constitutes, at the same time, a necessary prerequisite or means for the achievement of the strategic goal laid down for the next stage. In other words, every long- or short-range political action has simultaneously a strategic and a tactical aspect. Every action can, consequently, be characterized as partially strategic and partially tactical. Only the final stage in the long chain of development—the world revolution—is purely strategic in its character. On the other hand, only the first stage in the same chain —propaganda or attempts to influence certain individuals or groups of people, or whatever it may be—is purely tactical in its nature.

If we, in order to explain and illustrate further what has now been said, assume—and this assumption is in the case before us undoubtedly strongly motivated—that the strategic (that is the long-range) goal of the Soviet Union in Europe for the near or distant future is the incorporation of Western Germany in the "socialist camp," such an objective can certainly be reached only by stages. Its attainment supposes, among other things, the withdrawal of American troops from Germany, the disintegration or at least the weakening of N.A.T.O., and the political isolation and if possible neutralization of the Federal Republic. All these actions are different tactical means to be employed according to circumstances with a view to creating the necessary conditions for the achievement of the strategic goal: the incorporation of the Federal Republic sooner or later in the "socialist camp." At the same time, the political actions enumerated, as well as many others not mentioned, must be considered strategic objectives insofar as they, in their turn, presuppose the employment of other tactical means for their attainment.

The rulers in the Kremlin have in the past years resorted to different peaceful means in order to bring about the disintegration of N.A.T.O. or at least the weakening of this organization. The most promising has undoubtedly been the so-called Rapacki plan, which Poland by direction from Moscow or, in any case, in the interest of the whole world Communist movement has, in different versions, submitted for the consideration of the Western powers. Other suggestions recently made with the same purpose in mind have been the creation of atom-free zones and agreements on the mutual thinning out of the military forces of the two groups on both sides of the demarcation line in Germany or in other parts of Europe.

The tactical means to which at present the greatest expectation is attached are certainly the different proposals for the conclusion of a so-called European security pact, submitted to the Western powers from 1954 until recently. The drafts prepared by the Soviet government have, of course, nothing whatsoever to do with security in its traditional sense. The three first-mentioned proposals have not openly aimed at the destruction of N.A.T.O. Even if this is true they have, nevertheless, been drafted with a view to weakening this organization, particularly as they are destined to eliminate the Federal Republic as a first-rate political and military power.

The European security pacts, on the other hand, have been drafted with the declared purpose of dissolving N.A.T.O. It is true that the so-called Warsaw pact should, in such case, meet the same fate. This concession is, however, of scant importance—if of any. A close military collaboration between the Soviet Union and the Communist countries in Eastern Europe had been established a long time before the signature of the pact and can easily be continued in the same way after its formal dissolution.

The proposals previously mentioned have one characteristic feature in common. They are not ends in themselves. They have been produced in turns to serve as different tactical means for the achievement of the same strategic goal. Should the Soviet Union by exploiting such new diplomatic methods ever succeed in achieving its objectives, the disintegration of N.A.T.O. or the withdrawal of the United States from Europe, this strategic success will in turn serve as a tactical means for the attainment of a new strategic objective, and so forth, until the incorporation of the Federal Republic in the "socialist camp" can no longer be prevented.

If we continue to use the problem of European security for further illustration of Soviet strategic and tactical methods in foreign policy, it is evident that the rulers in the Kremlin can expect neither the summoning of a conference nor the conclusion of a pact with this object in view without the collaboration of the main capitalist countries. This seems a rather hopeless task as the pact, to judge by the Soviet drafts, is clearly intended to destroy the unity of the Western powers in order to weaken their position of strength as well as their future power of resistance. What the Soviet proposals amount to is, in other words, to invite the main capitalist countries to contribute to a result destined to hasten their own final destruction. Long experience has, however, taught the rulers in the Kremlin that the solution of this problem—difficult as it may seem—is far from impossible. Various particularly suitable tactical means have been employed to this end either separately or in combination.

It is in this connection that the previously analyzed, regularly recurrent peace offensives and other political actions for the "relaxation of tensions" must be seen. They belong to the most important tactical means intended to facilitate the seemingly impossible task of persuading governments, politicians, or public opinion in the Western world to act against their own interest. To achieve such a result it is, first of all, necessary to convince the Western world that the Soviet Union has definitely given up its aggressive aims and abandoned every thought of spreading communism in the world. The politicians, the press, and the public opinion must somehow or other be assured that, whatever their opinion about the internal situation, Soviet foreign policy has changed or is at least on the point of changing. If not yet, it will soon be more or less similar to the policy of any other democratic country. The conclusion influential personalities or groups of people are supposed to draw from such arguments is that alliances between the Western powers or other defensive measures adopted in order to prevent, if necessary by force, previously dreaded Soviet encroachments are no longer justified. If they do not answer their purpose anymore, they can safely be abandoned or at least softened up.

Aided by a continuous, skillful propaganda from fellow-travelers, by ignorant and easily influenced intellectuals, or by other people not aware of the real aims of Soviet foreign policy and the working of its strategic and tactical conceptions, the rulers of the Kremlin hope to be able to induce, as time passes, more and more important personalities of political, religious, industrial, or intellectual circles in the Western world to adopt the views they wish them to entertain. In such a way, an appropriate atmosphere in favor of—let us say—the conclusion of a European security pact will gradually be created. The next step is to provoke, with the assistance of sympathizers in as many countries as possible, an apparently general demand for the convocation of a conference on the European security problem. This demand must slowly be worked up to such strength that the conclusion of a pact on this subject will soon be considered by many governments almost as a moral obligation or at least as a problem of such importance for future peaceful relations between East and West, that the question of adherence to the pact can no longer be disregarded by any political party or government really aware of its "responsibility to humanity." It goes without saying that this analysis is only meant to illustrate the general pattern of Soviet strategy and tactics. The adherence of the capitalist powers to a European security pact can also be achieved by many other means. The same is true of the destruction of N.A.T.O. or the withdrawal of American troops from Europe which can also be attained by other "peaceful" means than the conclusion of a European security pact or the adoption of one or the other version of the Rapacki plan. The utilization of de Gaulle's idiosyncrasies and the tacit encouragement by appropriate and apparent Soviet concessions of his idea of a Europe from the Atlantic to the Urals is as valuable an instrument for achievement of the strategic goal just mentioned. The same would be true of attempts to support the organization of a public opinion inside the United States in favor of the abandonment of Europe to its fate.

It is always by a combination, according to circumstances, of several tactical moves that the "objective conditions" for a strategic success—to use Communist terminology—will slowly be created.

Heavy demands are made, however, upon the Communist leadership in charge of the application of the Party's strategy and tactics. One of their most important tasks is, as already pointed out by Lenin, to discover the weakest link in the chain when faced with a difficult tactical operation. When preparations were made during World War I for the overthrow of the government in Russia, Lenin, as mentioned in *The Foundations of Marxism-Leninism,* soon became convinced of the necessity to make use of the war weariness of the Russian population, whose intense longing for peace, as Lenin rightly assumed, was the weakest link of the chain in the then prevailing situation.

At the present time, the rulers of the Kremlin have, as clearly appears from the same book, attempted to take advantage of the strong fear of an atomic war in most countries. The struggle for peace in order to avoid such a war is now considered, in leading Communist circles, the weakest link. The purpose of the propaganda against an atomic war as well as of other similar campaigns is to instill in the populations in Western countries, as deeply as possible, the conviction that the leaders in the Kremlin are the only rulers animated by a sincere desire for peace. From this step, it is not far to believing that the only salvation from the horrors of an atomic war is always to support Soviet foreign policy whatever its aims may be.

We have now, in broad lines, summarized the strategic and tactical principles generally applied in revolutionary foreign policy. Its methods are essentially different from those used by traditional diplomacy. Traditional diplomacy has always attempted to solve its problems by negotiations, entered into with the tacit understanding of the partners sooner or later to reach a compromise by a mutual give and take. The main object of the negotiations has consequently been to obtain a result more or less satisfactory from the point of view of the interests of the negotiating partners.

Revolutionary foreign policy usually acts in a quite different way. It attempts to achieve the result it has set itself not by negotiations in the traditional sense, but by a combination of strategic and tactical stratagems carried out during a succession of years on the basis of a previously laid long-range plan. This rather complicated maneuvering is designed to put the adversary, step by step, in a position in which he has to give in, contrary to his better judgment, or preferably without even realizing either the real purpose of the demands made or the consequences to which their acceptance may lead.

For a successful result, revolutionary diplomacy is undoubtedly to a great extent dependent on its adversary's ignorance of the strategic and tactical principles on which its activity is based. And, above all, it is dependent on the maintenance in the Western world of the deeply rooted conviction that revolutionary diplomacy is acting according to the same rules and is in reality pursuing—behind a Communist screen —the same objectives as traditional foreign policy.

From what has now been said, it follows logically that the purposes of negotiations and international conferences differ considerably from each other in revolutionary and in traditional diplomacy. It is true that the former sometimes attempts, in the same way as the latter, to achieve a positive result by bilateral or multilateral negotiations. So it is first of all, as pertinently pointed out by Kurt London, when "the interests of the negotiators happen to coincide." This is, as will appear from the following chapters, the explanation of the Soviet decision in the last phase of the negotiations about the re-establishment of Austrian independence to sign the State Treaty and evacuate the country.

But also in some other contingencies revolutionary diplomacy can be interested in the attainment of a positive result by negotiation or conference. This is the case when the signature of a bilateral or a multilateral treaty has proved to be the most expedient method of legalizing either a status quo or territorial and other advantages already virtually acquired by peaceful or compulsory means. And, finally, negotiations are necessary when a rash and abortive action has to be given up or the Soviet Union or some other Communist state has to back out of a difficult or dangerous situation at the least possible cost and inconvenience for themselves or for the world Communist movement (the Berlin blockade in 1948–49, Korea in 1950, and Cuba in 1962).

It goes without saying that the cases cited do not exhaust

the subject. Whether mentioned or not, they have one thing in common. They are all exceptions to the general rule that in revolutionary diplomacy, negotiations and international conferences have mainly a tactical purpose to fulfill. They are an integral part in the long chain of strategic and tactical stratagems conceived with a view to preparing the ground, stage by stage, for more advantageous positions on the road to world revolution.

As the following chapters will show, few negotiations have been as valuable as those immediately preceding the conclusion of the Austrian State Treaty in throwing light on the purposes for which negotiations and international conferences are used by revolutionary diplomacy to further its near or more distant goals.

Before terminating this chapter, it may, however, be necessary to stress again one important point. Many misunderstandings regarding Soviet foreign policy can be explained by the failure of the West to realize that the Soviet Union, while safeguarding its national interests, at the same time still pursues the revolutionary goals of the world Communist movement.

As many, and maybe as grave, mistakes about Soviet foreign policy have, however, been committed because of a confusion by leading statesmen and politicians in the West of goals and means. Every now and then, they have taken for granted that a diplomatic action initiated by Moscow has been an end in itself, whereas in reality it has only been intended, as previously shown, as a tactical move with a view to preparing the ground for the attainment of a long-range strategic goal. The cordial and positive reception in many leading political and journalistic circles in the West of the Rapacki plan as well as of the numerous proposals for a European security pact submitted by the Soviet Union in recent years can be adduced as convincing proof of a rather frequent confusion of tactical means and strategic goals which in its turn leads to a complete misunderstanding of the real aims of Soviet foreign policy.

After these general and obviously far from exhaustive observations about Communist strategy and tactics, we shall proceed to a brief sketch of the fundamental traits of Soviet foreign policy from the end of World War II to the conclusion of the Austrian State Treaty in May 1955 in order to show how the previously analyzed strategic and tactical principles were applied by the rulers in the Kremlin during the negotiations of the Austrian State Treaty, particularly in the last stage from the conference in Berlin in January–February 1954 until the signature of the treaty on May 15, 1955.

When, for the sake of simplicity, the expression "Soviet foreign policy" is used in these chapters, I thereby mean the foreign policy of the "socialist camp" led by Moscow in the sense this policy has previously been interpreted. It is, therefore, necessary to remember, that the foreign policy formulated in Moscow has never been a great power policy in the traditional sense. After the creation of this camp, it should rather be characterized as the world-power policy of the international Communist movement.

5

Soviet Foreign Policy
at the End of the Stalin Era

With the unexpected German invasion of 1941, Stalin found himself involved in a life and death struggle which would determine not only the fate of the Soviet Union but also of the Comunist world movement. Since the Soviet Union could scarcely survive without substantial military and economic help from the Anglo-Saxon powers, a radical change of tactics toward them became necessary. From one day to the next, the "imperialist war," which according to previous pronouncements was being waged against Germany by the Anglo-Saxon powers, was transformed into a war of liberation led by the Soviet Union against fascism.

In this situation, Stalin had a compelling interest in uniting all population groups, regardless of their present or previous attitude, in a national effort. At the same time, he had to convince his new allies of his sincere desire to work with them not only during the war but also in the subsequent political and economic reconstruction of Europe. Stalin attempted, with some success, to delude his own people as well as the wishfully thinking British and Americans, with the hope that the Soviet regime might undergo a radical change. With understanding assistance on the part of the capitalist world, this change might gradually lead to the development of a new Russian social order more like Western democracy than the Communist system which had aroused the aversion of most Europeans and Americans. Primarily for this purpose, Stalin dissolved the Comintern during the war and assumed a positive attitude toward the Orthodox Church. The national and patriotic feelings of the Soviet population were also encouraged and strengthened.

In the field of foreign policy, the "soft line," as we can call it, lacking a completely fitting expression, was designed primarily to convince the Anglo-Saxon powers that after the end of the war the Soviet government would look after the interests of the Soviet state in a national spirit. In other words, plans for spreading communism would be given up or paid only lip service. This interpretation had a zealous and devoted advocate in Eduard Beneš, the exiled President of Czechoslovakia, who expended great effort to dispel the apprehension, which occasionally arose in the American and British governments and also among his own fellow citizens, that a Soviet victory could lead to a bolshevizing of Central and Southeastern Europe. He decried, even ridiculed, the thought that the U.S.S.R. planned social revolutions in that part of Europe which would belong to the Soviet sphere of interest after the victory of the allied powers. The warnings spread about this, Beneš declared, were only German propaganda.

"To imagine," he wrote from Moscow in December 1943 in a report to Foreign Minister Masaryk which is reproduced in Beneš's memoirs, "that the present outlook towards the International [Comintern], religion, *co-operation with the West,* Slav policy, etc. is merely tactical would be a fundamental error. A new Soviet Union will come out of the war," he continued. "Economically and socially it will retain the Soviet system in its entirety but will be quite new politically."

In the same report Beneš added that he regarded as certain that all treaties and agreements not only with Czechoslovakia but also with the British and the Americans would be kept. "Fulfilment of the promises made to the Anglo-Saxons in Moscow and Teheran," he asserted, "are regarded in Moscow as a matter about which there can be no doubt."

"Some changes in the Soviet Union which astonished the world recently," he continued in another report which he made in the same year after his return to London from Moscow, "were the natural outcome partly of the war, partly of developments already accomplished, partly of the changes in its whole position in the world. The dissolution of the Communist International, the new attitude toward the Orthodox Church, and toward religion in general, its profound Soviet patriotism and new national feeling, all this was not a mere game, not mere tactics which might perhaps be discarded again after the war."

He was confident that his voyage to Moscow and the agreement concluded with the Soviet government "might provide the best proof of what the real policy of the Soviet Union probably would be after the war." He, therefore, expected that the information brought back by him from Moscow would finally set the minds of the other allies at rest with regard to the aims of the Soviet Union.

Of course, Beneš had complete trust in the Soviet Union and, particularly, in Stalin. As he admits himself in his memoirs, he always accepted "at its face value what the Soviet Union was promising" because in his experience, as he added, he had "no reason to mistrust its word."

While Beneš was indulging in these illusions, the Soviet Politburo under the personal leadership of Stalin—as Rakosi revealed in a speech on February 29, 1952—was working on plans for communizing the countries occupied by the Red Army. This plan was partly based upon new tactics. Lenin, in his time, had counted on power being seized mainly by armed action of the working class organized under the leadership of a small but well-disciplined Communist elite. The new tactics, on the contrary, involved revolutionary change from above, which was to be achieved, step by step, with "peaceful means."

During the war, the strategic goal, as pointed out by Rakosi, was "the destruction of the German fascist conquerors." After the war the same goal was changed into establishment of the dictatorship of the proletariat. The most important tactical means to be employed for both ends was the creation of "anti-fascist coalitions" during the war, disguised as partisan movements under Communist leadership, and after the war as coalition governments. After such governments had been formed, "with the support of those Social Democrats and middle-class elements which were willing to compromise," infiltration became the foremost tactical means. Trusted people had to be installed in top positions; the police and other important departments were to be led by declared or disguised adherents of communism. At the same time, the open or latent opposition of the population had to be broken gradually, partly through acts of terror, partly through nationalization of industries and private banks, division of large estates, and other similar "reforms," by means of which the political influence and economic position of the moneyed class could be weakened to begin with and later entirely eliminated. Preparations for the eventual complete take-over should be made so thoroughly that, at a given time, any attempt at resistance was doomed to failure.

Of particular importance for the successful outcome was, as Rakosi pointed out, that the "reforms" should be introduced by stages in order to conceal, as long as possible, that their real purpose was political instead of social, as alleged by the party leadership. Consequently, nationalization was in the beginning limited to the mining and later extended to the engineering industry, and so forth, until the whole industry of the country had come into the hands of the state. The commercial banks were dealt with in a similar manner. As a first step, they were only put under governmental control. As a second step, the state assumed the management of the three biggest banks, and, finally, after two or three more stages, the whole banking system was nationalized.

The so-called agricultural reform was carried out in the same way. To begin with, only estates of more than 200 acres were divided among the peasants and the landless. Later the limit was extended by stages. The last stage came only after several years when the peasants, in their turn, were deprived of their property, what they had always possessed as well as the property they had acquired. The so-called collective system was thus created.

From the Communist point of view, the advantage of the tactics followed was that each stage of the "reforms," by which the new "Socialist" social order was gradually introduced, could be carried out without any opposition worth mentioning from those groups not yet affected by it. Blinded as they were by a skillful propaganda, it took some time before they realized or even suspected that they were confronted only with the first, or some of the first, stages of a long-range, carefully laid strategic plan. The turn of the majority of them would not come before the stronger and more influential groups had been eliminated as political and economic factors.

The tactics now described in general outline have often been referred to as "salami tactics" from a remark by Rakosi, who was inclined to boast of his own successful performances. Although he cautiously mentioned Stalin as the author, his remark has given rise to the belief that these tactics were more or less his own invention. They are, however, by no means characteristic either of Rakosi's performance or of the methods used in Hungary for the seizure of power.

What Rakosi called "salami tactics" is nothing else than the application of the new version of strategy and tactics already analyzed in the preceding chapter. The same principles apply and the same tactics are used in the foreign-policy field as well as in the preparations for the seizure of power in any country marked out for future bolshevization. In both cases, the rule laid down is to proceed by stages, whereby every stage has its own strategic and tactical aspect and every action successfully carried out is intended mainly to prepare the ground for the next stage. The strategy and tactics used at the present moment to achieve the withdrawal of American troops from Europe and prepare the ground for the attainment of the long-range goal of the bolshevization of the German Federal Republic and, later, of the whole of Europe are the same as those applied by Rakosi for the seizure of power in Hungary. The Rapacki plan, the European security pact, and other tactical stratagems fulfill, in other words, the same purpose as the different stages by which the "Socialist" social order was successively introduced in Hungary.

In 1944, with the German Army in full retreat on all fronts and the defeat of Hitler only a question of time, Stalin put the finishing touches on his plans. If luck was with him, he could bolshevize the whole or at least a great part of Europe in the course of a few years. The prevailing conditions were by no means unfavorable. The illusions blinding governments as well as public opinion in the West were so firmly held that only years of continued disregard of obligations entered into by the U.S.S.R. and repeated Soviet attempts at expansion could shake them.

Moreover, in the last stages of the war German propaganda spread the thesis that in the case of an allied victory the Soviet Union intended to bolshevize all or at least a great part of Europe. Any doubts about Stalin's honorable intentions and his newly discovered democratic views were, consequently, considered as proof that those who expressed such heretical opinions had become victims of German propaganda or, even worse, identified themselves with it. While en route to China in the summer and fall of 1944, I remember that British diplomats and officers with whom I spoke almost suspected me of having Nazi sympathies because I dared to doubt the prevailing notion that the politics of the Soviet Union had undergone a fundamental change, that it had given up its world-revolutionary aims and was only striving to expand its sphere of interest in Europe and Asia in the same way tsarist Russia had once done. In the fall of 1945 one of my Nordic colleagues surprised me with the comment that if the peaceful and unselfish intentions of any statesman deserved absolute trust, then that one was Stalin. He would be content to exert a certain political influence in Central and Southeastern Europe but would never think of supporting Communist revolutionary attempts.

Ideas of this type were firmly held in Sweden, also. When, during a visit to Stockholm in the spring of 1944, I maintained in conversations with friends and colleagues that the Soviet Union continued to pursue its revolutionary goals in spite of all nationalist declarations, I was met with pitying smiles. It appeared to me that much of this attitude could be attributed to the influence of Madame Kollontay, the Soviet Minister in Stockholm at the time, an intelligent person who was experienced in all tactical stratagems.

I met her only once. Obviously she had discovered that my appointment as minister to Moscow was being seriously considered, and, in the spring of 1944, invited me, through a mutual acquaintance, to lunch in Saltsjöbaden where she was taking treatments after a stroke. She was partially paralyzed and moved about in a wheelchair. Her intelligence, however, was in no way impaired. The conversation, which lasted several hours, showed that her main purpose, aside from a desire to form her own impressions, was to convince me before my expected assignment to Moscow that the Soviet Union was now developing in a democratic direction, and, above all, that its future foreign policy would more and more follow the conventional traditions of the time of the tsars. Fascinated, I listened to her tactically clever performance. Without in any way pleading for her cause or even giving the impression of wanting to convince me, she sought, by the expressions she used, by discreet allusions, by disclosing surprising and apparently confidential facts, to suggest the ideas which she wished me to form. By putting facts together in a skillful way, she hoped that I should be persuaded that I had arrived at her interpretation through my own observations and conclusions.

Through deliberately critical remarks about influential people in the Soviet Union or hints that some of her own subordinates were, unfortunately, not yet capable of adjusting themselves to the new situation, she tried to convey the impression that she could now express herself with greater freedom as well as act more independently than had ever been possible while Stalin pursued the old revolutionary aims. She wanted to instill the idea that conditions in the Soviet Union were on the verge of a thorough change, and that, in any case, her personal position in Moscow was so strong that I could rely on her opinions and ostensibly confidential hints about conditions in the Soviet Union. I must admit that Madame Kollontay made a strong impression. During the next few days, I often asked myself if I was, after all, completely wrong about Soviet foreign policy. After some weeks of reflection, however, I concluded that the opinions I had held since visiting Russia as a young student during the revolution in 1917 were still as valid as ever.

The misunderstanding of Soviet intentions and the ignorance of Communist strategy and tactics prevalent in Western capitals during and after the war was one of the main causes for the catastrophic political development in Central and Southeastern Europe. Once Soviet troops stood on the Hamburg-Trieste line, Stalin could hope to include the remaining capitalist states in Europe, or certainly the majority of them, in his sphere of interest. He was probably strengthened in this belief by the weak resistance offered by the Anglo-Saxon powers to his interference in the internal affairs of Poland, Rumania, and Bulgaria. Apparently what encouraged him, above all, was the precipitate withdrawal of American troops from Europe. Roosevelt had indicated that the interest of the American people in Europe, once the war ended, would soon wane and in the course of a few years would turn to pure isolationism. Indeed, the president stated in Stalin's presence that American troops could scarcely be kept in Europe more than two years after the conclusion of hostilities.

Influenced by Marxist-Leninist doctrines, Stalin was also convinced that the United States would face a serious economic crisis after its transition to a peacetime economy. That he entertained this idea is not surprising, since well-known economists in the "capitalist" states—among others, Professor Gunnar Myrdal in Sweden—had arrived at the same erroneous conclusion. Was it not possible that this impending crisis—Stalin certainly asked himself—might force the United States willy-nilly to leave Europe to its fate? Would the peoples of Europe, weakened by war, psychologically depressed, and without economic and military support from the United States, be able to resist a well-prepared Communist takeover?

Stalin had every reason to consider the situation favorable in the long run. He had no need to hurry. He could reach his goal by patience and careful action. Apparently the Western powers considered the alliance with the Soviet Union and seemingly good relations with it of greater importance than enforcing agreements; Stalin had every reason to utilize this attitude as long as possible. Without taking the slightest notice of timid Western remonstrances, he continued his patient preparations for Communist seizures of power in those states already occupied by the Red Army.

But the Anglo-Saxon powers finally began to recognize Stalin's true aims. Although Churchill undoubtedly shared the responsibility for many political mistakes, he was the first of the great Western leaders to realize the danger to Europe. In the spring of 1945, he and Eden had warned the Americans of Communist infiltration which was especially obvious in the Balkans. In powerful and clear words he had expressed his fear that the Soviet Union would gradually gain political and military control of the whole of Europe if the United States should withdraw its troops from the continent. Shortly before the Potsdam Conference, Churchill also expounded this view to the former American Ambassador in Moscow, Joseph E. Davies, then one of Truman's advisers. Davies, still a strong supporter of Roosevelt's appeasement policy, got very upset and reported to the President that the British Prime Minister—as he understood him—had advanced more or less the same arguments which Hitler and Goebbels had been using for the past four years in an effort to destroy allied unity. Davies felt that Churchill's attitude was responsible for much of the Soviet aggressiveness and for many unilateral actions since Yalta.* For his part, Churchill believed that he had to suppress his critical attitude toward Soviet foreign policy so as not to endanger unity among the allies. After leaving office, however, he repeated his warning openly, especially in the famous Fulton address in 1946.

But in a speech on February 9, 1946, several weeks before the Fulton address, Stalin himself had already intimated that cooperation with the Anglo-Saxon powers was only temporary and, for all practical purposes, had already ended. Stalin also asserted that the Communist regime had successfully passed the test of war. It had shown itself more stable than any non-Soviet system and superior to any non-Soviet social order. He reaffirmed the necessity of increasing the production of heavy industry in preparation for new wars which

---

* Admiral William D. Leahy, *I Was There* (London: Victor Gollancz Ltd., 1950), p. 442.

were inevitable so long as the capitalist system existed. Stalin's declaration evidently foreshadowed new plans for world revolution as soon as the Soviet Union was strong enough. But as the near future was to show, smaller and less risky enterprises could be undertaken earlier.

As Stalin's intentions became more and more obvious, the attitude of the Anglo-Saxon powers gradually began to harden. In 1946, President Truman opposed Soviet attempts to set up in northern Iran an independent Azerbaijan under Communist influence. Further, he rejected the extensive territorial demands which Stalin had already directed at Turkey. Finally, on March 12, 1947, President Truman made his famous address to the Congress of the United States in which, among other things, he gave notice of his firm determination to prevent the further spread of communism. The United States, he said, would support free people in their opposition to revolutionary attempts by external pressure or the action of armed minorities. Turkey and Greece, which appeared to be especially threatened, were to receive American help for this purpose if needed.

This declaration marked a decisive turning point in the postwar history of Europe. It showed Stalin that his aims were understood and that the moves which he had made in preparation for a Communist seizure of power in various countries would be strongly opposed by the United States. A few months later this impression was confirmed when General Marshall, then the American Secretary of State, in his famous speech at Harvard urged extensive economic aid, the so-called Marshall Plan, to a poverty-stricken Europe laid waste by the war. As later developments showed, this plan contributed decisively to frustrating the expansionist policy of the Soviet Union in Europe.

Now Stalin realized that he had nothing more to gain from the myth that he wanted to cooperate with the Western powers, and he decided to use clearly aggressive tactics. This decision had an additional justification from the Soviet standpoint, since preparations for bolshevizing Eastern Europe had already progressed considerably. The final transition to a Communist order could now be carried out so quickly and smoothly that the Western powers would be faced with a *fait accompli* which they could not prevent even if they wanted to.

It is from this point of view that one must consider the important conference which, on Stalin's initiative, met in September 1947 in the little city of Szklarska-Poreba near Breslau. Here gathered not only representatives of the six East European Communist parties which controlled their countries in reality, though not yet formally, but also representatives of the French and Italian parties; Stalin's chief lieutenant, Andrei A. Zhdanov, presided. Ostensibly, the most significant resolution adopted concerned the establishment of a new organization, the Cominform (Communist Information Bureau), embracing those parties participating in the conference. According to official announcements, the new "information" agency would arrange the exchange of experience and information in order to strengthen cooperation between the participating states and parties. The real purpose of the meeting was completely different; this was disclosed later by one of the participants, Eugenio Reale, the Italian Communist who belonged to his Party leadership at the time.

First, all the participating parties were to prepare for the important change in the foreign policy line which was soon to come. The distinct aggressive character of the new line was foreshadowed in the resolution released at the conclusion of the conference. It emphasized that World War II had resulted in the division of the world into two opposing camps —"imperialist" under the leadership of the United States and "anti-imperialist and democratic" under the leadership of the Soviet Union. The primary danger for the "working class" was that the Communist parties of Europe underestimated their own strength just as they overestimated the strength of the "imperialist" bloc.

The now so familiar emphasis on the opposition between two "camps" revealed Stalin's decision to liquidate the remains of the middle-class social order in the East European states and impose undisguised Communist dictatorships. According to the official Soviet interpretation, these countries had previously occupied an intermediate position between "capitalist" and "socialist" states. Since a "camp" presupposed the existence of several states, this expression would necessarily mean that the rulers in the Kremlin intended to establish more states of the type of the single existing "socialist" state, the Soviet Union, and join them in a common "socialist and anti-imperialist camp."

But a closer examination of the formulation of this resolution would have provided further valuable hints as to the future policies of the Soviet Union. Since the Communist parties had underestimated their own true strength and overestimated the strength of the "capitalist" bloc, they could now abandon the previous policy of reasonably good relations carried on according to instructions from Moscow. This did not mean that Zhdanov advised a military attack against Western Europe, but only that the opposition of the Western powers was still so weak that the Soviet Union could use tougher methods than before without seriously risking a world war.

And this was exactly how events unfolded. In the satellite states the new aggressive line expressed itself in a speeded-up sovietization. With few exceptions, the middle-class and Social Democratic parties, previously granted an apparent independence, were dissolved. In the same way the last remnants of the capitalist order were liquidated. The most sensational application of the new tactics, however, was the overthrow of the government in Prague in February 1948. Reale told this author that guidelines for the coup had been issued at the first Cominform conference.

The struggle with the Western powers changed. Hidden attacks became open battles which aimed mainly at the Marshall Plan. The opposition to this plan, however, was not, as generally assumed at the time, based entirely on the desire of the Soviet Union to prevent or make more difficult the economic recovery of Western Europe. Stalin was obviously convinced that the "permanent crisis" in which "capitalism" found itself, according to Marxist-Leninist doctrine, had not been overcome at all as certain Communist economists cautiously sought to imply. In his opinion, the crisis continued undiminished and would gradually lead to the collapse of the entire "capitalist" social order. It was therefore in the interest of the Soviet Union to encourage such a development as much as possible and to remove obstacles which could delay it. This was especially true for the United States where a serious and lasting depression was expected in connection with the transition from a war to a peacetime economy.

Stalin apparently assumed that Marshall was not interested primarily in the economic recovery of Western Europe but rather in creating new markets for American exports and in this way maintaining profits until the conversion problems of industry could be solved. Seen from this point of view, it would seem even more urgent to frustrate or at least obstruct the Marshall Plan. If it failed, the coming of the economic crisis in the United States would be speeded up and with it the unavoidable collapse of the capitalist social order in America and other industrialized countries. Thereby the problem of Communist expansion would be solved all at once and for good. This was probably one of the main reasons for the intensity with which the Marshall Plan was attacked. There were others, however.

According to the Marxist-Leninist interpretation, a state which received economic help became, by necessity, not only economically but also politically dependent on the donor country. The United States would, therefore, not only ward off its own economic crisis by means of Marshall Plan aid, but, at the same time, extend and strengthen its political influence in Europe. Aid to East European states would create the basis for American economic and political penetration, and could lead to liberation from political dependence on the Soviet Union. Accordingly, it is not strange that Stalin intervened vehemently in Poland and Czechoslovakia when those countries showed an inclination to accept Marshall Plan aid.

Stalin, moreover, did not limit his political activity to opposing the Marshall Plan. Without taking any serious risks, he used every opportunity to extend Communist domination. He probed carefully to ascertain the weakest points in the determination of the Western powers and avoided any measures of an irrevocable nature that could have led to an armed conflict with the United States. On several occasions, however, he made serious errors of judgment which might have involved the Soviet Union in warlike entanglements. Stalin probably never realized that the Anglo-Saxon powers had already made such far-reaching concessions that they no longer had room for maneuvering.

In Stalin's opinion, Berlin was the weakest point in the Western position. Its fall would have the direst psychological and political consequences for Western Europe. And once offensive tactics had been decided upon, a Soviet move against the German capital was not long in coming. Only six months after the first Cominform conference and a month after the overthrow of the government in Prague, the Soviet Union, under various pretenses—at first the improvement of railroads and highways, finally a currency reform by the Western powers—began a series of aggressive measures which culminated in the Berlin Blockade. After the approaches to the city had been sealed off, the sectors occupied by the Western powers were gradually completely blockaded; only the airways remained open.

The Soviet government undoubtedly counted on the Western powers capitulating and withdrawing their troops from the city which would then be incorporated in the Soviet zone. Stalin hoped at least to force the Western powers to give up the establishment of a West German state. In either case they would suffer a palpable defeat, and, in the face of this impotence and ineptness, the German people would be seized by a feeling of hopelessness. Citizens of other countries could also be expected to draw the proper conclusions, and the Communist parties of France and Italy, for example, would grow by leaps and bounds.

When Stalin initiated this encounter, he was certainly convinced that it would succeed. He overlooked several factors, however, that proved decisive. The first was the surprising determination of the Western powers; second, their military superiority in the air; third, the supplies of food, fuel, and industrial goods which the American occupation authorities had at their disposal; the fourth, finally, the ability to transport these supplies by air to West Berlin. For fear of a third world war, Stalin did not dare to give the command to attack the British and American transport planes. And after approximately a year it became clear that the blockade would fail sooner or later. In this situation the Soviet Union began to show its readiness for consultation with the United States which gradually led to the lifting of the blockade. Stalin's offensive tactics had failed.

The years of 1947–50 saw several other unsuccessful attempts, not less than three in Austria which I will discuss later. Preparations were made for a coup in Finland in 1948, but it was thwarted by premature disclosure. This offensive foreign policy of the Soviet Union led not only to one defeat after another but also caused a reaction completely different from that which Stalin had counted on: The Western powers, under the leadership of the United States, joined in organized opposition to Communist expansion. Scarcely had the coup d'état taken place in Prague, scarcely had the Berlin Blockade begun, than deliberations started concerning the creation of a North Atlantic alliance in which not only the West European states but also the United States and Canada took part. This led to an agreement signed in Washington on April 4, 1949, and, shortly thereafter, an extensive program of military aid for the member states.

The decision of the Soviet Union to withdraw from four-power control of Germany, and the Berlin Blockade which followed, facilitated the establishment of the Federal Republic of Germany as a sovereign state, something which Stalin had intended to prevent by the blockade. By the spring of 1949, the negotiations concerning this question had progressed so far that there was agreement in principle concerning delegation of the most important powers, which the Western allies had previously exercised together, to a new Federal Republic of Germany. And the establishment of this state in the fall of 1949 led to new consequences even more distasteful to the U.S.S.R.—but they were a direct result of the aggressive policy the Soviet Union had carried on since 1947.

It soon became clear that the defense of Western Europe would be almost hopeless without the rearmament of West

Germany. This question, with which the Soviet Union soon sought to link the negotiations concerning an Austrian State Treaty, dominated European politics in Stalin's last years as well as the years immediately after his death. It caused a serious conflict not only between the Soviet Union and the Western powers but also among the Western powers themselves.

In the face of these unforeseen developments, and under the influence of his repeated defeats, Stalin apparently considered it advisable to suspend for the time being his attempts to extend communism in Europe by force and threats. But this did not yet mean the abandonment of an aggressive diplomatic line. The opposition between the two power blocs became even graver. Although formal diplomatic relations remained intact, regular contacts between the foreign offices were interrupted on more or less convincing pretexts. From the fall of 1949 on, even discussions on such important questions as German reunification and the Austrian State Treaty, which had been carried on for a long time at the highest level, stopped almost completely. According to disclosures at a meeting of the Polish Central Committee in October 1956, Stalin was seriously worried about the possibility of a new world war in 1950 and the following years and forced the satellite states in Eastern Europe to increase their iron and steel production far beyond the powers of their economy.

In Europe, the Soviet Union had first concentrated its efforts on preventing the establishment of a West German state. And after this was an accomplished fact, it attempted to prevent the arming of the Federal Republic of Germany and its political, military, and economic integration in the Western bloc. Did Stalin really fear an attack by a rearmed Germany as was maintained in the West? Or did he have other reasons for this negative attitude?

The earlier Russian hopes for gradually sovietizing West Germany were based on two presuppositions: that the rearmament of Germany could be prevented, and that the Soviet Union would eventually bring about a neutralization of Germany and thereby its political and economic isolation from the Western powers. Given these conditions, sovietizing

West Germany would be a difficult but not impossible task in the foreseeable future. The U.S.S.R. wanted to preserve this possibility. Soviet opposition to the establishment of the Federal Republic of Germany and its rearmament was not based upon a vague fear of all Germans as claimed by the propaganda which was inspired by Moscow and willingly believed in West European capitals. This myth was rejected with contempt by no less a personage than Bulganin at the time of the Geneva Conference of 1955. The assertion that the mighty Soviet Union should entertain any serious fear of fresh German aggression was considered by the then Soviet Premier, not without cause, as an insult to his country.

German rearmament, however, would present perhaps insurmountable obstacles to the sovietization of the Federal Republic of Germany, while a disarmed and neutralized Germany or even a limitation of its armament would weaken the Atlantic Pact and perhaps make the defense of Europe impossible. In my conversations with Soviet diplomats in 1954 and 1955, I received the distinct impression that they did not have a high opinion of the inclination and ability of Great Britain to offer an effective contribution in this respect. About France they expressed the deepest disdain, and undoubtedly felt similarly about the smaller states in the north and west of Europe even though no direct remark was made in this connection. The United States and West Germany were considered in Moscow to be the two great supports of the Atlantic Pact. Their common participation was obviously sufficient to make N.A.T.O. a serious and dangerous obstacle in Soviet eyes.

Preventing the armament of the Federal Republic of Germany was so important in the European policy of the Russians in the fifties that other problems were subordinated to it. Thus, the Austrian State Treaty was put aside for several years: Apparently the Soviet Union wanted to retain the possibility of using it as a *quid pro quo* in order to persuade the Western powers to abandon, postpone, or limit the armament of West Germany.

After the failure of the Berlin Blockade, the Soviet regime soon found itself forced to change to largely defensive tactics in Europe. In Asia, however, the offensive continued for some years. But, as in Europe, this occurred only in areas in which no opposition or only slight opposition was expected from the United States. After Washington had realized the hopelessness of saving the corrupt regime of Chiang Kai-shek and suspended its support, the Communist conquest of China was soon completed with the indirect help of Soviet Russia. In Indochina, the revolutionary movement organized by the Communists also achieved great successes. In the Philippines, the Malay Peninsula, and Burma, Communist partisan activities were suppressed only after protracted fighting.

The most sensational Communist attempt began in the summer of 1950 in Korea. The immediate cause appears to have been the withdrawal of American troops a year earlier and statements by American politicians and high officials to the effect that South Korea was strategically unimportant and could be defended only with difficulty. Thus, Stalin assumed that a surprise blow by the well-equipped North Korean army would not lead to military hostilities with the United States. But he had erred again. The Communists achieved significant initial successes in Asia, but once halted in Korea they appeared temporarily to have exhausted their strength.

These repeated defeats forced a new examination of the situation. Even though the tactical line was changed only after Stalin's death, in the last years of his life he apparently recognized the necessity for a change and spelled out its theoretical justification in an article published shortly before the Nineteenth Party Congress.* One of the most important results of World War II, he wrote, was the disintegration of the former "single and universal world market" and its replacement by two great parallel markets opposed to one another: the "capitalist" and the "socialist." As a consequence, competition among capitalist states would become more severe, and their struggle for the "capitalist" market would over-

* "Ekonomicheskie problemy Sotzializma v sssr," *Pravda*, October 3, 1952; for an English translation see *Current Digest of the Soviet Press*, Special Supplement, October 18, 1952.

shadow the contradictions between the "capitalist" and "socialist" camps.

Apparently Stalin sought indirectly to dismiss the importance of repeated failures and at the same time present guidelines for new tactics. By his seemingly obscure formulation, he presumably meant that the "capitalist united front" which the United States was building up as a reaction to his aggressive policy was not necessarily as strong as many faithful comrades feared. Contradictions among the "capitalist states," between the United States and its allies and among the latter, would break out violently again sooner or later. Great Britain and France would once more find it necessary to look out for their own interests and to shake off their dependence on the United States.

Stalin was obviously convinced that the developments after World War I, increased differences between the victors and the vanquished and within both these groups, would now repeat themselves. Whether reunited or not, Germany would again take its place as a world power as it had after 1918. And such a development would necessarily bring about a new conflict between Germany and its former enemies. Evidently Stalin regarded developments in Asia from the same point of view. Once Japan had recuperated from its severe defeat, new discord would arise between the "capitalist states" and Japan, among other reasons because of the diminishing markets. It was important for the Soviet Union to utilize this discord to dissolve the "capitalist united front" which seemed about to spread from Europe to Asia.

Between the lines, one can discern the uneasiness over Western measures to preclude or make further Soviet expansion more difficult. Stalin may also have been conscious of how much he himself had contributed to the close ties between the Western powers. This unity, which Stalin represented in his article as fragile and not dangerous, had, nevertheless, convinced him that the period of "revolutionary floodtide" in Europe was nearing its end. A transition from offensive to defensive tactics was necessary. The first task was to split the "capitalist united front," and the European Communist parties should revive and stir up the dissension which had once existed among the great powers of Europe.

Although these defensive tactics were not applied during Stalin's lifetime, they were adopted by his first successors who generally followed the guidelines given by Stalin. It remained for Khrushchev to undertake a significant alteration in strategy and tactics after a serious disagreement with Molotov. It was this change, among other things, which made possible the conclusion of the Austrian State Treaty.

6

The Austrian Policy
of the Soviet Union, 1945–50

At the conference of foreign ministers in Moscow in 1943, the Allied powers had issued the first statement concerning their postwar policy toward Austria. In a communiqué published after the close of the conference, the governments of the United States, Great Britain, and the Soviet Union explained solemnly that they no longer recognized the annexation of Austria by Germany in 1938 and would establish a free and independent Austrian state after the war. But the Soviet Union added a fateful amendment against American and British opposition: Because of the participation of Austrian troops on the side of Hitler's Germany, Austria would not be completely absolved of responsibilities. This amendment later supplied a legal foundation for the war-damage claims which the Soviet Union put forward in the negotiations concerning a State Treaty. The Moscow declaration, however, stemmed less from concern about the future of Austria than from tactical considerations. By promising to restore Austria's independence, the Allies hoped to weaken the people's will to resist and induce them to take part in the fight against Hitler. Soviet propaganda broadcasts concentrated on encouraging Austrian nationalism and urged the creation of broad "fronts" embracing not only Communists and Socialists but also liberals and even anti-Nazi conservatives. Such "national fronts" were to play an important role in the early stages of the Communist takeover in the "people's democracies." That the same propaganda was carried on in the broadcasting to the Austrian population clearly indicates that the Soviet Union at the end of the war intended to incorporate Austria in the "socialist camp" in the same way as was done with the East European countries.

Even though Austria was not considered basically an enemy state, the Allied powers, nevertheless, decided on a joint occupation—after tedious negotiations on the boundaries of the individual zones. Unlike Germany, however, the country had a single government and civil administration almost from the beginning. Soviet authorities seized the initiative on April 27, 1945, with the creation of a provisional government under the leadership of the old Social Democrat, Karl Renner. In this first government, the Communists received several posts, including the key positions of Minister of Interior and Minister of Education.

At first, the new government inspired serious misgivings in Washington and London. The Western powers feared and the Soviet government hoped Renner would be the type of cooperative person found so frequently among both bourgeois and Social Democratic parties in other countries occupied by the Red Army. But, at the first opportunity, he expanded the government by including representatives from the Western occupation zones; this automatically diluted the Communist influence in the cabinet. Renner also urged elections for Parliament even before the end of the year. By this time the Western powers realized that he was no figurehead for a Soviet puppet regime, and on October 20 they recognized his government and extended its authority to their zones.

At this point, the Kremlin made a serious blunder in agreeing to free elections under impartial control, probably because the Soviet leaders and their Austrian Communist advisers were overconfident. After the overwhelming victory of the Red Army over the Nazi regime, they counted on a significant Communist vote; indeed, the first postwar elections elsewhere in Europe, for example, in Britain and France, had shown a strong trend to the left. And for tactical reasons the Communist Party in Austria, as in other "liberated" countries, was urging radical but not revolutionary reforms. The Communists indignantly denied that they intended to introduce a new social order modeled on that of the Soviet Union.

Nevertheless, judging from their later remarks, the Communists did not expect a majority but did believe they would win at least twenty-five per cent of the vote. With such a sizeable minority, the Soviet occupation forces could demand greater Communist representation in the coalition government and pave the way for an eventual takeover by a slow step-by-step infiltration.

But to the disappointment of the Soviet authorities, the Communist Party received only five per cent of the vote cast on November 25, 1945, and only four seats in parliament. Instead of improving its position, the Party had to give up the influential positions which it had held in the first coalition government. As a sop, however, the People's Party and the Socialists gave the Communists one cabinet post, the completely unimportant Ministry of Electrification. In November 1947, the Austrian Communist Party, after the rejection of the Marshall Plan by the Soviet Union and other Communist countries, withdrew their representation from the government. This was the result of the clever and farsighted policy of Renner who, in contrast to Beneš, had no illusions about Stalin's goals and knew how to frustrate them.

Stalin and his followers accepted their electoral defeat—probably because they believed it could be reversed later. At the time, the rulers in the Kremlin failed to realize how decisive the result of the election would be. "Only now do we understand that we had already conclusively lost Austria by the election of November 1945," a Soviet diplomat told me years later. But at the end of 1945 the U.S. forces in Europe were being precipitately demobilized; in less than a year, the few remaining American units were so thoroughly demoralized that even if token Western forces remained in Austria, the capital and government, being in the Soviet zone, were more or less at the mercy of the Soviet occupation forces.

In addition, even though the Communist Party had lost its fundamental influence in the Austrian government, it still occupied a strong position in the Soviet zone. As in the East European states, the Soviet occupation authorities had installed Communists in many important posts in the police forces and the local governments in their zone. And in the comparatively short time he held portfolio, the **Communist** Minister of the Interior, Franz Honner, with the help of the Communist head of the security police, Dr. Dürmayer, had filled the police of Vienna with so many Communists that the force could no longer be considered reliable by a non-Communist government. During the summer of 1947, however, the new, energetic Social Democratic Minister of the Interior, Oskar Helmer, cleaned out most of the known and secret Communist police functionaries outside the Soviet zone. In the course of this process, in which also Dr. Dürmayer had to leave his post, Helmer ran up against strong opposition not only from the Communists but also from bourgeois politicians who were paralyzed by fear of Soviet reprisals.

And in the summer of 1946 the Soviet representative on the Allied Council made a second major blunder which greatly reduced the Soviet potential for negative influence— at least in the Western zones of Austria. Until then every decree of the Austrian government and every law passed by parliament had to be unanimously approved by the Allied Council. Even the new government formed after the election of 1945 had to be submitted to the council for confirmation.

But a new control agreement, signed on June 28, 1946, brought an important change and practically abolished the veto power of the Soviet Union in the Allied Council. New laws or decrees would become effective after thirty-one days unless unanimously vetoed by the council. Only constitutional changes still required unanimous approval. Austria also received the authority to organize its own customs and border control. To be sure, this was often ignored by the Soviet occupation forces.

When one remembers how the Soviet Union used its veto power after the war in various international organizations, Moscow's acceptance of the new control agreement is surprising indeed. Probably officials in Moscow and Austria did not realize the full significance of the concession. Unfamiliar with Western legal terminology, they did not understand the difference between fundamental law and other legislation. And, in practice, they could always prevent the enforcement of unwelcome laws in their zone. When the Austrian government, for example, tried to nationalize certain so-called German assets in Austria which Soviet authorities had seized as reparations, the Soviet representative on the Allied Council asserted that the nationalization law was, in its nature, a fundamental law and, consequently, subject to Soviet veto. After the majority had rejected his claim, he finally declared that the law could not be applied in the Soviet zone.

Despite these reverses, however, the prospects, as seen from Moscow, of eventually securing and sovietizing all of Austria must have still appeared bright. At the Cominform conference in September 1947, the chief Soviet delegate, Zhdanov, declared that the only country which had emerged stronger from World War II, the United States, would experience a serious economic crisis in the near future. Thus, the only remaining strong capitalist power would lose its will as well as its ability to support the weaker capitalist states in Europe. Nevertheless, without waiting for this development, the Communists made three attempts at revolution in Austria in 1947–50. At the beginning of May 1947, shortly before the Communists took full control in Hungary, street demonstrations and strikes were staged by the Austrian Communist party which intended that they should culminate in an attack on and occupation of the offices of the Chancellor by a mob. A reconstruction of the government would be extorted in which the Communists should have a decisive influence. This plan was based on the assumption that the police were unable to offer serious opposition since they were to a large extent infiltrated by the Communist party; a regulation of the Allied Council had also severely limited their weapons and ammunition. Nevertheless, the Communist attempt failed completely. The leadership of the unions rejected concerted action and refused to be bullied into calling a general strike. When the intervention of American military police finally appeared possible, the order to retreat was apparently given.

After this unexpected defeat, the Communists turned to new tactics and approached several leading personalities, mainly in the People's party, who had lost their courage in the face of Soviet procrastination on the conclusion of the State Treaty and the apparently hopeless economic and political condition of the country. The only way out, warned the Communists, would be to organize a new government which could count on the support of the Soviet Union for the conclusion of the State Treaty. The government should be under the leadership of a well-known bourgeois politician who actually had pronounced Communist sympathies. Although the Communist Party would claim a number of key positions in the new government, the two large parties could continue to participate; their ministers, however, would have to be approved by the Communists. In other words, only disguised fellow-travelers or morally weak and easily influenced appeasers from the People's party and the Social Democrats would have been admitted to the government. Such a regime could undoubtedly have secured a State Treaty, but Stalin would have had Austria.

The plan was discovered at the last minute and completely ruined when Dr. Gruber, the foreign minister of the People's party, who had not been approached because of his anti-Communist attitude but had received information indirectly, informed the press about the secret negotiations. The resulting outcry caused the concerned or willing politicians to withdraw quickly and make light of the serious nature of the conversations. And shortly afterward, when the Austrian government stated it would participate in the Marshall Plan, the single remaining Communist member of the government, as already mentioned, resigned in November 1947 following the line then prescribed by Moscow. Hereby, the chances of the Communist Party to strengthen by legal means its position and influence in the administration had been definitely lost. The Communist party had to again resort to violent means in order to attain its goal.

Several years of relative quiet followed, however, before the most serious of the three revolutionary attempts, in September 1950. With the improvement of the economic situation as a result of the Marshall Plan, the Soviet Union apparently feared to lose soon its last chance to take over real power in Austria. A hardening in the attitude of the Soviet occupation forces was apparent several months earlier. Among other things, this showed itself in an increasing number of arbitrary arrests and in repeated attempts of local Soviet authorities to interfere in the domestic affairs of Austria. In addition, there were frequent demands, phrased in the forms of ultimatums, to remove or transfer police or other officials not in favor with the Russians. These measures were aimed at arousing anxiety among the populace and frightening Austrian officials, weakening their resistance in the coming test of strength. Later developments in the Far East in the summer of 1950 could also be expected to contribute to the success of the putsch. By mid-August, U.S. and South Korean forces had been driven back into a large bridgehead around Pusan. This demonstrated inability of the United States to protect South Korea should further discourage those who might wish to oppose the Communists.

The requirements for a successful revolution had already changed essentially by this time, however. The clean-up of the police had made great progress, and well-armed and organized gendarmery units were available in the Western zones. But the most important factor was the Social Democratic influence over the unions and the courage of the workers in the Soviet zone. The attempt at revolution began on September 26, 1950 with street demonstrations and strikes organized by the Communists. The aim was, in the first place, to force a change of the leadership of the unions which would permit a Communist takeover. The reorganized leadership should thereafter attempt to force through a reconstruction of the government in the same way and according to the same pattern.

The new government should finally, as in other countries where the Communist parties have taken over power by violent means, lay claim to representing the whole country. By Communist-organized demonstrations and riots, the Western powers should little by little be forced to give in and recognize the new government.

Although Soviet troops did not interfere openly in the struggle, they transported Communist goon-squads to strategically important points and prevented Austrian police from ejecting agitators and demonstrators from railway stations and other important points. Within a few days, however, it was apparent that the putsch could not succeed without direct Soviet support which Stalin did not dare give. On October 5 the Communist strike committee called off the action. The last and most serious attempt to bring about a change in Austria by force had failed.

7

First Negotiations Concerning
a State Treaty

Long before these events took place, the Western powers had proposed discussions with the Soviet Union concerning an Austrian State Treaty. These proposals, however, were rejected in Moscow under various pretenses. The principle reason may have been the Soviet desire to conclude peace negotiations with Hungary, Rumania, and Bulgaria before starting talks about an Austrian treaty. Once peace treaties had been signed with the first three countries, the Western powers had recognized the governments, and the Allied control commissions had been disbanded, preparations for a complete Communist takeover would be somewhat simpler. The Soviet Union, therefore, did not want the conclusion of peace treaties with Hungary, Rumania, and Bulgaria delayed by differences with the Western powers about an Austrian treaty. The Western powers either did not see through the Russian tactics or put up with them in silence.

Negotiations about an Austrian State Treaty finally began in January 1947, and, as expected, serious differences of opinion soon arose over the territorial claims of Yugoslavia and the unreasonable Soviet demands for "German assets" as reparations. When relations between the Yugoslav and Soviet Communist parties were broken off in the summer of 1948, the Kremlin continued for a time to support the Yugoslav demand. But apparently the Soviet Union would yield on this point in return for Western concessions on "German assets"; and indeed at a foreign ministers' conference in Paris in June 1949, Soviet Foreign Minister Andrei Vyshinsky agreed to recognize the Austrian-Yugoslav border of 1938. The Soviet

Union would receive two-thirds of the petroleum output of the Zistersdorf fields in Lower Austria, certain other oil rights, and 150 million dollars for those "German assets" which were to be given back to Austria. The government had accepted this compromise on the assumption that main difficulties had been solved and that the final draft of the treaty should be ready by September 1949. The signing of the State Treaty appeared to be only a matter of time. This optimism proved, however, to be rather rash. When negotiations between the foreign ministers were resumed in the autumn, after the deputies had not been able to reach an agreement, it soon became clear that the Soviet government had no intention of going any further. At the end of November 1949, its delegates presented new demands soon to be followed by others which had little or nothing to do with the re-establishment of Austrian independence. But what was the purpose of these tactics of delay?

It is impossible at present to answer this question for certain. The most plausible explanation is, however, to be found in political developments in Germany. As already mentioned, the Western powers had, after the Communist revolution in Prague, the Berlin Blockade, and the hurried bolshevization of the Eastern states, been forced into strengthening their political unity and military power. The Atlantic Pact had been signed on April 4, 1949, and the West German government was formed shortly thereafter. At the end of the year, discussions were initiated in the press about German rearmament, which soon were followed by deliberations between the governments. Considering these menacing prospects, the rulers in the Kremlin were constrained to concentrate their activities in Europe in the field of foreign policy upon preventing or at least delaying this development, equally dangerous from the point of view of Russian national interests as for the realization of the long-range goal of the Communist world movement. A means close at hand was to delay, for the time being, the conclusion of the Austrian State Treaty under different pretexts and later to use concessions in this question for bargaining purposes. The evacuation of Austria would be the price for the abandonment of the rearmament of West Germany if it could not be prevented in another way. Bulganin indirectly admitted this to an Austrian delegation in Moscow in April 1955. For "the last five years," he gave it to understand, the Party Presidium had constantly avoided serious negotiations about the evacuation of Austria in order to have a bargaining counter whenever it was necessary to entice the Western powers into negotiations about the German problem (source: the secret journal of president Adolf Schärf).

Whatever may have been the reason for the interruption of the negotiations at the end of November 1949, the delaying tactics of the Soviet Union in the following years were undoubtedly caused by considerations indicated by Bulganin.

8

Molotov and the Austrian Policy of the Soviet Union, 1953–54

After Stalin died in March 1953, a collective group assumed power. But the "collective leadership" was merely a way of dealing with the fact that, in the first years after Stalin's death, no single member of the Party Presidium was strong enough to be recognized by his colleagues as undisputed leader. Malenkov, for example, was initially both Premier and Party First Secretary. As a result of the struggle for power within the Party Presidium, he was forced, after only a few days, to resign the office of First Secretary in favor of Khrushchev, who was comparatively unknown at that time. A similar situation still prevails after the removal of Khrushchev when the "collective leadership" was proclaimed anew.

During the fight for power which broke out after Stalin's death, the contending groups needed quiet in the area of foreign affairs and agreed on a temporary policy of relaxation. As Molotov later indicated in his speech of February 8, 1955, they wanted to re-establish the direct contact with the Western powers which had been practically broken off in the last years of Stalin's rule. Without such contacts no concessions from the Western powers could be expected. The senseless provocations of that time stopped almost entirely. Diplomatic communication began to assume a more normal and polite character, and the new "collective leadership" even made a few concessions in questions of secondary importance. But concessions on more important subjects only involved abandoning demands which would not have been met in the near future. With respect to important long-term objectives no concessions could be made. In this respect the new "collective leadership" was just as stubborn as Stalin.

The relaxation of tensions was only aimed at undermining the resistance of the Western powers against Soviet claims. Consequently, diplomatic relations were re-established with Israel and the Soviet government accepted a new Secretary General of the United Nations and abandoned its territorial claims on Turkey which could not be met in the near future anyway. Armistice negotiations in Korea were also accelerated and finally concluded on July 27, 1953. But the Soviet Union refused to consider the reunification of Korea as an independent state outside the "socialist camp." This outcome did not surprise me at all. The Polish Ambassador in Prague had predicted it to me two years earlier. The armistice negotiations would indeed be of long duration, he explained, but, nevertheless, successful. On the other hand, a political agreement which could lead to the reunification of Korea through free elections was completely out of the question. Such concession would have meant the abandonment of a long-range goal: the expansion of the socialist camp in this part of the world.

Only the negotiations about the cessation of hostilities in Indochina in the spring of 1954 led to Communist concessions, which from the beginning seemed to be of primary importance. But, in this case, the Communists must have considered the settlement only a desirable truce. Moscow did not want to prematurely alarm India, Burma, and other countries of Southeast Asia. It was desirable for the present, therefore, with Western help to secure the important gains already won by the Communists. Once they had consolidated their regime in the north, and once the French had departed, the Communists thought it would be a simple matter to take over the rest of the peninsula. The resumption of the "national liberation war" in Vietnam some years later proved that the settlement of 1954 had only been a truce.

The policy of relaxation was also extended to Austria. The tedious and time-consuming control of traffic between the Eastern and Western zones was eliminated or eased. Mail and telephone censorship was officially abolished in the Soviet zone even though still practiced—in more discreet forms to be sure. In August 1953, using all propaganda media, Soviet authorities announced that the U.S.S.R. would assume the expenses of its occupation forces. After six years, the Soviet Union had followed the example of the United States whose government had given up its share of occupation costs in 1947. But these and other minor concessions did not in any way limit the real power which the Soviet Union had obtained for itself in Austria in the first postwar years. In addition, they could be withdrawn at any time by a unilateral decision in Moscow.

The new attitude of the "collective leadership" made a stronger impression on leading circles in the West than one might have expected. Many leading statesmen and politicians were only too ready to believe that the "new men" who now held the fate of the Soviet Union in their hands had decided to break with the policies of Stalin. The new men, they maintained, would eventually be ready for sincere cooperation with "capitalist" states. Influential individuals and groups in Great Britain, France, and West Germany soon began to pressure their governments to adopt a more friendly attitude toward the Soviet regime, to sieze—so it was said everywhere in the West—what was perhaps the "last chance" for an agreement with Moscow and lasting peace in the world.

A few passages from the British press give ample evidence of this type of thinking. The Moscow correspondent of the *Times* reported on conditions in the U.S.S.R. at the beginning of April 1953: The former almost reverent praise for Stalin had suddenly as good as ceased. *Pravda* seemed to be interested only in world peace and in internal problems such as defects in the irrigation system and lower prices for bread, sugar, tobacco, textiles, and vodka. The anti-American campaign continued but with noticeably less intensity. From these observations, correct in themselves, the newspaper reached the surprising conclusion in a lead article that the change apparently extended deep "into the structure of the system itself."

In a speech in April 1953 a certain British politician

claimed that Foreign Secretary Eden and his predecessors had helped transform Russia into a democratic state. Their firmness had "contributed to the good that now seemed to show itself." Even Churchill was inclined to regard the dramatic although unimportant concessions the "collective leadership" had made in the field of internal and foreign policy as a sign of an approaching thorough transformation, if not of the Communist system at least of its foreign policy. In a speech in Glasgow on April 17, 1953, he spoke enthusiastically of "sudden hopes that have sprung in the hearts of the peoples under every sky." Cautiously he added: "May be that another chance has come. Perhaps it will come. We cannot tell." In a later speech in the House of Commons on May 11, 1953, Churchill explained that it was "a mistake" to assume that no agreement of substance could be reached with the Soviet Union without a general agreement. He suggested, therefore, a summit conference as soon as possible at which the leaders of the three Western powers, without an agenda, would attempt to determine in informal discussion whether the new collective leadership in Moscow was prepared for real concessions. "At the worst," he summed up his opinion, "the participants in the meeting would have established more intimate contacts. At the best we might have a generation of peace." He left his listeners at rest in assuring them that there was insufficient evidence that the Soviet Union had inspired the Communist offensive in Laos. The *Times* commented: "the Prime Minister spoke with the reflective wisdom of an elder statesman."

These random examples are typical of the atmosphere produced by the policy of relaxation. According to his memoirs, Eden, however, appears to have judged the situation far more cautiously. He did not share the optimistic views of his Prime Minister that the death of Stalin could lead to a final solution of the conflict between the two blocs. Still he did not oppose Churchill's idea of a summit conference. The prospects for an agreement with the Soviet Union about Central Europe appeared slight indeed, but he considered them "worth exploring." On the other hand, the British Prime Minister received strong support from the opposition in his own country and in France where influential groups were trying to prevent ratification of an agreement on a European Defense Community and German participation in the defense of Western Europe. The chamber would never approve this agreement, warned Georges Bidault, if the government ignored the "basic changes" introduced by the "new course" in the Soviet Union. A new attempt must therefore be made to settle through negotiations the actual differences between the Soviet Union and the Western powers. Public opinion in France, Bidault added, must be convinced that Soviet policy had not changed decisively. Only then would the chamber agree to the rearmament of West Germany.

In Washington, a realistic rather than sentimental policy had prevailed since the death of Roosevelt, and these illusions gained little ground. The U.S. government was firmly convinced that the Soviet Union only wanted a summit conference to delay or prevent ratification of an agreement on a European Defense Community, a supranational army which would include German units. Consequently, the United States at first emphatically opposed the conference suggested by Churchill. Until the Soviet Union presented more convincing evidence of a change in policy, a conference would be senseless. In spite of its doubts about the alleged transformation of the Soviet regime, however, the U.S. government, in the interest of Western unity, eventually agreed to a new four-power conference, though only at the foreign ministers' level.

Even if the atmosphere of relaxation brought no direct and immediate gains, Moscow hoped for other advantages. The various interpretations of Soviet policy could themselves provoke serious differences among the Western powers and the political groups in each country. Latent disagreements between capitalist states, social classes, and interest groups might be aggravated as Stalin had prescribed in his last tactical guidelines. The United States might even be isolated from its allies. In a speech on August 8, 1953, Malenkov claimed that the Atlantic bloc was already torn by inner disagreement at a time of great international strain. With the relaxation of this strain, he added, the Atlantic bloc might fall apart completely. And indeed in Great Britain and France the ostensibly new and conciliatory Soviet policy produced exactly the illusion the Communist rulers hoped for.

For its part, the United States aimed at saving the European army or undertaking the rearmament of the Federal Republic of Germany in another form. American diplomats considered it their primary task to prevent the Soviet Union from using a conference for the further division of the Western powers. As soon as Soviet representatives had demonstrated that they lacked any real will to negotiate, the conference should be broken off and its failure exploited to hasten ratification of the agreement concerning the European army.

According to information from a Western diplomat in Moscow with strong Communist sympathies, the top conference suggested by Churchill entirely met the wishes of the "collective leadership." Encouraged by the disagreement among the Western powers, the Soviet attitude, however, stiffened perceptibly. In this way, Moscow hoped to further accentuate the differences. Soviet newspapers praised Churchill and the governments in London and Paris. Attacks were **now concentrated** specifically on the United States which was declared to be the sole obstacle standing in the way of true relaxation between the East and West. Moscow evidently hoped that either Western unity would be severely strained, or domestic public opinion would force Britain and France to recommend concessions which they might even persuade the United States to accept. Now there followed a long and fruitless war of diplomatic notes between the Western powers and the Soviet Union.

Soon the leaders in the Kremlin put forward special conditions for participation in the conference. They demanded a conference covering all differences between the two blocs. They also called for the invitation of Communist China, rejected free elections in all of Germany as a basis for reunification, and opposed putting the Austrian State Treaty on the agenda. Finally Molotov declared that before the conference met the Western powers would have to abandon the rearmament of Germany. Molotov had gone too far, however. This demand provoked such strong resentment in London and

Paris that the Soviet Union finally agreed to discuss the reunification of Germany along with its own proposal for a European security system, and it was agreed that the conference should begin in Berlin on January 25, 1954 without a firm agenda. For this reason, on January 5, 1954 in a note to the four occupation powers, the Austrian government urged that they grant the Austrian question an important position on the agenda. Some days later, to the surprise of all, the Soviet government agreed to do so and also suggested that an Austrian delegation take part in the deliberations about the State Treaty. This answer aroused a faint hope in Austria but no great expectations of a satisfactory outcome. And indeed the Soviet Union had not the slightest intention of concluding a general agreement involving any real concessions.

9

The Berlin Conference, 1954

The Berlin Conference began on January 25 and ended on February 18, 1954. Although it lasted considerably longer than Washington had originally wished, the negative results abundantly confirmed that no fundamental change had occurred in Soviet foreign policy. Soviet participants had only sought to weaken the will to resist of the Western powers. As on previous occasions when the reunification of Germany was discussed, the Soviet Union agreed, in principle, that it should be based on "free elections." But "free elections" do not mean the same thing in the Soviet Union and the Western world. As prerequisites for "free elections" in a communist sense, all industrial "monopolies and combines" must first be completely liquidated. The property of "war criminals"—a very classic notion—must be confiscated and turned over to the people, that is, socialized. All property of the so-called Junkers must be given to the "poor" peasants in a "democratic" land reform. Finally, and not the least important, the civil administration must be purged.

Once this program had been carried out, the elections would be "free." Moscow would then have no reason to worry about the outcome—Germany would already have been to a great extent sovietized in exactly the same way Soviet-imposed regimes had transformed the "people's democracies." Even these four points, however, were not enough. Before the "election" the U.S.S.R. demanded the creation of an all-German government composed of equal numbers of representatives of the parliaments of both the "German Democratic Republic" and the Federal Republic of Germany "with the extensive participation in both cases of the democratic organizations," that is, Communist front associations. An equally important requirement was that the Western powers should abandon plans for rearming the Federal Republic.

The Austrian question, the last item on the agenda, was not dealt with until February 12. And in his first speech on the subject, Molotov submitted proposals which indicated no relaxing of the Soviet attitude toward the State Treaty. The 1952 Paris agreement concerning the European Defense Community, although not yet ratified, Molotov maintained, had created a new situation. The Soviet Union had basically nothing against the signing of the State Treaty. After it went into effect, however, the four occupation powers should maintain troops in their zones until a peace treaty had been concluded with Germany. Consequently, the evacuation of Austria should be postponed until the Soviet conditions for a German peace treaty had been accepted, in other words, until the Western powers had agreed to "free" elections in the Communist sense. This meant that even if the state treaty had been signed, the occupation of Austria would continue indefinitely.

The military units, however, would no longer have the character of occupation troops or function as such. Their disposition should be regulated by special arrangements between Austria and the occupation powers. Molotov confirmed our conclusion shortly before the conference ended, also rejecting an Austrian suggestion that the occupation troops be withdrawn by June 30, 1955. He merely offered to examine the question again before the end of 1955.

Aside from the conclusion of a German peace treaty, Molotov named two further conditions for evacuating Austria. The country must never participate in any coalition or military alliance aimed at a state that had taken part with its fighting forces in the war against Hitler (for example, the U.S.S.R.) and could not allow foreign military bases (for example, of N.A.T.O.) on its territory or accept foreign military instructors or specialists. In this case, the demands found no opposition from the Austrian side; as Foreign Minister Figl emphasized in a speech during the conference, his government had never had any intention of joining alliances or allowing foreign powers to establish bases.

Great Britain and the United States, on the other hand, had from the very beginning evidently hoped that Austria, some time after the restoration of its sovereignty, would of its own free will adhere to the Western alliance or at least establish close political and—maybe—military relations with the powers belonging to this group. Therefore, the British and the Americans—and particularly the former—were rather reluctant to accept provisions restricting the freedom of action of the Austrian government in the way required by the Soviet Union. The Austrians on their side were convinced that if the Soviet Union should ever agree to the evacuation of their country, a firm promise of neutrality and non-adherence to great power blocs would be one of the main conditions required.

However, as they did not dare to jeopardize the support of the Western powers in the future, they finally agreed to meet their wishes to some extent. They, consequently, refused the inclusion in the State Treaty of the provisions suggested by the Soviet Union while stating at the same time that they had no objection in principle to any of these and never intended to participate in military alliances or allow foreign military bases on their territory. The Austrian government wished, in other words, to avoid tying its hand by obligations in the State Treaty but had already decided to choose neutrality of its own free will as the only possible foreign policy.

Secretary of State Dulles agreed: Austria had the complete right to decide voluntarily on such a policy after the State Treaty went into effect, but should, on the other hand, not be forced to adopt neutrality by provisions in the State Treaty. The United States did not want to deprive Austria of the possibility to decide by itself upon the policy to be pursued.

Because of the opposition Molotov met, he proposed a *pro forma* modification shortly before the close of the conference. The prohibition of foreign bases and participation in coalitions and military alliances need not be included in the actual text of the State Treaty, but could be embodied in a special protocol added to the treaty as an appendix. Naturally enough, this "concession" was refused by Austria as well as the Western powers.

It has often been said that the Soviet Union had already at the Berlin Conference offered a neutrality clause which the Austrian government, however, under strong pressure from the Western powers had rejected. This is a mistake. Neutrality implies not only obligations but also rights. The two clauses suggested by the Soviet Union had imposed certain obligations upon Austria without conferring any corresponding rights to the country. Being one-sided they cannot be characterized as neutrality clauses. Their sole purpose was to prevent Austria from joining coalitions or alliances which the rulers of the Kremlin—rightly or wrongly—considered as being directed against themselves or from granting other countries military advantages which could be detrimental to Soviet interests.

First, after more than a year—or at the end of March 1955—the Soviet Union intimated, as we later shall see, that it would be willing to evacuate the country against a guaranty of Austrian neutrality. But before this point was reached, many other proposals had been submitted and for some reason or other abandoned.

What the Austrians at the Berlin Conference primarily objected to was the idea that the withdrawal of the occupation troops should not take place at the same time as the signature of the State Treaty. Without a simultaneous evacuation, the situation of the country would have been worse than before. For one thing, the control agreements, the most effective obstacle to Soviet interference in the domestic affairs of the country, would lapse. Not only would the Allied Council disband, but troops of the Western powers, predominantly American, would leave Vienna while Soviet units remained on the outskirts of the city. If Communist-inspired riots broke out as in September 1950, Soviet troops could occupy the city to "restore order," and the Western powers could do nothing without risking direct hostilities with the U.S.S.R.

The "solution" proposed by Molotov reminded many people of the fate of the three Baltic states after the signing of the so-called mutual assistance treaties with the Soviet Union in the fall of 1939. The Russians—just as Molotov now suggested—had secured the right to station troops at certain locations in these countries. Just as now planned for Austria, these units were not considered as occupation troops. And on October 31, 1939, in a speech in the Supreme Soviet, Molotov had solemnly declared that the Soviet Union by these treaties had expressly recognized the sovereignty of the Baltic states and guaranteed them against interference in their domestic affairs. Less than a year later he proposed to the same body to incorporate the Baltic States as union republics in the U.S.S.R. They still are, but since 1940 a large part of the population has emigrated to Siberia and Central Asia—involuntarily.

True, the Austrian government wanted to free the country from the control agreement's limitation on its sovereignty. But, on the other hand, this agreement helped prevent Soviet encroachment. The government, consequently, believed that it could not abandon this protection unless the occupation forces were withdrawn. Too, the economic provisions of the State Treaty would be a heavy burden to the people for years ahead, a burden worth assuming only if accompanied by complete deliverance from foreign troops. If, from time to time, in Austria one played with the thought of bringing about an evacuation without a State Treaty, it now appeared that the Soviet Union offered the opposite—a State Treaty without evacuation.

10

Austria after the Berlin Conference

During the spring of 1954, nothing important developed in Austria's international situation. The more animated was the speculation in the diplomatic corps in Vienna about the failure of the Berlin Conference. Why had the Soviet Union clung so stubbornly to the demand that Austria should remain militarily occupied even after the State Treaty took effect? The great majority of the uninitiated cited stipulations in the peace treaties with Hungary and Rumania allowing the U.S.S.R. to keep military forces in both countries to maintain lines of communication with the Soviet troops in Austria. In the case of a withdrawal from Austria, the Soviet Union would also be obliged to evacuate Hungary and Rumania. The most popular view was that this would scarcely be possible considering the weak position of the Communist parties in those countries. In notes made at the time, I granted this argument little credibility since the Soviet government could always conclude bilateral agreements which would entitle it to station military units in Hungary and Rumania.

This opinion was shared by a young Indian diplomat whom I had met in my Budapest years and had run into again in Vienna. He had strong Communist leanings and maintained active connections with the leading officials of the Soviet Embassy in Vienna. Because of his sympathies, he wanted to convince me that the negative attitude of the Soviet Union toward the Austrian State Treaty was justified. Since he realized, however, that he could not use the official arguments, he repeated the reasons he had heard from his Soviet friends which undoubtedly represented the current opinion in higher Soviet diplomat circles. So I learned that Moscow feared that withdrawal from Austria might be interpreted in Eastern Europe as a serious political retreat and have dangerous moral repercussions in those countries. As a result, the faith of local Communists in the strength of the Soviet Union would be weakened, and, simultaneously, disaffected elements, actually most of the population, would be encouraged. Disturbances of the type which had broken out in 1953 in East Germany and Czechoslovakia were unlikely, it is true. Still, any measures interpreted as a sign of weakness might encourage passive resistance. And after all I had witnessed and experienced during my five years behind the Iron Curtain, I knew that the tacit opposition was already extremely strong and could easily get still stronger.

The second reason was that the government in Vienna might attach itself more closely to the Western powers, politically if not militarily, after the end of the Soviet occupation. I remarked that the Austrian government had already stated at the Berlin Conference that it would neither participate in alliances nor allow foreign powers to establish military bases on Austrian territory. Austria intended to carry on a neutral policy, once the occupation had ended. Why did not the Soviet Union consider Austrian neutrality a sufficient guarantee against the country's political attachment to the Western powers? In such an important question as this, my informant immediately retorted the Soviet Union could not rely on promises. The only sure guarantee against Austrian adherence to the Western bloc was the presence of Soviet troops in the country.

My Indian friend then came to the obviously decisive argument in his opinion. The leaders in the Kremlin considered their occupation zone in Austria a valuable pawn that must be kept until a time when major Soviet interests were at stake. Why should the Soviet Union evacuate Austria just now, he asked, when the German question was not yet solved and negotiations about it were bound to be taken up again sooner or later? Even if the arguments repeated by my Indian friend did not suffice, subsequent developments showed that they reflected the official opinions prevailing in Communist diplomatic circles at the time.

At the end of April and the beginning of May 1954, serious friction arose in the Allied Council between the Western powers and the Soviet Union. The Austrian government had submitted a list of requests to the council. The most important ones concerned removal of the visa requirement for travel between Austria and a number of countries such as Sweden, Denmark, Norway, and the Federal Republic of Germany; accession of Austria to the so-called fugitive agreement which was signed at that time in Geneva; and, finally, eliminating the existing limitations on civilian air travel. The last was a prerequisite for establishing an Austrian flight safety service.

To the surprise of all, the Soviet representative opposed these moderate requests. If no visas were required, he claimed, citizens of the Federal Republic of Germany could enlist support for the idea of a new *Anschluss*. And the proposed flight safety and the purchase of a few helicopters necessary for this service was "an easily penetrated camouflage for the re-establishment of an Austrian air force."

An interlude of a more serious nature happened in mid-May at a meeting of the Allied Council when Soviet Ambassador Ilyichev charged that the Austrian government had failed to eliminate "fascist" and "Nazi" organizations and thereby disregarded the control agreement. When challenged by his colleagues, the ambassador could present no concrete evidence. Instead he summoned the chancellor and vice-chancellor and read them a long document drawn up in threatening terms. It maintained that the two coalition parties had, on various occasions, invited actions hostile to the Soviet Union even though the control agreement expressly prohibited any activity aimed at the occupation powers. Too, the press published almost daily articles which decreased respect for the Soviet Union. The "occupation [that is, Soviet] authorities," therefore expected, declared the ambassador, that the Austrian government would take the necessary measures to prevent a continuation of such subversive activity hostile to the Soviet Union. If this were not done, Soviet authorities would be forced to take steps to restore order. The gravity of this warning was accentuated when the official Soviet news agency TASS immediately published the text. The Austrian government did not think it could leave this challenge unanswered. Chancellor Raab made a detailed report about the conversation to Parliament where the auditors galleries were bursting. The accusations made by the Soviet Ambassador were sharply rejected by all the parties represented except the Communists. Loud applause greeted this action, an overwhelming demonstration of the unity of the political parties in the face of Soviet threats.

Against this background, it is not surprising that when Soviet officials shortly thereafter again introduced a limited control of traffic at the zonal demarcation line, the populace considered it the prelude to a generally more severe policy in the Soviet zone. Fortunately the fears proved exaggerated. The measures adopted by the Soviet authorities had no serious political implications and did not, as had been feared, foreshadow either a hardening of the Soviet attitude or preparations for the integration of the Eastern zone in the "socialist camp." Soviet military officials limited their interference mainly to seizing brochures and pamphlets which they considered "friendly to Anschluss" or "hostile to the Soviet Union." The explanation may have been that the Soviet leaders, after Molotov's stubborn performance in Berlin, feared that the Western powers might integrate their zones of Austria economically and militarily with West Germany. Propaganda about the danger of a new *Anschluss* should make such a move difficult, however, and threatening gestures toward the Austrian government should remind the West that the Soviet Union still held eastern Austria as a hostage.

Conversations with Austrians from various levels of society during those first months after the Berlin Conference left a strong impression of deep disappointment, particularly in the large mass of the population. Although no one had harbored exaggerated hopes, the result was worse than anyone had feared. Most Austrians had been reluctant to abandon the hope that some unforeseen occurrence might cause the capricious rulers of the Kremlin to discontinue the policy of procrastination and consent to the conclusion of the State

Treaty on conditions acceptable to Austria. The tactic of relaxation of tensions adopted by Moscow shortly after Stalin's death had largely contributed to the propagation of this idea. As matters now stood, the Austrian government had no choice but to try to find new or not earlier considered solutions. During the second half of March, the leading members of the government discussed exhaustively what they could do to maneuver the State Treaty out of the deadlock of the Berlin Conference. They were, first of all, convinced that the Soviet Union would oppose not only the evacuation of the country but also any reduction of the occupation forces on a large scale. It was evident, furthermore, that it would be a long time before the Austrian question could again be raised to the level of a meeting of foreign ministers.

The first task—as the Austrian government saw it—was to prevent the Western powers from removing the Austrian question from their immediate program and from leaving further discussions with the Soviet Union to the indefinite future. For this reason a special effort was made to create a new forum for continuous negotiations between the occupation powers and Austria. After long discussions the government decided to propose an idea suggested by Bruno Kreisky: a permanent commission in Vienna consisting of the four ambassadors and one or more representatives of the Austrian government.

In numerous and lengthy discussion with me, Kreisky developed his basic idea before he submitted it to his government. His idea was that the re-establishment of Austrian sovereignty need not wait for the conclusion of a State Treaty. As long as this treaty could not be had on conditions acceptable to Austria, other solutions must be found. Through negotiations with the great powers, one might conceivably regain, step by step, the essential sovereign rights while maintaining the authority and powers of the Allied Council until the conclusion of the State Treaty. Through the proposed five-power commission, Kreisky hoped to eliminate those limitations on sovereignty which would automatically have been removed by the State Teaty. A few examples: (1) restoration of air rights, (2) Austrian control over Austrian borders, (3) repurchase of the industrial enterprises (U.S.I.A.) seized by the Soviet Union as "German assets," (4) admission of Austria into the United Nations, (5) equality, in principle, of Austria with the occupation powers in negotiations over the State Treaty.

Points 2 and 3 require further explanation: Soviet occupation officials frequently allowed duty free import and export between their zone and the neighboring "people's democracies" and also allowed foreign citizens to cross the border without Austrian visas. Finally, Soviet authorities forced the Austrian police in their zone to hand over political fugitives from Czechoslovakia and Hungary, a notorious violation of the right of asylum.

The question of "German assets" was also important. These included enterprises originally owned by Germans as well as allied property taken over illegally by the Nazis. The idea was to obtain the restitution to Austria of those "assets" before the total amount of compensation had been fixed by the State Treaty. In return, Kreisky contemplated offering the Soviet Union merchandise worth sixty million dollars to be delivered over a six-year period. Immediately after the conclusion of the State Treaty, the amount already paid would be counted toward the total sum of the compensation established by the State Treaty.

At the end of March 1954, Foreign Minister Figl sounded out the representatives of the three Western Powers in Vienna. He emphasized that the five-power commission should not replace the Allied Council or assume any of its functions. The two institutions should work side by side and handle quite different questions. The new commission would be limited to problems connected with the State Treaty. As Figl expressed it, Austria wanted the Western powers to deliberate with, not about, Austria. On the American side the proposal was received with noticeable skepticism. Was not the negative Soviet attitude at the Berlin Conference proof enough that no real concessions could be expected from Moscow? Washington also feared that the Soviet Union would use the proposed commission for its own propaganda. By making more apparent rather than real concessions, the rulers in the

Kremlin might try to convince public opinion and influential politicians in the Western world that they were inspired by a desire for results by way of negotiations which they actually lacked. This might delay still further the ratification of the treaties on the European Defense Community and the armament of West Germany, particularly as the latter question was a matter of extreme difference of opinion, especially in France.

Nevertheless, the Austrian government expressed its wishes in an informal memorandum to the American, British, and French governments. After a long delay they gave it to understand that they were prepared in principle to support the proposal as soon as it was presented to all four occupation powers. The Austrian government, however, decided to await the results of the Geneva Conference on Indochina which had already been called and would meet on April 26, 1954.

When the official *démarche* was finally made, the British government was the first to answer, at the beginning of August, that the proposal was basically acceptable, and they instructed the British Ambassador in Vienna to begin preparatory discussions with the three other occupation powers and the Austrian government regarding the five-power commission. The British stressed, however, that their positive attitude did not imply any change in policy. Great Britain still considered the re-establishment of the sovereignty of Austria as primary and was ready to take up negotiations concerning the State Treaty as soon as the Soviet Union had declared itself willing to withdraw its military forces from Austria immediately after enactment of the treaty. The answers of the United States and France shortly afterward were basically the same.

Since Dulles, however, had declared, at the end of the Berlin conference, that he considered further negotiations useless as long as the Soviet government was unwilling to set the time for the withdrawal of occupation troops, the Austrian government had been anxious to avoid the impression that their proposal was opposed to his view. They feared that the U.S. government, in such a case, could feel called upon to reject the whole idea of setting up the commission. For this reason the Austrian government purposely did not define the activity of the commission as a continuation of treaty "negotiations." Instead it should mainly be concerned with "alleviation of the current situation in Austria," that is, with a relaxation of the occupation regime. This unfortunate formulation offered the Soviet Union a pretext for distorting the real sense of the proposal. A lead article in the *Volksstimme,* the central organ of the Communist Party of Austria, on the same day that the Austrian government published the contents of its note to the four occupations powers, foreshadowed the attitude of the U.S.S.R. The newspaper tried to make its readers believe that "alleviations in the occupation rule" meant that the government wished to avoid further negotiations about the State Treaty, even though Molotov, at the conclusion of the Berlin Conference, had offered such negotiations at a later date. This offer had purposely been vague and had given rise to different interpretations. As far as I myself and most of the members of the Austrian government could understand, Molotov had only meant that the Soviet Union was willing to resume the negotiations on the basis of the proposals submitted at the Berlin Conference, in other words, on the basis of a continued occupation. In such case, the only task of the negotiations would have been to make an agreement about the size of the troops to be left in Austria, their legal status and permanent stations, and so on.

Many influential people had, on the other hand, taken the opposite view. They believed, or entertained the hope, that the Soviet Union after some time would be prepared to take up negotiations on a new basis and consent to the evacuation of the country on conditions which—although hard—would nevertheless be acceptable to Austria.

The article in the *Volksstimme* scattered these illusions. It declared, certainly inspired by Moscow, that when Molotov offered to resume the negotiations at some later date, he had only meant that they should be based "on the proposals presented by the Soviet government in Berlin." In an article published a few days later, the Communist newspaper expressed itself even more clearly. Because of German rearmament, Austria's independence was threatened, the newspaper declared, by a new *Anschluss*. "With the disinterested intention" of protecting Austria from this danger, the Soviet Union demanded a continuation of the occupation until "a peaceful solution" of the reunification of Germany could be achieved. After the publication of these two articles, it could no longer be doubted that the Soviet Union would reject the procedure suggested by the Austrian government.

The official Soviet answer was delivered to the Austrian Ambassador in Moscow on the afternoon of August 12, 1954 and was published in full the next day by TASS. As the Austrian government had not been informed in advance of the intended publication, it had no possibility of commenting on the Soviet note at the time of the announcement. The text confirmed the impression given by the *Volksstimme*. Molotov had presented "concrete proposals" at the Berlin Conference, the note declared, and the Soviet Union wished to convoke an ambassadors' conference and continue the discussion of these proposals for the purpose of concluding a State Treaty. Austria, on the contrary, wanted to limit the discussion to "alleviations in the occupation rule." In other words, Moscow was only willing to discuss the questions which from its point of view were still unsolved, for example, the status of the occupation forces, the number and location of garrisons, the end of the control agreement, and the return of Austrian property requisitioned for the control commission or for troops billeted in Vienna.

If the Austrian government did not accept the program thus outlined or, as a Communist newspaper expressed itself, "refused to pay the price" which has been asked, the Soviet Union would oppose not only the evacuation of the country but also every alleviation of the occupation regime.

Although there can be no doubt about the aim of the negotiations proposed by Moscow, Communist propagandists immediately began to spread the idea that the Soviet note of August 12 meant that the Kremlin was prepared to resume these under conditions acceptable to Austria. But the Austrian government, inspired by the Western powers, had failed to answer the Soviet promptly and positively. Even intellectuals, industrialists, and experienced Austrian diplomats, who could not be suspected of any Communist leanings, communicated to me their serious worry that, as a result of regrettable subservience to the Western powers, Austria had again missed a favorable opportunity to conclude the State Treaty.

These critics were, of course, right about the rulers in the Kremlin being prepared to sign the State Treaty within the shortest possible time, but on Soviet and not, as they imagined, on Austrian conditions; in other words, provided that the occupation forces could remain in Austria for an indefinite time.

In a noncommittal answer on October 12, the Austrian government regretted that the Soviet Union had rejected its proposal but expressed pleasure that the Soviet government was favorably inclined toward the conclusion of a State Treaty. Austria hoped, therefore, that the four occupation powers would convene a conference in Vienna for this purpose. Still, no positive result could be expected unless the four powers accepted the idea that enactment of a State Treaty necessarily meant withdrawal of occupation troops.

Apparently, differences of opinion had existed even within the Austrian government, although mainly about the wording of the Austrian note to Moscow. At first some of its members, including Chancellor Raab, had toyed with the idea that a very few small occupation units from all the four powers might be allowed to remain in the country indefinitely provided they were concentrated in a few localities. The soundings made showed, however, that such a suggestion would meet with serious misgivings, especially on the part of the Social Democrats. The chancellor, therefore, soon abandoned his idea and declared upon several occasions that the withdrawal of the occupation troops was an indispensable prerequisite for Austrian acceptance of the State Treaty. And this was also indicated in the text of the Austrian answer.

But Raab's willingness to compromise reflected no overall inclination to make concessions. It can only be explained as a result of the utter despondency which had seized not only the population in general but also leading politicians after the Soviet Union had now given a new proof of its intractability. It must be added that Raab was an experienced, careful man who followed the old proverb, a bird in the hand is worth two in the bush. In the prevailing atmosphere the repeatedly confirmed obstinacy of the Soviet Union caused him as well as many others to take too pessimistic a view of the future. He was certainly convinced that he acted in a "realistic" way and according to his country's interest when he considered a limited number of military bases preferable to an indefinite prolongation of the existing situation.

This shows, on the other hand, how efficient the Soviet tactics had been. In the preceding month one of their main purposes had been to create an outlook as pessimistic as possible in Austrian political circles in order to soften up their power of resistance to the Soviet demands.

The Western powers were aware of the chancellor's discouragement and it caused them serious worry. When Raab paid an official visit to Washington a short time later, American leaders—to judge by the text of a communiqué published at Raab's departure—considered it their most important task to persuade him to pledge his government to demand the complete evacuation of Austria as a requirement for a State Treaty.

11

The Soviet Union and West Germany's Admission to N.A.T.O.

In the year following the Berlin Conference, February 18, 1954 until February 8, 1955, Austria was never a major factor in Soviet calculations. True, it was kept "on the shelf" as a possible pawn to be used at some future date, but the Soviet regime apparently felt it could achieve its aims by other means, mainly by skillful propaganda or relaxation of tensions. And, of course, the chief aim was preventing the rearmament of West Germany, the neutralization of this country, the breaking up of N.A.T.O., as well as the withdrawal of American troops from Germany.

These aims were pursued simultaneously: the first by attempting to influence in different ways the French Parliament not to ratify the agreement on the European Defense Community, the three others by proposing European treaties of collective security. Already in Berlin on February 10, 1954, Molotov had proposed a "General European Treaty on Collective Security in Europe."

This treaty which should replace the agreement on the European Defense Community had nothing to do with security in the conventional sense of the word. As the draft submitted by Molotov ruled out any coalition, alliance, or agreement, the objectives of which were contrary to the purposes of the treaty, neither the maintenance of the N.A.T.O. nor the conclusion by West Germany of any other political or military agreement would have been compatible with the proposed treaty. Another draft agreement on European security submitted by Molotov on the same day provided—with the exception of limited contingents—for the simultaneous withdrawal within six months of the occupation forces from both East and West Germany.

Had the two treaties been accepted, the Soviet Union would have arrived at the result desired without a peace treaty with Germany. This would, above all, have been the case if the treaty on collective security, as at first intended, had been confined to European states. Had this happened, the United States would have been excluded but could together with the Chinese Peoples Republic (Red China) be invited to send representatives in the capacity of observers. The purpose was evidently to bring Germany and other European states under Soviet control with the consent of those nations. When Molotov read his proposal at the Berlin Conference, it seemed so preposterous that laughter rippled around the Western sides of the table to the dismay of the Communist delegation. Molotov understood that he had made himself and his country ridiculous, and in a note to the governments of France, the United Kingdom, and the United States of March 31, 1954, he modified his proposal. Considering its "participation in the common struggle against the aggression of Hitler during the Second World War," the Soviet government, Molotov now declared, had no objection to the United States' adherence to the treaty on collective security in Europe. In the same note the Soviet Union expressed its willingness to join N.A.T.O. With his customary lack of humor Molotov declared that this organization "would lose its aggressive character if adhered to by all the Great Powers who had belonged to the anti-Hitler-coalition." But this polite hint by the wolf of willingness to join the sheepfold was not taken seriously. Its purpose was to transform N.A.T.O. into an organization similar to the one to be created by the treaty on collective security in Europe.

The next move was made in notes to the Western powers on July 24. The Soviet government, encouraged by the result of the Geneva Conference on Indochina—the peak of its successes after Stalin's death—as well as by the favorable prospects for rejection of the treaty on the European Defense Community by the French Parliament, urged an early conference of European states and the United States "for the purpose of exchanging views on the question of setting up a system of collective security in Europe." And on August 4 Moscow proposed a four-power conference in August or September as a preliminary to the general conference.

In these circumstances it is hardly surprising that the Soviet Union found it possible to modify slightly its attitude to the Austrian State Treaty during the summer 1954. Although rejecting the Austrian proposal for a five-power commission, it declared that the conclusion of a peace treaty with Germany was no longer an absolute prerequisite of the evacuation of Austria. The adherence of the Western powers and of Western Germany to the treaty on collective security in Europe would also make the evacuation possible. Both would, of course, have achieved the same purpose: the abandonment of the West German rearmament, the disruption of the N.A.T.O., etc.

During August, the Communists mounted an intense propaganda campaign against the European Defense Community which was finally rejected by the French National Assembly on August 30, 1954. In Moscow this vote was interpreted as proof that the campaign of relaxation had been the right tactic. Apparently the rulers in the Kremlin were now convinced that they had succeeded in putting the question of West German rearmament "on the shelf," if not indefinitely, in any case, for a long time to come. The vote in the French Chamber was a major defeat for American policy in Europe, declared an Austrian of high station who sympathized with communism and had close connections with the rulers in Moscow. One of the cornerstones of American policy in Europe had tumbled down, he continued. American policy had been discredited for a long time to come. Indeed, it appeared from the same report that the Soviet Union expected a general dejection throughout Western Europe after the United States had so clearly shown its inability to prevent the Soviet Union from reaching its tactical goals. After this diplomatic victory, Moscow hoped that many influential political circles would soon be convinced that the advance of communism could no longer be prevented. A number of governments would be more inclined to meet Soviet demands.

But the jubilation in the Kremlin did not last long. On September 11 Sir Anthony Eden, the British Foreign Secretary, set out on a quick tour to consult the European governments involved and organize a nine-power conference which met in London on September 28. At London, the Western powers agreed on a more conventional military alliance with separate national armies, including a new West German army, to replace the supranational army envisioned for the European Defense Community. Agreements on this concept were signed in Paris on October 23. In contrast to the European Defense Community, the negotiations had been finished within a short time. But it was by no means certain that the agreements would be approved by the French Parliament. By making the right propaganda moves, Soviet leaders might still wreck the Paris agreements just as they had the European Defense Community.

For the Soviet Union the most promising gambit was still to urge international conferences, to give the impression that the Soviet Union worked without pause—even if in vain— for a *détente* between East and West. And hints of possible concessions might increase the reluctance to present the Soviet Union with a *fait accompli*. "There were no questions contested," Malenkov had declared in his speech of August 8, 1953, "which could not be solved in a peaceful way on the basis of a mutual understanding." No differences of opinion were so complicated that they could not be resolved by discussion, argued Soviet propagandists in accordance with this line.

The expectations in which the Soviet leaders had indulged were far from unfounded. As Molotov later hinted in his speech of February 8, 1955, "certain oscillations had then manifested themselves in the French Parliament which could create new difficulties for the supporters of the Paris agreements." As judged from Moscow, the situation was certainly bad but still far from desperate. The confidence in the power of international conferences to work miracles, to prevent and settle serious conflicts, or to smooth out existing antagonisms between East and West was growing from day to day. The Soviet tactic succeeded sooner than anyone could suspect in inducing influential political figures in Great Britain, France, and West Germany to believe that no irrevocable decisions should be made with regard to the rearmament of the Federal Republic before a conference between the heads of governments of the great powers had met again. This conviction was particularly strong in France as well as in the Socialist parties and some liberal circles in Great Britain and West Germany. In these quarters it was thought absolutely necessary to postpone, for the time being, the ratification of the Paris agreements unless the Western powers, as the saying went, wished to gamble away "the last opportunity" to solve the conflict between East and West in a peaceful way.

In the United States, on the other hand, no one in the government indulged in any illusions about the real meaning of the Soviet conference proposals, and Washington continued to reject them or postpone discussion until the Paris agreements could be ratified by all the signatory powers.

As early as October 23, the same day the Paris agreements were signed, the Soviet Union, in order to prevent their final approval, repeated its previous proposal for an international conference on a European security pact to replace any defense treaty between the Western powers. The Soviet government was, as always, willing to discuss the reunification of Germany "on peace-loving and democratic," that is, on Communist, foundations and to consider the withdrawal of occupation troops from both East and West Germany. Of greater interest was that the Soviet Union also declared itself prepared "to examine anew the proposals for holding all-German elections submitted by Britain at the Berlin Conference supported by France and the United States." This statement caused many people inclined toward wishful thinking to believe that the Soviet Union had finally decided to give up its opposition to free elections as a basis for German reunification. But the wording of the note showed clearly that the Russians merely wanted to *discuss* free elections on the basis of the British *as well as* the Soviet proposals already submitted at the Berlin Conference. Discussions had taken place at past conferences without causing the Soviet Union to change its standpoint. Why should it do so now? Moreover, the note indicated that the rejection of the European Defense Community had been the main reason for the willingness of the Soviet Union to reopen the discussion of "free elections." Consequently, the note promised nothing else than another repetition of the performance of Molotov at the Berlin Conference.

At the time for the debate on the Paris agreements in the French Chamber moved nearer, the rulers in the Kremlin were getting more and more nervous. On November 13, 1954 the Soviet Union invited the United States and all European countries to an international conference to convene on the 29th of the same month in order to consider the establishment of a collective security system for Europe. In the text, Moscow for the first time made no secret of the real purpose of the conference: "As in some European countries the debates on the ratification of the Paris agreements should begin already in December," the notes emphasized, "a postponement of the conference" after November 29 "would not be suited to its purpose."

"The development of Europe," the notes continued, "should not follow the disastrous path of restoring German militarism, and creating in Europe opposing military groupings of states." Ratification of the Paris agreements "would greatly aggravate the entire situation in Europe, and would undermine the possibility of the settlement of outstanding European problems, and of the German problem in particular."

Despite this threat to postpone indefinitely not only German reunification but also the signature of the Austrian State Treaty, Austrian political circles appraised the Soviet proposal realistically. It was assumed that the Soviet government could scarcely have expected Western participation in a conference before ratification of the Paris agreements. The proposal, therefore, must first of all have propaganda goals and purposes. A conference might also formalize the cooperation which already existed between the East European states, and this could take place without the participation of the Western powers.

Soon thereafter, this suspicion was confirmed by an article

in *Pravda* which was extensively quoted and paraphrased in the Austrian Communist newspaper, the *Volksstimme*. The Soviet government had counted on two possible answers to its note of November 13, indicated *Pravda*. The Western powers would either participate in the conference, which the newspaper scarcely considered possible anymore, or take a negative attitude. In the latter case, *Pravda* stressed, it was more than possible that the conference would meet on the previously determined day in Moscow. All countries that desired could participate, and the East European states would, it was implied, create their own security organization which would, however, be open to all countries.

As expected, the Austrian government stated that it could not take part in any conference at which all the occupation powers were not present. Since several of the invited countries had already refused, it was not in a position to participate. The conference opened on schedule in Moscow with only the U.S.S.R. and its satellites represented.

As the time passed without any tangible result of its intensified propaganda against the ratification of the Paris agreements, the Soviet government was obviously getting still more alarmed. Its attitude became threatening. In a new note to the Western powers on December 9, 1954, it referred to the declaration adopted at the Moscow Conference in which the participating governments had threatened to take the "necessary measures to safeguard their security" if Germany were brought into N.A.T.O. Since the satellite armed forces had been taking orders from Moscow for years (Poland even had a Soviet marshal as defense minister), this "threat" aroused little anxiety. What seemed to be more serious and, as I remember, caused some anxiety in Austria, was that the note also warned that ratification of the Paris agreements would not only prevent further negotiations on the reunification of Germany but also "not contribute to an agreement on the Austrian State Treaty." Molotov expressed the same idea even more bluntly in a public speech: ratification of the Paris agreements, he declared, would render further negotiations on the German as well as the Austrian question completely useless.

Toward the end of the year the actions of the occupation authorities seemed to confirm that the Soviet attitude had hardened, an impression which Molotov undoubtedly had hoped to create by his threatening speech. First of all, Communist propaganda against the alleged danger of a new *Anschluss* was intensified. Soon a new theme was added: that the Western powers, above all, the United States, were developing the provinces of Vorarlberg, Tirol, and Salzburg into a so-called Alpine fortress in order to protect the lines of communications between West Germany and Italy in case of war. And at a meeting of the Allied Council at the end of November, the Soviet High Commissioner developed the same line of thought and maintained that Austria was rearming secretly. Along with regular police, purely military units were being organized in the gendarmery schools located in the Western zones. According to the information which the Soviet Union had at its disposal, the ambassador said, these units were being armed with machine guns, anti-tank guns, and tanks. In contrast to the other accusations, this one contained a germ of truth. As early as 1949 the Austrian government had begun to organize mobile gendarmery battalions in the Western zones; some of the officers eventually constituted the cadre of the Austrian military forces raised after the signing of the State Treaty.

The Soviet High Commissioner now called upon the four occupation powers to prevent what he characterized as the "rearmament of Austria." Even if this demand was rejected by the Council, the Soviet intervention was successful insofar as it created new anxiety and a fresh feeling of insecurity in Austria. This was undoubtedly its purpose.

Several weeks later a new sensational incident occurred which deeply alarmed the population. On December 20, 1954 the Soviet High Commissioner suddenly called a special session of the Allied Council for the next day. The anxiety increased as he refused to disclose the questions which he intended to put on the agenda. A regular meeting was already scheduled for two days later, but apparently the idea was to call the council together under dramatic circumstances and, thus, secure as much publicity as possible. When the council convened, the Soviet High Commissioner charged that the American occupation authorities had committed illegal actions and violated the control agreement. American military units had been moved to the Tirol in the French occupation zone to secure communications between American Forces in West Germany and those in Italy. Military repair shops and weapon and munition stockpiles had also been established in the Tirol and were guarded by American troops. These measures, the Soviet High Commissioner continued, represented a conscious attempt by the United States to enlarge its occupation zone at the expense of France and to prepare areas in Western Austria "for the ends of the aggressive Atlantic bloc."

Arbitrary measures of this kind, the High Commissioner added in a threatening tone, could easily endanger the unity of the Austrian State. It was the last sentence which aroused the greatest sensation and caused the greatest anxiety. The performance closed with the submission of a resolution which termed the presence of American troops in the French zone an offense against the control agreement. The Allied Council should therefore order the American occupation authorities to withdraw their units and remove the military stores immediately.

In their answers the French and American commissioners denied any violation of the control agreement. True, a few small American units, about three hundred men altogether, had been transferred to the French zone. But this had been known for a long time by the Soviet Union as well as the other occupation powers. As this troop move had taken place with the consent of the French government, the control agreement had not been broken in any way.

The Allied Council had never passed a resolution permitting the United States to have troops in the Tirol, the Soviet High Commissioner replied. The size of the units was irrelevant. As nobody could deny that American troops had been moved, the agreement between the allies had been violated. In a more threatening tone the High Commissioner repeated once more: "These offenses are inadmissible and of great consequence because they could, as an end result, endanger the unity of the Austrian state."

Die Österreichische Zeitung, the organ of the Soviet occupation forces, reported this discussion of the Allied Council in a prominent position with large headlines. Although the Austrian press sought to discount the incident, it caused extreme disquiet in the government in Vienna as well as among the people. Although the unexpected action was probably connected in some way with the Soviet campaign against the arming of West Germany, it might also indicate a decision in the Kremlin to use the insignificant American troop transfer as an excuse for terminating the control agreement. The termination of this agreement would in its turn allow the occupation authorities to make arrangements which would finally lead to the division of the country into two sections as had already happened in Germany.

Several days before the Soviet High Commissioner called the Allied Council to the special session, a strange event took place, the significance of which I did not understand at the time. I had invited a number of guests for lunch. A Soviet diplomat, L., was one of them, and after the meal he asked if he could remain after the other guests had gone. When we were alone, he asked whether I had noticed an interview which Vice-Chancellor Schärf had given a short time before to a Dutch newspaper. Among other things, Schärf had maintained that several members of the People's Party had not completely rejected the idea of a division of Austria along the Enns. The interview had attracted considerable attention in the country and provoked vehement retorts by People's Party spokesmen who accused Schärf of slandering his political rivals.

After I had answered that I was acquainted with the interview and the newspaper polemics, L. asked an astonishing question: Did I believe that there existed very strong feelings among the people for a division of Austria along the demarcation line?

The question appeared so absurd, I replied, that it scarcely deserved an answer. "Not a single Austrian can be so foolish."

"Oh, let me tell you," L. retorted with a sly grin, "many Austrians are often very stupid."

By his question and his own reply he had undoubtedly intended to indicate that a division of Austria was being considered in Moscow. He was testing my reaction to the argument which would be used to justify such a step. Later information has confirmed that the misgivings that the Soviets had such designs were not unfounded. During the Moscow negotiations between the Austrian and Soviet delegations in April 1955, Mikoyan stressed in a private conversation that his government had been afraid that the rearmament of West Germany would, besides other unpleasantnesses, sooner or later cause the Western powers to organize their own occupation zones in Austria as part of their general strategic plan. In order to meet this danger, different alternative solutions had been considered. One of these was to forestall the plans of the Western powers by incorporating the Russian occupation zone in the Eastern bloc.

The nervousness of the rulers in the Kremlin before the approaching ratification of the Paris agreements, clearly reflected in the menacing notes to the Western powers and the hardly disguised threat to terminate the control agreement and divide Austria along the river Enns, was far from surprising. After the rejection of the treaty on the European Defense Community, the ruling circles in Moscow had been firmly convinced that the campaign for the relaxation of tension had succeeded in removing the danger of the West German rearmament for good.

So much greater was the disappointment with the course events had taken during the fall. Why had the campaign for the relaxation of tensions now suddenly failed after its great success only a few months earlier? This was to all appearances the grave problem which occupied the minds of the rulers of the Kremlin in the last month of 1954. Obviously, Soviet diplomats who enjoyed the special confidence of the Politburo had been instructed to try to find a clue to this disappointing development during conversations with some of their Western colleagues. This was certainly the reason why one top-ranking member of the Soviet Embassy, whom I knew fairly well, hinted, when we met at a cocktail party in December, that he would like to have a talk with me.

Before I enter into the details of the interesting conversation which followed at a small dinner party, to which I invited him and one of his colleagues at the Soviet Embassy, I must first mention that I had, during the early fall of 1954, become more acquainted with two high Soviet diplomats K. and L. Later I was to meet both of them often with State Secretary Bruno Kreisky. To judge by the diplomatic registry, K. had a higher rank than L. How the matter actually stood is difficult to say. Both, however, exercised an influence far beyond their ostensible function in the embassy and undoubtedly enjoyed the confidence of the Kremlin. In the preparatory negotiations concerning the State Treaty, which took place in the first months of 1955 in Vienna, all important feelers were undertaken by either K. or L. or both together. They were obviously the only ones who were empowered to express themselves relatively openly. They appeared to be inseparable. Very rarely did one go out without having first made certain that the other was also invited. When they themselves invited guests, they appeared together as hosts. K.'s attitude appeared to be more realistic. He apparently never allowed himself to be influenced by preconceived opinions and was interested mainly in the solution of practical political problems. L., on the other hand, had a more doctrinaire attitude and obviously possessed a more thorough theoretic knowledge of Marxism-Leninism. He had at his disposal an impressive supply of appropriate quotations from the works of the classic writers of communism. K. was a clever and worldy-wise diplomat who, in contrast to his colleague, moved easily in all circles. L. was more reserved and inaccessible at first. Both were educated, intelligent, congenial, and knew German perfectly. Both improved on closer acquaintance.

Thanks to my friendly connections with Kreisky, of which K. and L. were aware, I was often invited that winter together with Kreisky to private discussions on the question of the State Treaty. Both the Russians apparently had to inform their superiors how the Austrian government would react to various suggestions which were being tentatively discussed on the Soviet side before the decision had been taken if they should be presented officially. When the probing assumed a more serious character I realized that the main reason why they invited me together with Kreisky and sometimes wished to see me alone was that they had been instructed to double-check the reactions of the Austrian government or of Kreisky personally to different suggestions which had been made to them. Obviously the two Russians took for granted that I was quite familiar with Kreisky's opinions, his general line of thought, and had also been informed of the attitude of his government. In bringing up the same topics or asking the same questions in separate conversations with both of us, they could easily find out if we expressed the same opinions or gave the same answers to the questions put to us. It was typical that when we were invited together our hosts always managed to avoid general talks on important problems and tried to have separate conversations with each of us. None of us had any objection to this course of action as none of us had any intention of telling anything else but the truth. I enjoyed these conversations. They were especially interesting and almost always contributed to illuminating and completing the often unsure conclusions derived from an analysis of official Soviet notes and other documents.

After this interlude I shall now go back to the dinner party to which I had invited K. and L. and in addition to them my able and experienced secretary of legation, Gunnar Lorenzton. When the dinner was finished, the two Russians immediately set about to expatiate on the armament of West Germany. It was, however, soon clear that this was only the pretext they had chosen to explain the reason for their wish to see me. After they had dutifully recited their propaganda piece and had painted in glaring colors the frightening dangers which rearmament would bring to Austria and the rest of Europe, the conversation turned gradually to the question which really interested them. K. now took over the conversation; the main task L. had to fulfill was apparently to keep Lorenzton occupied.

The first question K. brought up as soon as we were alone was the Soviet policy of relaxation. He complained bitterly that it had not had the success expected in Moscow. This policy, said K., had obviously not been understood in the leading circles of many Western countries. The Soviet attitude to a great number of important political questions had softened. When I asked what he meant, K. referred to the Paris agreements. The measures adopted by the Soviet Union to promote a relaxation of tensions had to all appearances not influenced the attitude of the signatory powers. These measures had, in any case, not, as had been hoped in Moscow, removed the danger of the ratification of the Paris agreements. He, thereafter, enumerated some of the fruitless concessions made by the Soviet Union: "Didn't we accept the cost of the occupation in Austria?" he asked. "Didn't we waive control at the demarcation line for all practical purposes; didn't we grant an amnesty, release political prisoners, and so forth? Are we not the ones who made the truce in Korea possible?" The enumeration continued for a few minutes, then he added: "And in spite of all these concessions we have not been able to convince any of the Western powers that our foreign policy has undergone not just a tactical but a real and sweeping change. What should we do then," he continued in a bitter tone, "in order to finally convince the politicians in the West that our desire for the easing of tensions is honestly meant? What do you think?"

In my opinion, I answered, none of the measures which he had mentioned could make any significant impression in the West. "Obviously you do not understand the psychological situation in capitalist countries, just as it is often difficult for us to understand your train of thought or the motives that are at the bottom of your procedures. I will give you a few examples which make clear what I mean.

"When the Soviet Union accepted occupation costs in Austria, every politically informed person in the West knew that the United States had done the same thing several years earlier. The only thing noteworthy in this Soviet decision was that it was so long delayed. How could such delay convince the West that your foreign policy had changed?

"That the senseless and irritating control at the demarcation line was finally discontinued is naturally also gratifying. But every Austrian knows that the three other occupation forces haven't exercised such control for years. The Soviet Union has only followed the example earlier set by the three other occupation powers and established a system we in the West consider as normal. Why should the abolishment of conditions, which to us seem absurd, make an especially strong impression in the West?

"Add to this that when you examine the concessions made by the Soviet Union, in Austria as well as in other countries in order to promote the relaxation of tensions, you will soon realize that they all are unilateral. As, consequently, they don't constitute an obligation for the Soviet Union they could easily be reversed by another unilateral decision in Moscow. How can you imagine that the abolishment of utter absurdities or minor unilateral concessions without real political significance should be accepted by responsible statesmen as evidence of a basic change in Soviet policy?

"There is less reason for doing so as one even receives the impression," I continued, "that the Soviet Union, in practical political questions, often follows a course in clear contrast to the officially announced policy of relaxation. Under such circumstances how can anyone believe that the ostensible policy is honestly meant?"

K. appeared surprised and depressed by what I had said. After a few moments of silence, he asked what I had meant by my last remarks.

Before I continue the narrative of the conversation, I must explain the reasons for the reply I now made. In every private discussion of a serious nature I had had with Soviet diplomats of such high standing that they had permission to talk freely, I had always noticed that arguments which usually carried weight with peoples of the same category in the West never seemed to make the slightest impression on my Soviet partners. It soon became clear that the only way to influence them was to convince them that one or the other measure the Soviet Union could adopt would contribute to the realization of the goals of the Communist world movement or facilitate the achievement of one of the tactical objectives at that time considered a condition for promoting one of these goals. The only argument likely to stir up an interest in the conclusion of the State Treaty was, therefore, one which could make him believe that the evacuation of Austria would contribute to convincing Western governments of a basic change in the Soviet foreign policy.

"Just think of the stubborn refusal of the Soviet Union to withdraw its troops from Austria," I answered. "How can anyone reconcile this negative attitude with the alleged policy of relaxation? This refusal to withdraw from Austria has contributed more than anything else to discrediting the relaxation policy. If your government is really anxious to convince the Western powers that its policy of relaxation is not only a tactical move but a real and sweeping change, the least you could do would be to evacuate Austria without any conditions."

My guest was quiet for a few minutes, reflecting. Then he asked: "Tell me honestly, do you really believe that agreement on our part to the evacuation of Austria would make such a strong impression and finally convince the public in the West of our serious desire for relaxation?"

This question surprised me. I answered that such a move would certainly convince many people, probably most.

My guest again sat in silence for awhile and then asked again: "Would it really have such a powerful effect if we were to withdraw our troops from Austria?" When I repeated: yes, undoubtedly, he asked: "Would you also be convinced?" I replied: "What does it matter to the Soviet Union if I and a few others who, like me, are without any political influence should not be convinced? What is important for you is that governments, influential politicians, journalists, and high officials in the foreign ministries in London, Paris, Washington, and perhaps in a few other countries should firmly believe that Soviet foreign policy has changed for good.

"If you waive control at the demarcation line in Austria, grant an amnesty, release political prisoners, and admit, as in the case of the Jewish doctors in Moscow, that you have imprisoned innocent people, you may convince a large section of public opinion and some politicians and journalists in the Western countries who are inclined toward wishful thinking. But if you want to deceive responsible governments or politicians you must at least make *one* concession of *real* political significance. Up till now you have made none. So, why complain that you have not succeeded to convince the West that your desire for easing the tensions is honestly meant? If you have not succeeded you have only yourself to blame."

As my guest was still silent, I continued: "With the present state of affairs, no Soviet concession of political significance could make a bigger impression in the West than a clear and unequivocal declaration that the Soviet Union is ready to evacuate Austria without any unseemly conditions." I had told K. nothing but the truth. By what I said I had, of course, hoped to stir up his interest in the conclusion of the State Treaty. But at the same time I was convinced that the Soviet readiness to evacuate Austria would be interpreted—if not by all—in any case by most Western governments as a proof of a real change of the Soviet foreign policy. The conclusion of the treaty would be considered as the "deed" Dulles had for a long time called for.

"As far as I can see," I continued, striking the same note, "a declaration of your willingness to sign the State Treaty as it now stands would at the same time be a concession you could easily afford in order to ensure confidence in your desire for relaxation. As a matter of fact," I added, "I have always wondered how the occupation of a country of the size and geographical position of Austria could give the Soviet Union any political or military advantage. I must therefore, in my turn, ask: Which are the real reasons of your stubborn refusal to evacuate Austria?"

As I had expected, K., to begin with, repeated the customary argument about the danger of a new *Anschluss* which would increase considerably if the Paris agreements were ratified. When he noticed that this argument made no impression, however, he immediately changed his tactics and added another that obviously seemed to him to carry more weight: A withdrawal from Austria would cost the Soviet Union more, militarily speaking, than it would the United States. I answered that the case seemed to be rather the reverse. If Austria is evacuated, the line of communication between the N.A.T.O. troops in Germany and Northern Italy will be completely cut.

"But, nevertheless," K. replied, "the evacuation of Austria will be of greater advantage to the United States than to the Soviet Union. In such a case, the Americans need to pull their troops only a few kilometers back from Salzburg to Bavaria. If they should consider it necessary, they can reoccupy their zone in a few hours, and the Soviet Union can do nothing to prevent it."

"What you have just said," I objected, "is equally true for the U.S.S.R. Soviet units can be moved in the same way to Hungary and Czechoslovakia and from there they can also reoccupy Eastern Austria within a few hours. Your military argument appears neither tenable nor convincing."

K. declared that he had not finished his reflections which I had interrupted. "Certainly it is true," he said, "that we could arrange to transfer our troops to Czechoslovakia and Hungary without great difficulty. A withdrawal from Austria would, nonetheless, put the Soviet Union in a less favorable position than the United States."

"How is that?" I asked, surprised and interested.

"The Austrian government and people have a clearly pro-Western outlook, which you know as well as I do," K. answered. "So what would prevent the United States from making a secret agreement in which Austria pledged itself to prepare suitable bases? In case of war, American units would have supplies, quarters, and air fields waiting for them."

"But," I rejoined, "Austria has already declared that it will not allow foreign military bases on its territory. Wouldn't the Soviet Union attach the slightest meaning to such a promise?"

"It is, of course, correct," K. answered, "that we have demanded such a promise from Austria. We wanted to avoid a situation such as I have just described. But what if the government, after the evacuation of the country, is exposed to strong pressure from the United States as well as from a rearmed Germany? The only effective guarantee that we have is occupation. With troops in the country, the threat of retaliation in our own zone, which could mean the partition of Austria, prevents the United States even now from carrying out military preparations in the three Western zones."

"But wouldn't the troops which you have stationed in Hungary," I objected, "be just as effective in restraining the Americans from violating the State Treaty?"

"No," K. answered. "If the Austrian government ignored a more or less covert American violation of the State Treaty, it would, of course, never consent to the return of the Soviet troops in Czechoslovakia or Hungary to Eastern Austria. After the Austrian sovereignty has been restored by the State Treaty, Soviet military measures without such consent would be considered aggression under international law. For the United States, however, the situation would be completely different. The American government can easily—because of the pro-Western outlook of the country—induce Austria, for its own use, to establish military bases which American troops could occupy immediately in case of a threat of war. True, this would in fact violate the State Treaty, but it wouldn't be aggression under international law. We could only protest but not retaliate with military countermeasures. This is what I referred to when I said that a withdrawal from Austria would cost the Soviet Union more than it would the United States."

I had followed K.'s exposition with interest. As I had been entirely frank myself, he had apparently stated with complete frankness the political and military considerations which towards the end of 1954 still prevailed in Moscow and had prevented the consent of the Soviet Union to the evacuation of Austria.

It was only some years later when Khrushchev and Mikoyan during their visits to Vienna had revealed to Kreisky the background of their conflict with Molotov about Austria that I fully understood to what extent K. had told the truth.

The arguments he had advanced during the conversation with me in December 1954 reflected as a matter of fact the reasons which had prompted Molotov to oppose the evacuation of Austria. The conversation consequently proves that as late as at the end of the year, he still exercised a considerable influence in Soviet foreign policy.

One thing Molotov dreaded was, as also confirmed by a careful study of the Soviet propaganda, that the American military high command would, after the signature of the State Treaty and the evacuation of Soviet troops, establish bases and perhaps build fortifications under the cover of the Austrian government. Generally speaking Molotov and his friends were convinced that because of the pro-Western attitude of the Austrian government and population, the country would, as soon as it had recovered its independence, be in fact, if not in form, politically, militarily, and economically integrated in the Western bloc. The danger would increase as West Germany rearmed and regained its earlier predominant political influence in Central Europe. This is what the Soviets had in mind when they were talking about the danger of a new *Anschluss*.

But there was also another side of the coin. Why had the Soviets not earlier dropped the iron curtain along the demarcation line at the river Enns? The same considerations K. had mentioned also prevented the Soviet leaders from isolating Eastern Austria. They feared an immediate reaction by the United States followed by the development of fortified bases in Salzburg and the Tirol.

Toward the end of the conversation, I finally mentioned the earlier Soviet proposal in the note of August 12 of an ambassadors' conference to examine the unsolved questions connected with the State Treaty. "What did Molotov mean by that?" I asked. "As far as I can recollect, only one single unresolved question of very great importance still remains, the withdrawal of the occupation troops. Since this question must be answered with either 'yes' or 'no,' I cannot understand what should be discussed in the proposed negotiations."

K.'s answer completely confirmed my own analysis of the

Soviet notes. He explained that the Soviet Union had never considered discussing anything but the status of the occupation troops, for example, the strength and quarters of units. The Soviet Union would also be willing to accept a mutual reduction of occupation troops. Whether the remaining units should be moved to a smaller number of stations or whether the occupation would, as now, include the whole country, could be one of the subjects of the negotiations. At the Berlin Conference, the Soviet Union had proposed withdrawal from Vienna. If the Western powers persisted in their objections to this suggestion, the Soviet side would agree to the maintenance in Vienna of small units of the four occupation forces.

K. concluded the exchange with a summary of the Soviet attitude toward the Austrian State Treaty: A withdrawal of troops would be out of the question until the Western powers had either agreed to the European security pact proposed by the Soviet Union or concluded a peace treaty with Germany which effectively neutralized and disarmed the Federal Republic. If the Western powers were unwilling to accept either of these alternatives, the Soviet Union was prepared to make new arrangements about the status of the occupation troops. This question—but only this, he stressed—could be discussed at the proposed ambassadors' conference in Vienna.

On December 30, 1954 the French Chamber approved the Paris agreements with a bare majority. But they still had to face the Council of the Republic and also considerable opposition in West Germany. As Chancellor Adenauer, however, disposed of a strong majority there was no doubt about ratification when the agreements would come before the Bundestag on February 24, 1955. The Soviets, therefore, set their hopes on the French Council of the Republic, where several members were hesitant and irresolute, and could, as K. declared, probably be persuaded to vote for the rejection of the agreements, once they were convinced that Soviet foreign policy had basically changed, and that, consequently, the rearmament of the Federal Republic was not as necessary as had been earlier thought.

From the beginning of the new year and till the end of

March 1955, when a positive vote in the Council of the Republic was no longer doubtful, the tactics of the Soviet Union must be judged against this background to be fully understood. Before undertaking any political action, the rulers of the Kremlin certainly asked themselves if or how far it could be expected to influence or sway the still doubtful members of the French Council. In any case, this was the impression I got from my talks with K. and L. in the following months.

The first action initiated after the approval of the Paris agreements by the French Chamber was a statement by a Soviet foreign ministry spokesman on January 15, 1955. He still stuck to the old tactical line. Ratification of the Paris agreements, he warned, "will establish the division of Germany for long years to come and be an obstacle to the restoration of German unity in a peaceful way." In case the rearmament of the Federal Republic was abandoned, however, there were still "untried possibilities" for achieving the reunification of Germany. To make the new bid more attractive, the spokesman added that the German people should be offered the restoration of a united Germany in its previous position as a great power through free elections. There was, however, an important condition which apparently most people overlooked. Such elections would have to be held according to a new electoral law based on the regulations then in force. As this meant that the laws of both the Federal Republic of Germany and the "German Democratic Republic" would be taken into consideration, the Soviet suggestion would hardly be compatible with free elections in the Western sense. The Soviet government, the spokesman added, also "considers it possible, in the event of assent by the governments" of both East and West Germany, "to come to an understanding regarding the establishment of the appropriate international supervision over the holding of the all-German elections." This offer was, at first sight, surprising as the Soviet Union had previously energetically opposed any such supervision. On closer inspection, however, it could be seen that the statement, as tempting as it seemed, was not really binding. The Soviet Union could always count upon the East German government to reject, in the end, the supervision of the elections. As is clear from this short recapitulation, the concessions offered by the Soviet Union were more apparent than real. They could at any time be restricted, withdrawn, or interpreted as best suited the rulers of the Kremlin. Their main purpose was to entice the Western powers into negotiations in the hope of thereby postponing the ratification of the Paris agreement. This purpose was, moreover, plainly emphasized by the spokesman who, in a threatening tone, added that the ratification of the Paris agreements would prevent further negotiations. The same I concluded from a conversation I had with L. a few weeks before the statement was published.

When I asked him if the Soviet Union was really prepared to allow free elections in the Soviet zone of Germany if the Western powers would abandon the arming of the Federal Republic and agree to the neutralization of a reunited Germany, he answered right away with an unconditional "yes." This answer surprised me, and I asked, therefore, whether the elections would be "free" in the Western or in the Communist sense.

"In the Western, naturally," L. answered without hesitating even for a moment.

"Is the Soviet Union prepared, then, to sacrifice its occupation zone," I continued, "to prevent the armament of the Federal Republic of Germany? For free elections in the Western sense will certainly lead to a catastrophic defeat for the Socialist Unity Party" (the Communist front organization in East Germany).

"That result is not so certain," L. answered. Admittedly, the bourgeois parties and the Social Democrats would probably acquire a decisive majority, but the result would hardly be as catastrophic as I obviously assumed on the basis of "misleading accounts" which I had supposedly "received from Berlin." As he refused to express himself more clearly, I first thought he wished to hint that the Communist regime in East Germany was sure to bring such pressure to bear on the electorate to enable it to win at least sufficient mandates to claim a few key positions in an all German government.

However, when L., some minutes later, added that the most recent election in the Soviet zone had been completely "free" in the Western sense, I realized that Moscow did not even intend to go as far as that. The same, he added, could, unfortunately, not be said about the election of the West Berlin city council. This election, L. pretended, had taken place "under heavy pressure by the American occupation force." The Communist Party had indeed received a very small number of votes in West Berlin. Since, however, the majority of the population undoubtedly realized the superiority of the Communist system but, nevertheless, had not voted accordingly, this was, L. declared, proof that the occupation forces, above all, the Americans, had prevented the voters from expressing their true convictions. The reluctance to vote for the Communist list had, in other words, demonstrated that the election had not been "free" even in the "Western sense."

This sophistic explanation finally convinced me that any Soviet offer of "free" elections could not be seriously meant. It merely aimed at misleading the public in order to bring about negotiations. Thus, the conversation entirely confirmed the impression I had acquired from the analysis of the text of the Soviet declaration of January 15, 1955, published a few weeks before.

But even if the governments of the Western powers had not been impressed by this statement and still refused to negotiate before ratification of the Paris agreement, the seeming offer of the Soviet Union had not been entirely without success. The opposition had been considerably strengthened in many countries, particularly in West Germany, where the Socialist Party, although an analysis of the text proved the contrary, was firmly convinced that the Soviet desire of "free" elections in the Western sense was genuine, provided the Federal Republic was neutralized and refused to join N.A.T.O. The leaders of the party characterized the Soviet declaration as sensational and warned the government not to treat the new offer by Moscow as the usual propaganda.

12

The Negotiations on the State Treaty Enter the First Decisive Phase

If Soviet policy toward Austria had shown absolutely no sign of change during the first month of 1955, the Kremlin had achieved nothing of substance in its struggle against the rearmament of the Federal Republic and its political and military integration in the Western bloc. Since the conclusion of the Paris agreements, the campaign for the relaxation of tensions had been of no avail. As soon as the statement of January 15 proved to be equally unsuccessful, it did not take very long before the Kremlin finally realized that the governments of the Western powers could hardly be convinced of a basic change in Soviet foreign policy without at least one concession of real political significance.

Sometime at the end of January or the beginning of February 1955 the Politburo decided to use the Austrian State Treaty for this purpose. The concession the Soviets were prepared to make would, however, still not be unconditional. It had to be connected in some way or other with the German question. If the Soviets should consent to the evacuation of Austria, they hoped to achieve, by this concession—or perhaps only by the offer of it—two purposes: render their desire for a relaxation in the traditional sense of the word more credible and, at the same time, prevent German rearmament.

A new large-scale plan with this aim in view was initiated in a speech by Molotov to the Supreme Soviet on February 8, 1955. In his introductory remarks Molotov stressed that the Soviet Union attached great importance to the re-establishment of the independence of Austria and considered further delay on the State Treaty unjustified. Nevertheless, this question could not be considered apart from the German problem. In view of an increased danger of an *Anschluss* mainly created by the plans for rearming the Federal Republic of Germany, the four occupation powers must agree on suitable "guaranties" to prevent any such occurrence in the future. In the event of an agreement on the guaranties, all troops could, however, be withdrawn from Austria without waiting either for a peace treaty with Germany or for the conclusion of a European security treaty.

Secondly, the Austrian government must pledge itself not to grant military bases on its territory or join coalitions or alliances directed against a country that had taken part in the war against Hitler. These conditions were not surprising. The Soviet Union had demanded the same pledges at the Berlin Conference, and Austria had agreed, in principle.

Only Molotov's third condition revealed—as later became clear—the true purpose of his speech: "For the earliest settlement of the Austrian issue, a four-power conference must be called without delay to examine simultaneously the German problem and the conclusion of a State Treaty with Austria. . . . It should, however, be borne in mind," he added, "that if the Paris agreements, which open the way for the resurgence of militarism in West Germany, are ratified, a serious danger of an *Anschluss* arises and, consequently, a threat to Austria's independence."

Now, fourteen years after the event, it is evident that the Soviet qualified consent to an Austrian State Treaty had, first of all, a tactical purpose. It was put forward mainly as bait to bring the Western powers to the conference table and thus delay ratification of the Paris agreements. But during the weeks immediately following Molotov's speech, this purpose was far from clear, the more so as Soviet diplomats apparently had instructions to play down as much as possible the importance of this third condition. Instead they tried to draw the attention of the Austrian government and public opinion to the guaranties against an *Anschluss,* the meaning of which they stubbornly refused to disclose. As Molotov, however, had abandoned two earlier alternative demands, a peace treaty with Germany or the signature of a general European security agreement as a condition for the withdrawal of Soviet troops, his speech caused a great sensation in Austria, which evidently was also intended by Moscow.

In the following weeks, Soviet diplomats commented on Molotov's speech in official as well as in private conversations. In their statements the possibility of concessions was, as in the speech, only indicated in general terms; no binding promises nor any hints on the nature of the desired guaranties were ever made.

The Austrians should apparently be held in suspense and kept guessing as long as possible or, in any case, until they had of their own initiative proposed the calling of an international conference and prevailed upon the occupying powers to get them to accept their demand.

When I met K. for the first time after his Foreign Minister's speech, he, in accordance with his instructions, confined himself to restating Molotov's position. He particularly stressed that the U.S.S.R. no longer demanded a peace treaty with Germany before withdrawing from Austria. Instead the occupation powers must agree on a "formula" which would prevent a new *Anschluss*. Consequently, even if the peace treaty had been abandoned as a prerequisite, the connection between the German and the Austrian questions was still retained. K. added, however, that both questions need not be settled fully at the same time. This meant, as he implied, that the Soviet Union would agree to withdraw occupation troops if only some of its demands regarding Germany were approved at the proposed conference. As Kreisky told me, a high official of the Soviet Foreign Ministry—Semenov—had made the same point in his talks with the Austrian Ambassador in Moscow. Both were acting on the same instructions.

When I pressed K. for more information it appeared from his remarks that the Soviet government attributed more importance to the meeting of the conference than to its agenda. He even stressed that the conclusion of the State Treaty not only depended on the willingness of the Western powers to cooperate in a four-power conference but that the conference itself must take place before the debate about ratification of the Paris agreements in the French Council of the Republic.

The question the Austrian government kept asking itself the following weeks was: Did the Soviet Union really intend to evacuate the country on certain not yet specified conditions? Or did it only dangle its signature on the State Treaty temptingly in the hope of preventing the ratification of the Paris agreements in France and perhaps in Germany? In the first alternative, what were the terms? Would the Kremlin insist on the abandonment of German rearmament altogether or be satisfied with something else? What would happen if the conference were never called or if ratification of the Paris agreements was rejected or indefinitely postponed before the conference had met? Would the Austrian question once again be removed from the agenda? In any case, the first thing to do was to find out what kind of guaranties would be satisfactory to Moscow.

Therefore, in the weeks after Molotov's speech, members of the Austrian government as well as high officials of the Foreign Office tried to prevail upon the Soviet Ambassador and his colleagues to define more precisely the "guaranties" they desired against an *Anschluss*. But the ambassador was either not informed or not empowered to give any explanations. Although he was the official representative of the Soviet government, perhaps he was not the right man to talk to about such an important question as the State Treaty. The dialogue between the ambassador and the representatives of the Austrian government always followed the same pattern. The following reconstruction would have been typical:

AUSTRIAN: What guaranties would the Soviet Union consider necessary to prevent a new *Anschluss?*

RUSSIAN: Molotov's statements were so clear and precise that it seems unnecessary, indeed foolish, to clarify a single point.

AUSTRIAN: Since, however, I am unaware of exactly what guaranties Molotov had in mind, I would appreciate a more detailed explanation.

RUSSIAN: It is completely incomprehensible that you did not understand what Molotov meant. He is famous for his clear and simple style of presentation.

AUSTRIAN: Molotov's statements may present no difficulty for you, but they do for me. Don't you want to comment upon them and give me your interpretation as well as an explanation of the guaranties he desires?
RUSSIAN: I have nothing to add to what Molotov has already said.

Corresponding feelers in Moscow evoked answers just as evasive. Soviet Foreign Ministry officials hoped that the Austrian government had not misunderstood Molotov's speech. He had never made the signature of the State Treaty dependent on a full agreement on Germany. He had only pointed out that the differences about the treaty must be solved in "connection with" discussions on Germany. But why didn't the Austrian government itself attempt to bring about a four-power conference? That would be in its interest. Hadn't Molotov made it clear that agreement on the few unresolved questions could easily be reached at such a conference? Did the Austrians really believe they could achieve anything by hanging on to the apron strings of the Anglo-American powers? The latter opposed a four-power conference fearing that it would prevent or make more difficult the ratification of the Paris agreements. But what interest did Austria have in these agreements? The Austrian government would have to decide whether it might not be more advantageous to seek agreement with the Soviet Union instead of constantly identifying its interest with those of Britain and the United States. And Austria had no time to lose. Once the Paris agreements were ratified, the situation for Austria would "develop in a by no means pleasant way." Soviet representatives in Austria followed a similar line in their conversations with individual politicians and diplomats.

The Kremlin had evidently believed that as soon as Molotov dangled possible concessions, be they ever so vague, the Austrian government would immediately implore the Western powers and particularly the United States to withdraw their opposition to a conference. As, however, nothing of the kind happened, Molotov summoned the Austrian Ambassador quite unexpectedly on the evening of February 25. He opened the conversation by referring to his speech of February 8 and asked if the ambassador had read it. In such a case, the ambassador had probably noticed, Molotov continued, that the Soviet attitude toward the State Treaty had undergone a fundamental change. Although the Soviet government did not fear an *Anschluss* in the near future, it must, nevertheless, have certain guaranties, especially as the danger would increase in the event of the rearmament of West Germany. Therefore, Molotov continued, there must be agreement as soon as possible on a "formula" for such guaranties. After that the Soviet Union would be prepared in principle to withdraw its troops from Austria. He personally believed that an agreement could be achieved most easily if Austria and the U.S.S.R. first discussed between them the meaning of the guaranties and then notified the three Western powers of the understanding they had reached. These powers could not reject an agreement already accepted by Austria. But Molotov again avoided spelling out what guaranties he wanted. Apparently his main concern was that Austria had not yet reacted to the vague Soviet overtures. He had, therefore, thought it necessary to stress more clearly the importance the Soviet Union attached to the conference. And something he *failed* to say was especially encouraging: the Austrian Ambassador *reported that he didn't repeat that a four-power conference on Austria must meet before ratification of the Paris agreements.*

On the basis of this statement, which was in striking contrast to what Soviet diplomats in Vienna had earlier said, the Austrian government instructed its ambassador in Moscow to stress that it had just as great an interest as the Soviet Union in avoiding a new *Anschluss*. As desirable as they were, however, Austria could only accept guaranties presented jointly by the four occupation powers. The government could not negotiate about them with the Soviet Union alone. In order to lead to a positive result the negotiations must be carried on between all four occupation powers and Austria. The ambassador should also ask again for an exact statement of the guaranties the Soviet government had in mind.

In the next conversation on March 2, 1955, Molotov again

refused to give even the slightest hint of the kind of guaranties he desired. They could not be disclosed, he said, until it was reasonably certain that a conference would be held. As a first step, the Austrian government must officially agree in principle to the conditions in Molotov's speech of February 8. *As the Austrian government had declared that it could not negotiate with the Soviet Union alone, Molotov wanted to stress that he had no objection to the Western powers being informed* about the views of the Soviet Union. The Soviet Union had never intended to deal with Austria behind the backs of the other occupation powers. On the contrary, it wished to bring about a conference of the four powers and Austria as soon as possible.

Two days later, on March 4, 1955, the two Soviet diplomats K. and L. invited Kreisky, Bruno Pittermann, the parliamentary leader of the Social Democrats, and me to dinner along with our wives. Another Soviet diplomat whom I will call M. also participated. He had arrived shortly before and played an important role, especially in the last phase of the negotiations over the State Treaty. He had, for many years, been stationed in Stockholm and spoke fluent Swedish. When he became excited, as frequently happened, he changed into German which he spoke even better than Swedish.

It was an excellent meal with caviar and the customary Lucullan Russian dishes. At the table the conversation touched only on unimportant affairs. Since the Russians, in contrast to the English, cannot be considered masters of "small talk," the conversation was kept going with great effort and strain mainly by the guests. Immediately after the meal, which appeared more of a burden than a pleasure to the hosts, the ladies were disposed of in a great hurry. As my wife later told it, after a long trip through empty or sparsely furnished rooms with glaring electric lights, they finally landed in a remote wing of the embassy where the dinner conversation was renewed and dragged out over many hours, about children and servants, occasionally interrupted by long intervals of silence.

The gentlemen were conducted into an enormous room in the opposite part of the building. As we entered, I was struck by the sight of three tables, each with two chairs, in three of the four corners of the room, evidently to prevent conversations from being overhead. Otherwise the room was completely empty. The hosts obviously had a carefully established plan. K. invited me to sit down with him, and L. took care of Kreisky, M. of Pittermann. Scarcely had the coffee been served, scarcely had the servants left the room, when K. took up the question of the Austrian State Treaty. After only a few minutes I became aware that he followed the line Molotov had adopted during his last talks with the Austrian Ambassador in Moscow, whose reports I had read shortly before.

K. opened the conversation, as Molotov had, by inquiring whether I had read the speech of his Foreign Minister. After I had confirmed this, the next question followed immediately. Had I also understood that the conditions mentioned by Molotov meant a fundamental change in the Soviet attitude toward the State Treaty? "Naturally," I answered. K. thereupon complained vigorously that the important concessions Molotov had spoken of had not called forth the reaction which Moscow had counted on, either among the Western powers or from Austria.

"What can be the reason for this?" K. asked. As a personal friend not only of Kreisky and other influential Austrian politicians but also of the British and American ambassadors in Vienna, perhaps I could give an explanation.

"Before I answer your question," I replied, "I would first like to know what you mean by saying that 'the expected reaction' was lacking. To what reaction do you refer?"

"I mean the fact," K. answered, "that in spite of Molotov's indication of the readiness of the Soviet Union for meaningful concessions, neither the Western powers nor Austria has shown the slightest interest in the four-power conference at which these concessions would be presented and clearly defined."

"The explanation appears to me to be right at hand," I replied. "No one knows what guaranties Molotov intends to demand. You can scarcely ask a government to participate in a conference without the slightest hint of the proposals it will have to consider."

The answer obviously did not satisfy K. and he changed to an argument which I now heard for the first time but which would constantly be repeated later to Kreisky and myself: Of all the parties concerned, Austria had the greatest interest in the State Treaty. It was, therefore, the business of the Austrian government to indicate what type of guaranties it believed it could offer. The negotiations could not begin until a concrete proposal had been made.

I answered that naturally I could only express my personal opinion, and when K. still wanted to hear it, I asked, "Did the Soviet Union not offer to evacuate Austria upon receiving certain 'guaranties against annexation,' and did it not propose to take up negotiations about these guaranties?" "Yes, certainly," K. replied.

"Then it appears to me to be the business of those making the proposal," I said, "to be the first to give an exact summation of their wishes before they can expect the Austrian government to support their demands for a conference."

K. had certain objections to this interpretation; one could hardly expect the Soviet Union to give its conditions in detail before it had been assured that a four-power conference would take place. If the Austrian government wished to push negotiations on the State Treaty, then it should persuade the Western powers to agree to a conference. The Soviet government realized, he continued, that the Austrian question must be disposed of somehow or other. It was also prepared to make the necessary concessions to bring about an agreement. A prerequisite was, however, that the Western powers as well as Austria make up their minds and relinquish their opposition to the calling of a conference for this purpose.

The tactics employed by K. were far from new. It was characteristic of the Soviet diplomacy to try to force the opposite party to take the initiative to submit concrete proposals as a basis for coming negotiations. Molotov had already made use of the same tactics in August 1939 when he did his utmost to persuade the German Ambassador, Count Schulenburg.

to state in advance on what terms Hitler would be prepared to make an agreement on the partition of the neighboring countries in spheres of interest between the Soviet Union and Germany. At that time Molotov had also clearly hinted that the proper negotiations could hardly begin before the German government had in more detail defined the territorial concessions it was prepared to offer at the expense of the neighboring countries.

As the Soviets, on the other hand, as a rule have never insisted on concrete proposals unless they honestly desire an agreement satisfactory to both partners, K.'s urgent demand that the Austrian government should be the first to put its cards on the table was undoubtedly a good omen. The more I thought the matters over, the more inclined I was to believe that the Soviets were already considering a change of tactics, even if no definite decision had yet been made. Had not K. during our conversation also declared that his government now realized that the Austrian question somehow had to be disposed of? If this was the case, the conclusion of the State Treaty might, after all, still be possible even if the Paris agreements should be ratified.

It was now my turn to ask questions. Would the Soviet government still be interested in a conference after ratification of the Paris agreements?

K. hesitated a moment and then answered that the Soviet Union might conceivably participate in a conference even after this event. He hastened to add, however, that in such a case Austria would have to accept more unfavorable conditions than before the conference. The Soviet government would require substantially stronger guaranties against *Anschluss* after the French debate.

I now wished to find out if Moscow had entirely abandoned the hopes it had earlier set on the French Council. I, therefore, mentioned that the recent reports I had from Paris tended to show that the Council would take a positive attitude. Was the Soviet government, I asked not without irony, still fooling itself that it could prevent ratification of the Paris agreements?

K. became extremely incensed. He replied in a furious

tone that the Soviet Union had better information about the situation in Paris than I did. Was I aware, he asked in his turn ironically, that the agreements would be rejected if only six or seven senators who had not yet taken a firm position voted against ratification? The same would happen if they only succeeded in passing an amendment. "This latter possibility which is not at all as unlikely as you seem to imagine," he continued, "would send the agreements back to the chamber. If you still believe that the Paris agreements have the slightest chance of being passed for the second time by the chamber considering its present mood, then it is you who are fooling yourself about the situation and not the Soviet Union.

"I hope you understand," he continued, "that if the proposals are sent back to the chamber, such a long time will pass before the next vote that we will never have to trouble ourselves about the question you just asked, that is to say, if we would be willing to take part in a four-power conference even after ratification. Should the agreements not be approved or the ratification be postponed indefinitely, then I doubt that the Western powers can agree a third time on a new formula for the armament of West Germany. If you believe that is possible," he added, still furious, "then you are not only poorly informed but also rather naive."

As this conversation established, the Soviet government had at the beginning of March not yet given up hope that the French Council would reject or at least insist on some amendment to the Paris agreements which would postpone the ratification. If the Western governments should agree to a conference and enough French senators were convinced that only the outcome of a new summit meeting could prove conclusively if the German armament could be left to the future without great risk, the Soviet Union would have achieved its aim.

On March 12, eight days after this dinner, the Soviet Foreign Ministry, without consulting the Austrian government, published a detailed account of the conversations of February 25 and March 2 between Molotov and the Austrian Ambassador in Moscow. Some of Molotov's remarks were left out, however: for example, his admission on February 25 that there was no immediate danger of an *Anschluss* and that the Soviet Union wanted "guaranties" mainly for the future. But on one very basic point the facts were completely different: According to the communiqué, Molotov had, contrary to what the Austrian Ambassador had reported, added that in the opinion of the Soviet government it was essential to convene the conference of the four powers *before* ratification of the Paris agreements. As the Soviets never without a purpose pass over in silence that which they earlier have considered important, the Austrian government had concluded from its ambassador's reports that the Kremlin had already tacitly abandoned the connection between the Austrian and German questions. Molotov's silence would consequently have meant that the Soviet Union no longer made the evacuation of Austria conditional upon the abandonment of the German rearmament. If Vienna had not considered this a *sine qua non,* the reason was that the government believed that the apparent Soviet readiness to negotiate stemmed from apprehension, exaggerated in propaganda but, nevertheless, genuine, that an indefinite delay in the evacuation of Austria might tempt the Western powers to include their own zones in their strategic planning. Austrian officials had hoped that whether the conference met or not, the Soviet government would be satisfied at the last minute with token "guaranties" against an *Anschluss.* But now the publication of the communiqué had shattered these illusions. Even though the Soviet apprehension was not all pretense, it was not as important at this time as was assumed in Vienna.

Furthermore, the communiqué now aroused fear that neither Molotov's earlier statements about the desire of the Soviet government to conclude the State Treaty nor his vague hints about possible concessions had been meant seriously. And a lead article published in the Communist newspaper, the *Volksstimme,* four days before the Soviet communiqué, now took on a completely different meaning. As a closer scrutiny of the text showed that it had apparently been translated from Russian into German, Austrian government circles considered it a semi-official commentary on the later

communiqué. Among other things, the writer maintained
that those Western circles who had ceaselessly demanded that
the Austrian question be solved before all other international problems had now suddenly lost interest in the State
Treaty. Instead, they now demanded priority for the arming
of West Germany. Apparently this should, the newspaper
added, be carried out at any price, if necessary even at the
cost of the State Treaty. The author finally warned that the
re-establishment of "German militarism" would, in any case,
make the conclusion of an Austrian State Treaty extremely
difficult. It might even prevent it altogether for a long time.
*True, such warnings were nothing new. When, however, re-
peated over and over again, the impression arose that the
"guaranties" demanded by Molotov meant nothing else than
the complete abandonment of the rearmament of the Federal
Republic.* If this was the only "guaranty" acceptable to the
Soviet Union, the prospects of the signature of the State
Treaty were indeed gloomy.

Although the Soviet attitude seemingly hardened and the
Austrian government directly and indirectly received repeated warnings about the serious consequences of ratification of the Paris agreements, there was still a gleam of hope.
Several Soviet hints had indicated that the Kremlin might
not reject negotiations on the State Treaty even after ratification. As we have seen, K. had told me as much on March 4.
Furthermore, the communiqué referred to a moment ago
had particularly stressed that Molotov had told the Austrian
Ambassador that bilateral discussions of a preliminary nature between the Soviet Union and Austria would largely
contribute to a positive result. The same would be the case if
personal contacts could be established between the leaders of
both countries. Finally, about the middle of the same month,
Molotov expressed himself in a way which seemed to indicate
that he would not entirely dismiss the thought of a conference after ratification of the Paris agreements. The *Volksstimme* gave some similar intimations. It suggested that the
"re-establishment of German militarism" need not prevent
realization of the State Treaty forever, but would make it
much more difficult. The two different propaganda lines

adopted by the Kremlin were not, as it might have seemed, conflicting. As long as it was uncertain if the Paris agreements would be ratified, Soviet spokesmen naturally had to stress their hard line even if an important change of tactics already was under consideration.

Simultaneously with these hardly noticeable signs of a new orientation of Soviet policy, I realized that Molotov and other Soviet diplomats were exerting themselves more and more zealously to get the Austrian government itself to make known what kind of "guaranties" against an *Anschluss* it would accept. As already mentioned, these inquiries had a special purpose. This purpose was particularly noticeable during another conversation between Molotov and the Austrian Ambassador in Moscow. In a note of March 14, the Austrian government had formally replied to Molotov's remarks of February 25 and March 2. It stressed that it would naturally welcome any effective guaranty of the independence of the country and, consequently, against the danger of an *Anschluss*. The note also recalled how clearly and unequivocally Austria had emphasized that it did not intend to join military alliances or allow military bases on its territory. It was, therefore, willing to negotiate about the form of such a declaration. Austria also agreed that all the questions connected with the State Treaty could only be settled as a conference. Nevertheless, these questions should first be so thoroughly clarified through diplomatic channels that negotiations could quickly lead to concrete results. In conclusion, the Austrian government stressed that the business of the conference should be limited to the State Treaty.

The answer basically meant that a conference should be postponed until the Soviet Union had made known what guaranties it wanted. But Molotov seized on the term "effective guaranty" and asked the Austrian Ambassador what type of guaranty his government had thought of when it used this expression. The ambassador answered that in Vienna the danger of an *Anschluss* was not considered at all acute; the general prohibition in the current draft of the State Treaty was considered sufficient.

The Soviet Foreign Minister then repeated once again that

he himself could not give an exact summation of Soviet desires until he knew what guaranties the Austrian government would accept. Nevertheless, he wanted to emphasize that the Soviet Union would not be satisfied with oral assurances. The two governments should consequently endeavor to determine what "guaranties" would be considered effective and acceptable.

The expressions used by Molotov once again proved that even if the rulers in the Kremlin had not entirely abandoned their hopes of a rejection or postponement of the ratification of the Paris agreements, their doubts about the outcome increased more and more as the date of the debate in the French Council approached. If the agreements were ratified and the rearmament of West Germany could no longer be prevented, then Austria had lost its usefulness as a pawn. It was, therefore, necessary to prepare in time for a new tactical line. As many of the leaders in Moscow apparently considered the earlier intransigent attitude towards the evacuation of Austria as an unfortunate obstacle to the success of the campaign for the relaxation of tensions, the Politburo had probably already decided in principle to enter into negotiations on an entirely new basis in case the Paris agreements should be ratified.

The adoption of a new line in Soviet foreign policy is, however, a serious decision. Before a definite agreement within the Politburo could be reached, it was necessary to find out through cautious soundings how far the solutions envisaged on the basis of the new line were acceptable to Austria. Once the new line had been definitely adopted, the Politburo and particularly its members who had insisted on the change could not risk the loss of prestige they would have incurred through a rejection of their proposals by the Austrian government.

Already at the March 4 dinner with the three Soviet diplomats mentioned earlier, one of them had made a cautious feeler. He asked Kreisky if Austria might conceivably grant the occupation powers the right to reoccupy a small number of bases in their former zones in the event of an immediate threat of an *Anschluss*. As Kreisky told me when we drove away together that evening, he had assured the Russian that his own party would withdraw from the government before giving the Soviet Union the power to exert pressure by the threat of reoccupation. Because of other hints by Soviet diplomats, Kreisky and I concluded that other Soviet proposals were being considered, possibly an evacuation of the country in stages to be rigidly specified in the State Treaty.

These were the principal features of Soviet policy toward Austria up to mid-March 1955. To see the whole picture, however, we must consider how the Anglo-American powers —above all, the United States—judged the situation. My conversations with their representatives in Vienna showed that they—at least the Americans—had received Molotov's assurances and obscure proposals of February 8 very skeptically. They doubted that the Soviet Union was prepared for meaningful concessions; in the event of negotiations, the withdrawal of Soviet occupation forces from Austria would in any case be made dependent upon abandonment of the rearmament of West Germany. And most American officials felt this was too high a price.

Thus, a four-power conference seemed rather senseless from the standpoint of the Western powers. And even if the Soviet Union should declare its willingness to limit the negotiations to the Austrian State Treaty, a discussion in some form or another about the arming of West Germany could scarcely be avoided. The Americans were convinced from the beginning that Molotov merely wanted to convene a four-power conference to prevent the German rearmament. If, at the last minute, the Soviet Union hinted at important concessions, some French senators might demand amendments to the Paris agreements which would send them back to the chamber. Just as the Russians, the Western powers were convinced that a new delay could make the arming of the Federal Republic of Germany impossible for a long time to come.

13

The Negotiations in the Second Decisive Phase

The Soviet diplomatic activity from Molotov's speech on February 8, 1955, until the signing of the State Treaty on May 15 of the same year was more complicated than anybody at that time believed. To be fully understood it must be divided into two clearly separated phases. We have already examined the first phase which lasted until the latter part of March. During this period the Soviet Union was seeking to use the Austrian question to prevent the rearmament of West Germany. If before the debate in the French Council of the Republic on the Paris agreements it had been decided to call a four-power conference to deliberate at the same time on the German and the Austrian questions, the Soviets were convinced that the ratification would be rejected or at least postponed. "If we can only win time," one of the Soviet diplomats explained to me, "then nothing is lost yet."

After mid-March, however, the situation in France became clear. As one of my Soviet acquaintances reluctantly admitted, there was no longer much doubt about the outcome of the coming debates. The time for a radical change on the Austrian question was approaching.

The second phase was initiated by a note of March 24, on which I shall comment later in this chapter. This note was the result of a fundamental change of the general line, which after a bitter struggle within the Politburo had been approved at the time of Malenkov's defeat and Khrushchev's rise to power. However, as long as the Austrian question could be used in the struggle against the rearmament of West Germany and the ratification of the Paris agreements by the

Council of the French Republic still was undecided, the new line which we shall analyze in a following chapter, could not yet be applied.

The first sign of an approaching reorientation of Soviet policy I noticed at a dinner which Kreisky gave on March 17. Only a few people had been invited: Vice-Chancellor Schärf, Josef Schöner, then chief of the political department of the Austrian Foreign Office, two Soviet diplomats, one of them K., and the French *chargé d'affaires*.

After the meal had ended, Kreisky immediately took up the question of the State Treaty and with Schärf and Schöner sought to talk the two Russians into spelling out the contents of the "guaranties against an *Anschluss*" demanded by Molotov. K., the main spokesman for the Russians, skillfully avoided answering Kreisky's question by mentioning, among other things, that he had received no new information since the last meeting of Molotov with the Austrian Ambassador on March 14. Then K. took the offensive and complained that the Austrian answer of that date "had failed to take a position" on a four-power conference.

Kreisky replied that his government had never been against a conference but had only emphasized the necessity of careful preparation through diplomatic channels. When the answer was written, Kreisky added, it was assumed that the Soviet government had already understood that Molotov's demand for a conference *before* the ratification of the Paris agreements was unrealizable at that time. Quite independently of Austria's position, the Western powers had decided not to participate in such a conference until *after* the approval of these agreements by the parliaments of all the countries which had signed the agreements. If the Soviet government made the resumption of negotiations about the State Treaty conditional upon the acceptance of an impossible demand and at the same time refused to specify what guaranties it considered necessary against "*Anschluss*," it must be inferred that Molotov's proposal of February 8 had never been serious and had only been made in order to prevent the ratification of the Paris agreements. K. made an effort to disprove this assumption and convince us of the sincerity of Soviet intentions. Among other things, he reminded us that on February 8 Molotov had stressed the Soviet desire not only to resolve the Austrian question but also to resolve it swiftly. I was struck by the phrase "resolve swiftly," which K. had never before used in his conversations with me about the State Treaty. I concluded that he wished to give us as clear a hint as he dared, that, contrary to what had earlier been the case, the Soviet Union now had a real interest in arriving at an agreement. Why this change of attitude had occurred and what it implied, I could not guess at that time.

My impression of an approaching reorientation was confirmed sooner than I had expected. When Kreisky for the second time the same evening made an attempt to induce K. to explain the real meaning of the guaranties, K. adopted the same tactic Molotov had used during his latest conversations with the Austrian Ambassador. He declared that the Soviet Union had no reason to indicate what kind of guaranties would be necessary. It was up to the Austrian government to make proposals in this respect.

Despite the heavy pressure which was put upon him from all sides, K. repeated the same reply again and again. At that time I did not understand what he was after and considered his replies merely an empty evasion. Now, in retrospect, I think it is clear that what K. hoped to achieve by his reiterations that it was up to Austria to submit offers was to get Kreisky himself to propose a declaration of Austrian neutrality. This explanation seems to me the more likely as I now remember that the Soviets had shortly before made cautious soundings in this respect in different quarters.

In the course of the following conversation, K. gave us the interesting information that next week Molotov intended to answer the last Austrian note. What he referred to was the Soviet note of March 24, which later proved to have marked the beginning of the second phase of the negotiations and finally led to the conclusion of the State Treaty.

If, however, those present at Kreisky's dinner party considered K.'s information of great interest, there was another reason. He had thereby intimated that, contrary to the threat expressed in the Soviet note to the three Western powers of December 9, 1954, the Kremlin wished to continue the talks about the State Treaty although it was now certain that the Paris agreements would be ratified and the Federal Republic rearmed. That the Soviet Union had no intention to postpone the conclusion of the State Treaty once again was confirmed when K. spontaneously added that his government would prefer to discuss, at the beginning, with the Austrian Ambassador in Moscow the problems raised by Molotov in his speech of February 8.

For the third time during the evening, Kreisky now invited K. to explain the real meaning of Molotov's demand for "guaranties" against an *Anschluss*. As K. once more repeated that it was up to the Austrian government to tell the Soviet Union what kind of guaranties it could accept, Kreisky stepped over to a bookshelf and took out a volume which contained the diplomatic documents signed at the Congress of Vienna in 1815. In a loud voice he read the declaration in which the permanent neutrality of Switzerland was recognized and collectively guaranteed by the eight powers which had participated in the war against Napoleon. He then turned to K. and asked if the Soviet Union would consider permanent neutrality after the Swiss model an adequate guaranty against a new *Anschluss*.

Although K. had listened with noticeable interest, especially when the "perpetual neutrality of Switzerland" was mentioned, I had expected him either to give a negative answer or turn to another topic with some polite noncommittal phrases. To our surprise, however, K. answered positively: "Yes, this or a similar proposal could at least be the basis of further discussion." But the State Treaty would still have to allow the occupation powers to take certain steps in case West Germany should threaten the independence of Austria. This was obviously an allusion to the earlier proposal he had made to Kreisky that the occupation powers should have the right to reoccupy their zones in case of an "imminent danger of *Anschluss*." Kreisky, vigorously supported by Schärf, repeated what he had said on that occasion, namely, that the

Austrian government could never grant the occupation powers the right to decide whether the independence of Austria was threatened. Still less could it accept the authority of these powers to reoccupy their zones. With that the discussion of this question ended. When the State Treaty was again taken up later in the evening, K. asked whether the Austrian government was prepared—as Kreisky's remarks indicated—to declare that it would adopt perpetual neutrality after the Swiss model. Kreisky and Schärf answered that their party would greet such a solution with satisfaction. They could not speak for the People's Party, of course, but they were convinced that it would also share this opinion. I returned home convinced for the first time that the Soviet Union seriously desired an agreement on the State Treaty. The following day I visited Kreisky in his office. We discussed thoroughly what had happened the preceding evening and both arrived at the same conclusion. Whatever the intention of the Soviet Government had been at the time of Molotov's speech on February 8, it was now willing to evacuate the country in exchange for a declaration of a perpetual Austrian neutrality.

On March 20, Chancellor Raab explained the political situation in a radio speech. He reported first on the exchange of notes with the Soviet Union and recalled, among other things, that Article 4 of the draft treaty prohibited any *Anschluss*. If the Soviet government considered further guaranties necessary, it was their business to make concrete proposals. In his opinion, however, the four occupation powers should together guarantee the inviolability of Austria's borders. I was surprised that, although three days had passed since Kreisky had suggested neutrality after the Swiss model, the chancellor did not allude to this proposal or to neutrality at all. Had he been informed? Or didn't he attach the importance it deserved to K.'s declaration?

At our dinner on the 17th, K. had mentioned that Molotov would reply to the Austrian note the following week. And on March 24, when I met him by chance at a reception in the Italian Embassy, I asked if he had anything new to tell. He smiled, glanced at his watch, and said: "At this moment the

Austrian Ambassador is arriving at the Foreign Ministry in Moscow where Molotov has summoned him to receive an especially important communication. The foreign minister is going to deliver that note to which I referred at Kreisky's dinner a few days ago." K. emphasized several times the importance of the note without giving the slightest hint of its contents. That night the long text arrived at the Austrian Foreign Office where it was assumed that the contents would be kept secret for the time being. The time-consuming task of deciphering was still not finished on the morning of March 25, however, when the newspaper of the Soviet occupation force, *Die Österreichische Zeitung,* in its first edition published the complete text in a German translation obviously authorized by the Soviet government.

The debates in the French Council of the Republic had started on March 23, and the Paris agreements were finally approved on the 27th. In releasing the note on the morning of March 25, the Soviet government may have made one last desperate effort to influence the outcome. In any case, the note of March 24 marked a decisive turning point in the negotiations over the State Treaty.

The Soviet government referred first to the Austrian statement welcoming any effective guaranty of the independence of the country. Measures must be agreed upon which would effectively protect this independence; at the same time the plans for rearming West Germany must be taken into consideration. In connection with this, two further questions arose: the amount of time for withdrawing occupation troops, and actions which the occupation powers could take in the event of a direct danger of an *Anschluss* in the future. The last sentence hinted at the idea which K.—obviously on instructions from his government—had already brought up twice, the last time at Kreisky's dinner party when he declared a reoccupation under such circumstances to be a necessary complement to an Austrian declaration of neutrality. The note then referred to the previous Austrian declaration disavowing any intention of joining military alliances or permitting the establishment of military bases. This was completely acceptable to the Soviet government. Finally, the only new point and the most important one, the U.S.S.R. now agreed that the proposed conference should deal only with the Austrian State Treaty.

At the Berlin Conference in 1954, the Soviet Union had agreed to the immediate conclusion of a State Treaty but made, on the other hand, the evacuation of Austria conditional upon the signature of a peace treaty with Germany; in other words, upon an agreement of the Western powers to preparatory measures for the future bolshevization of the Federal Republic. After the delivery of the note to the Western powers about collective security in Europe on July 24, 1954, the Soviet Union changed its attitude insofar as it made the evacuation of Austria dependent upon either the signature of a German peace treaty or the adherence of the Western powers as well as the Federal Republic to the proposed European security pact. Consequently, if the Soviet Union should consent to the evacuation of Austria, the Federal Republic should at least be disarmed and neutralized.

Finally in his speech on February 8, Molotov made a more ostensible than real concession. He declared that Austria could be evacuated even before the conclusion of a German peace treaty provided satisfactory guaranties against an *Anschluss* could be obtained. As the never-revealed "guaranties" certainly included the disarmament as well as the neutralization of the Federal Republic, the concession—compared to the attitude at the end of July 1954—was not as great as it seemed. The evacuation of Austria was still conditional upon some not yet specified concessions of the Western powers in regard to German rearmament.

If the Soviet note of March 24 has been described as the real turning point, the reason was that in this note the rulers in the Kremlin for the first time consented to the separation of the two questions: the evacuation of Austria and German rearmament.

If I have thought it necessary particularly to stress these rather obvious facts, the reason is that many important people I have talked to still seem to believe that the German and the Austrian questions had been separated already by the speech of Molotov on February 8.

When I met K. at a reception a few days after the publication of the note of March 24, he asked immediately if I had read this note. After I had told him that I certainly had, the next question followed: "Did you also understand why this note is so important and which of the points enumerated in it is the most essential?"

I answered that although I had not yet had time to examine the text carefully, even a quick reading had given the impression that the last point was without doubt the most important. For the first time, the Soviet government had declared itself willing to take up negotiations about the Austrian State Treaty detached from the complex of German questions. Logically, this must mean that the Soviet Union no longer considered the abandonment of the rearmament of West Germany an indispensable condition for withdrawal from Austria.

As this concession, however, seemed rather sensational, I wondered whether I had understood the note correctly or overlooked some important detail. "Do you really mean," I added, "that you no longer insist on the abandonment of West German rearmament as a condition for withdrawal from Austria?" "Of course we don't," K. replied in a rather angry tone. "What else should we mean?"

On the same day the Soviet note was published, *Die Volksstimme* in a lead article had, however, again repeated the demand for guaranties against an *Anschluss.* This had given me the impression, I continued, that abandonment of German rearmament might still be considered the only effective "guaranty against an *Anschluss.*" "How can this contrast between the Soviet note and the interpretation of the *Volksstimme* be explained?" I asked.

"I doubt that you understand as much about Soviet foreign policy as you imagine," my acquaintance answered in a slightly annoyed tone. "In interpreting our policy, one should not attach any special importance to the explanations and comments of local Communist newspapers. For example, in today's issue of the organ of the Soviet occupation force, the *Österreichische Zeitung,* which you have probably read, did you see a single word about the arming of West Germany?" I admitted that I had not.

"There you see it," the Russian answered. "To judge Soviet foreign policy correctly, one must, first of all, carefully study the lead article in *Pravda* and pay attention to every nuance of the presentation. It is just as important to notice what the newspaper has passed over in silence as to analyze what it actually says. If *Pravda* is not available, then in Austria you should stick to the *Österreichische Zeitung*. When it no longer deals with a question which was previously the object of ceaseless attention, as is now the case, this is of the utmost importance and should be considered as a proof that we have changed our attitude. What the *Volksstimme* says is immaterial."

"But the *Volksstimme* has often published articles based, as far as I have been able to ascertain, on exact information from official Soviet sources," I objected. "Its comments on official statements from Moscow have often proved to be correct and have helped illuminate obscure points of Soviet foreign policy."

"Often the local Communist press is given information," my acquaintance agreed. "But we do not always have the time or the inclination for this."

Significantly, just when Moscow offered a real concession, anti-*Anschluss* propaganda began to be stressed in the "people's democracies"—at least in Czechoslovakia, Hungary, and East Germany. The *Österreichische Zeitung* took part in this propaganda by frequently quoting the newspapers of these countries. According to the general propaganda line, the United States secretly favored an *Anschluss* and sought to prevent, at almost any price, the conclusion of the Austrian State Treaty. For example, an East Berlin newspaper claimed that the U.S. Ambassador in Vienna had been informed by Washington that fresh negotiations on the State Treaty were no longer desired. The same newspaper had also learned from a "trustworthy source" that the American commander-in-chief in Austria had been ordered to prepare for an amalgamation and a consolidation of the American, British, and

French zones. This would secure military communications between West Germany and Italy; the United States also wanted the Western occupation zones incorporated in the Atlantic bloc.

The main Communist organ in Prague, *Rude Pravo,* had learned from other "well informed persons" that the United States intended to oppose any effective guaranties against an *Anschluss.* Finally, "a dependable source in Salzburg" had informed the newspaper *Nepszava* that the American commander-in-chief had told his allied colleagues that Western troops in Austria must be put under the control of one headquarters. (By this time, for reasons of economy, Great Britain had reduced her occupation troops to a single battalion, and French forces consisted of a few hundred men. These symbolic occupation forces could hardly have contributed very much to the strength of a unified command.)

The Communists spread similar propaganda in Austria. The Western powers were allegedly preparing for an eventual *Anschluss* after a slow and careful economic as well as military infiltration. This infiltration had already begun, claimed the Communists; as a result of strong American pressure, Austrian industry was adapting its production to the demands of German armament.

It can scarcely have been a coincidence that such propaganda was intensified and in part carried on in a new vein directly before publication of the first really important Soviet concession. The main aim was evidently to mask fresh additional concessions. A withdrawal from Austria might, as had already been pointed out by the young Indian diplomat previously mentioned, be considered a sign of weakness in the neighboring "people's democracies"; it could weaken the self-confidence of the Communist cadres and encourage passive opposition on the part of the non-Communist populations. It was important, therefore, to convince the public in the "people's democracies" that the United States was working against the State Treaty, whereas the Soviet Union was working for it. Its conclusion could then be portrayed as a noteworthy Soviet victory and a withdrawal from Austria as confirming the power and strength of the Soviet Union.

Already at Kreisky's dinner party on March 17, K. had pointed out that the Soviet government to begin with preferred to discuss with the Austrian Ambassador in Moscow the problems raised by Molotov's speech of February 8. When the Russian Foreign Minister delivered the note of March 24 to the Austrian Ambassador, he mentioned that as far as he understood, Chancellor Raab was favorably disposed toward the idea of a personal visit in Moscow. Since the Soviet government had announced that it regarded personal contact between leading statesmen of the two countries as desirable, Molotov had extended a formal invitation to the Chancellor and other representatives of the Austrian government. By March 29, the Austrian government had already accepted this invitation and had decided to send a delegation to Moscow for preparatory discussion on the State Treaty. When the delegation left Vienna, it had no intention of assuming any binding commitments; these would have to wait for more comprehensive negotiations involving the other three powers. It only wanted to discover if, as Kreisky was already convinced, the Soviet Union now seriously desired the conclusion of the State Treaty on conditions acceptable to Austria. If their hopes should prove well founded, the Austrian delegation counted on getting a definite statement of Soviet conditions for the evacuation of Austria.

At the same time, it was quite obvious that the Soviet Union for some reason of its own was very anxious to discuss some problems related to the State Treaty with the Austrians without the presence of any representatives of the Western powers.

It is easy to understand that this desire seemed rather strange to the Western powers. They suspected that the main reason for the invitation of an Austrian delegation to Moscow was that the rulers of the Kremlin intended to set a trap of some kind which the Austrians, rather inexperienced as it was feared they were, would not in time detect or be able to avoid. They might under strong pressure make concessions detrimental to the Western powers as well as to themselves. As the situation had developed, these powers were to some extent bewildered. That the Soviet Union intended to make real concessions was, considering earlier experiences, too good to be true.

I well remember that, when I discussed the situation with my friend the American Ambassador, even he was rather skeptical. He could hardly believe that I could be right when I told him that the discussions at Kreisky's dinner party on March 17 as well as my subsequent conversations with K. had definitely convinced me that the Soviet Union, for some reason at that time unknown to me, sincerely desired a speedy conclusion of the State Treaty. They were certainly now prepared to evacuate the country on conditions acceptable to Austria.

The same skepticism prevailed in some Austrian governmental circles. True, nobody wanted to assume the responsibility of declining the invitation. Chancellor Raab suggested as a precautionary measure sending to Moscow, to begin with, only Figl and Kreisky. The two party leaders should follow later if the prospects of a favorable result should prove to be greater than he now dared hope. He soon, however, abandoned this idea.

To illustrate the prevailing mood, I think it should also be mentioned that Figl told his colleagues on leaving Vienna that he feared they had committed a serious blunder in accepting the invitation to go to Moscow. They would probably return without having achieved any result.

My conversations with Kreisky before the departure of the delegation proved, however, that he himself as well as Schärf had both been strongly impressed by the pronouncements of K. at the dinner party on March 17. They were now both convinced that the Soviet government had decided to make some interesting concessions. How far these would be extended was, of course, impossible to foresee.

At the time of the departure of the Austrian delegation for Moscow, I could certainly not guess what was behind the rather strange Russian idea of inviting representatives of the Austrian government to Moscow without taking the trouble to inform them or the Western powers of the real purpose of the visit. Now, after the lapse of almost fifteen years, I think that the explanation is quite clear. To fully understand the purpose of the invitation of the Austrian delegation to Moscow it is necessary to go back to the Berlin Conference of 1954. The Soviet government had undoubtedly been informed of the reluctance of the Anglo-American powers to admit, in principle, an Austrian neutrality. They certainly also knew, or at least suspected, that the two powers had secretly hoped to be able, sooner or later, to persuade the Austrian government to join the N.A.T.O. or to collaborate in some way or other with this organization. Suspicious as they are, the Soviets had obviously been afraid that the United States and Great Britain might be tempted to put pressure on the Austrian delegation in order to convince it of the desirability of not binding its hands into the indefinite future by a declaration of perpetual neutrality.

Such a declaration was, on the other hand, of the utmost importance to the new rulers of the Kremlin if the new general line in their foreign policy should bring the favorable result they expected. At the same time, they knew that both parties who together formed the Austrian government would only be too happy to accept the status of perpetual neutrality in exchange for the long-hoped-for evacuation of the country by foreign troops. The Soviet government, therefore, doubtlessly thought that it had better, as a precautionary measure, present the Western powers with a *fait accompli*.

If the Austrian delegation could be persuaded to undertake an obligation to declare its perpetual neutrality at a meeting with representatives of the Soviet government alone, it could hardly later revoke its promise. Nor could the Western powers oppose an agreement the Austrian government had made with the Soviet Union entirely of its own free will.

As regards other still unsolved questions of a comparatively lesser importance, the Soviet Union had no objection to their being negotiated at the conferences of ambassadors and foreign ministers.

Even if the Western powers apparently had great doubts about the utility of the Austrian delegation's journey to Moscow and were rather inclined to believe that it would soon return without any tangible result, they did not want to bring pressure to bear upon the Austrian government or make any serious attempt to persuade it to decline the Soviet invitation. They wished, however, to reserve their rights in case the Austrian delegation should be forced to make concessions which the Western powers considered to be contrary to their own interests.

Consequently, the American, British, and French ambassadors, shortly before the departure of the delegation, delivered a joint declaration in Vienna, in which they recalled how the Western powers had striven for years to bring about agreement over the State Treaty. At the Berlin Conference in 1954 they had even accepted the wording of the articles not yet agreed upon in accordance with earlier Soviet proposals, but the Soviet Union had rejected this offer and introduced new, unacceptable demands. Now, however, it appeared from the exchange of ideas which had taken place between the Austrian and the Soviet governments that the latter was prepared to clarify more exactly than earlier the conditions for its consent to the conclusion of the State Treaty. The three governments further declared that they had a sympathetic understanding of the decision of the Austrian government to accept the Soviet invitation to Moscow. At the same time, they wished to stress that the "questions relating to the conclusion of the State Treaty were of the same concern to the governments of all four responsible powers, as to the Austrian government."

With this declaration the Western powers had emphasized that they also had a word to say in the matter. The Soviet Union would not be permitted to make an agreement with Austria on its own or present the Western powers with a *fait accompli*.

14

The Austrian Delegation in Moscow

The Austrian delegation, consisting of Chancellor Raab, Vice-Chancellor Schärf, Foreign Minister Figl, and State Secretary Kreisky, arrived in the Soviet capital on April 11, and negotiations began the next day. A cordial reception seemed to indicate that the Soviet government was sincere in its desire to dispose of the Austrian question "as quickly as possible," and arrive at a solution acceptable to all parties, as Molotov had expressed it. At the first meeting, the Soviet Foreign Minister was anxious to dispel the misgivings of the Austrians that the Western powers should suspect them of seeking an agreement with the Soviet Union behind their back. He therefore stressed that the negotiations would only have a preparatory character and should rather facilitate a later agreement between the four occupation powers and Austria. Molotov also emphasized the importance which his government attached to the composition of the Austrian delegation. Since it consisted of the leaders of both parties which made up the coalition government and had an overwhelming majority in Parliament, one could count on wide popular support for any agreement.

Two questions were especially important, said Molotov: first, ending the occupation depended on "decisions being made which served the interests of peace in Europe." The "question of peace" had, in recent time, assumed such an importance that it was now the most essential factor in the "solution of the State Treaty." With this purposely obscure expression, the Soviet Foreign Minister doubtlessly referred to the great weight which the Soviet Union for some time attached to an Austrian declaration of neutrality as "a factor of peace." The second condition was that the Soviet Union must receive assurances that Austria would not be used as an area for deploying troops of states "inclined toward hostility."

Before I proceed further with the narrative of the meeting in Moscow, I think it is necessary to mention that the importance the rulers of the Kremlin attached to neutrality at this junction was twofold. If the movement in favor of a policy of neutrality was gaining ground not only in Europe but also in Asia and Africa, many countries which recently had acquired or soon would achieve their independence would be prevented from joining "aggressive blocs" under the leadership of the United States. At the same time, several small or middle-sized states in Europe which already belonged to such groupings could probably be convinced of the advantages of neutrality and be induced to withdraw from these groupings. In such a way the "aggressive blocs" would be weakened and might finally disintegrate. By proclaiming its neutrality, Austria would constitute a model for other countries in a similar situation and thereby serve the interests of peace, or, in other words, serve the interests of the Soviet Union in the field of foreign policy.

In reply the chancellor affirmed anew that his government had not the slightest desire to join military alliances, East or West. It was also prepared, Raab added, to place a special law before Parliament which would establish more firmly the position of the country as an independent state. The chancellor then asked exactly what guaranties against an *Anschluss* the Soviet government had in mind and mentioned his earlier proposal, presented in his radio address: that the four occupation powers jointly guarantee the independence of Austria. He stressed that his government would welcome an agreement between the occupying powers to this end. Judging from these remarks, Raab realized neither the importance of K.'s remarks at Kreisky's dinner on March 17 nor that the main desire of the Soviet government at the moment was for an Austrian declaration of neutrality after the Swiss model.

By this time the Soviet government was not particularly worried about any new *Anschluss*. The rearmament of West

Germany was now agreed upon. The cautious Soviet feelers about permitting the occupation powers to repossess their former occupation zones had also led to a negative conclusion. Consequently, the "guaranties" which Molotov had demanded in his speech of February 8 were no longer relevant. Molotov stressed that the guaranties against an *Anschluss* he had earlier insisted upon would cause no difficulties at all if only the two demands he had made in his introductory statement were met. In the subsequent meetings he limited himself to insisting on the maintenance of the article in the current draft of the State Treaty in which an *Anschluss* had been prohibited. Austria had as little reason to oppose this as the Western powers later had.

Since the Soviet Union had entirely lost interest in guaranties against an *Anschluss*, Austrian neutrality instead appeared to be the central question. Before this problem had been solved in a satisfactory way, the Soviet government refused to discuss other questions on which differences of opinion had arisen. As an absolute condition for Soviet agreement on the State Treaty, Molotov demanded a declaration by the Austrian government of its intent to observe perpetual neutrality. The four great powers should also guarantee the independence and territorial inviolability of Austria as Raab had proposed. Molotov did not believe that his first demand would cause difficulties. He recalled how President Körner had, in an interview in the *Journal de Genève* in 1952, characterized Swiss neutrality as worthy of imitation by Austria. He doubted that the Western powers would oppose such a declaration. At the Berlin Conference in 1954, Dulles had emphasized that neutrality was honorable if it came about as the result of a voluntary decision. Molotov suggested, therefore, that the Austrian declaration of neutrality be made after enactment of the State Treaty, that is, as a decision freely arrived at.

It soon also became apparent that the Soviet Union placed special importance on use of the word "neutrality." Considering the important part neutrality—as a following chapter will show—would play in Soviet foreign policy after the adoption of the new course, this is not hard to understand.

The propaganda for neutrality was directed not only at the small and middle-sized countries in Europe belonging to N.A.T.O. but, to an even greater degree, at the newly independent states in Asia and Africa which should be prevented from joining any political and military organizations under the leadership of the United States. To achieve its greatest effect, such propaganda must avoid any confusion of ideas in the mind of the leaders of these states; it must stress a single term—neutrality—as the good example to imitate.

Since the Austrian delegation was unaware of the new Soviet line, some of its members were unsure how to react to the Soviet desire that only the word "neutrality" should be used. Because of the vague meaning of "neutrality" and "policy of neutrality," Schärf and Kreisky preferred the expression "freedom from alliances," since it portrayed more clearly the goal of both coalition parties. And in their opinion Austria should pledge itself only in a very general way to the principles of such a foreign policy. On this question a serious difference of opinion arose within the Austrian delegation. Raab, with his more practical political outlook, attached little importance to juridical niceties. He was rather indifferent as to which word would be used in this connection. If the Russians, for one reason or another, preferred "neutrality," why oppose such a modest demand? Austrian interests would in any case not suffer from the acceptance of the word "neutrality."

After some discussion Raab and Schärf agreed, however, first to suggest the expression "freedom from alliances" as a substitute for "neutrality." It was characteristic of the purpose of the Soviet demand that Molotov immediately and categorically rejected this offer. The Austrian delegation then suggested a "foreign policy based on the principles of neutrality" which met with the same negative reception. The Soviet government adhered stubbornly to its demand that only the word "neutrality" and no other expression should appear in the Austrian declaration. "If what you are offering is really neutrality," Molotov said, "then I cannot understand why you do not want to use the right word for it." The Austrian delegation soon received reliable information which indicated that the fate of the entire State Treaty might depend on acceptance of the word "neutrality." Under these circumstances Schärf and Kreisky, after careful consideration, agreed to accept the Soviet wishes on the condition that "neutrality" should be defined in some way. Therefore, they suggested the addition of "after the Swiss model." If differences of opinion should arise concerning the meaning of "neutrality" or "policy of neutrality," then the Austrians could always refer to the Swiss interpretation of the conception of neutrality.

As soon as agreement was reached on neutrality, the negotiations proceeded at a swifter pace. The only political question which still caused some difficulties was the amount of time for withdrawing the occupation troops. Molotov did not demand as much as the Austrian delegation had feared, for example, that the withdrawal take place in a long series of stages. He first proposed a time limit of six months after the State Treaty came into force. When the Austrians rejected this proposal categorically, Molotov suggested that the six months be calculated from the ratification of the treaty. Since the treaty came into force upon ratification, this was hardly a concession. And as Kreisky had foreseen earlier, and later stressed in conversation with me, the Soviet Union could delay ratification of the State Treaty in order to keep troops in Austria. Now Molotov added: not later than July 1, 1956. The Austrian delegation, however, resisted any change in the draft of the treaty under consideration which stated that withdrawal should be completed ninety days after the treaty came into force or at the latest by December 31, 1955. The Soviet Union finally gave way in this matter and accepted the Austrian position, and on April 15 the negotiations in Moscow were concluded with the signing of a memorandum covering those points on which both delegations agreed.

The memorandum consisted of two main sections. The first covered the obligations assumed by the members of the Austrian delegation, while the second enumerated the concessions made by the Soviet side. A difference existed insofar as the members of the Austrian delegation had only pledged themselves personally to secure the approval of their government and Parliament. The Soviet pledge, on the other hand, was made in the name of the Soviet government and thus had a binding character.

The Austrian government was to promise, in an "internationally binding form," to observe perpetual neutrality after the Swiss model. Immediately after ratification of the State Treaty, the government was to present a declaration which Parliament would approve in conformity with the rules of the constitution. But this declaration of neutrality had a wider scope than what was originally proposed by the Soviet Union. In his speech of February 8, 1955, Molotov had limited himself to demanding confirmation of the statement by the Austrian government at the Berlin Conference that it would neither join alliances nor allow military bases on its territory. The declaration provided for in the Moscow memorandum specified perpetual neutrality without any qualifications.

Neither in Moscow nor later did the Soviet Union propose a four-power guaranty of Austrian neutrality. It was only suggested that the Austrian government should secure the recognition of its neutrality by all states, not only by the great powers. In addition, both parties agreed that Austria should receive a guaranty of its independence and territorial integrity from the four great powers. For reasons which I will mention later, however, the last guaranty was never given. The Soviet Union declared itself willing to sign the State Treaty, withdraw its troops not later than December 31, 1955, and finally to recognize and respect Austrian neutrality. The Soviet government was also willing to delete a small number of articles from the draft treaty since they had lost their pertinency or appeared superfluous, for example, stipulations about the extradition of certain categories of war criminals and the duty of Austria to expel German nationals under certain circumstances. The Soviet government was also prepared to support Austrian wishes for other changes in the text of the treaty if such changes caused no unnecessary delay.

After the close of the negotiations in Moscow, the Western powers and the Soviet Union agreed to call an ambassadors'

conference in Vienna on May 2, 1955. The ambassadors, together with Austrian representatives, should once again go
through the draft treaty and propose any changes which
seemed necessary. The foreign ministers of the four occupation powers would then meet in Vienna to pass on the work
of the ambassadors and, hopefully, sign the State Treaty.

15

The Ambassadors and Foreign Ministers in Vienna

The most important question the ambassadors' conference had to deal with was without doubt the declaration of neutrality to which the Austrian government had pledged itself. In the years before the Berlin Conference, the Western powers had, as already mentioned, assumed that after the end of the occupation Austria would have complete freedom to join N.A.T.O. At the Berlin Conference they wanted to avoid restrictions in the State Treaty which would have prevented such a development. The Soviet government, on the other hand, had obviously feared that a free Austria would join N.A.T.O. or provide it with military facilities of one kind or another. This was one of the reasons for its reluctance to withdraw from the country.

Although developments during 1954 and at the beginning of 1955 had forced the Western powers to abandon the idea of Austrian membership in N.A.T.O. and they were now willing to recognize and respect the neutrality of Austria, they could not allow the Soviet Union to regulate this question bilaterally. The Western powers opposed any wording of the declaration which would prevent Austria from joining non-military organizations such as the European Payments Union, the European Coal and Steel Community, the Council of Europe, or the Organization for European Economic Cooperation. As the Moscow memorandum proved, the Soviet Union had nothing against Austrian membership in the United Nations, but its attitude to Austria's adherence to the other organizations remained uncertain for a long time.

Raab's proposal that the four occupation powers should

guarantee the independence and territorial inviolability of his country posed another difficult problem. The American and British leaders feared that the Senate and the British Parliament would not be willing to grant such a guaranty for an indefinite time. When the conference met, it was still unclear how this difficulty would be solved.

Another and still more important question was whether the whole draft treaty should be reviewed again or only the comparatively few articles on which agreement had not already been reached. The Western powers insisted upon a complete review since they wanted to delete articles which ran counter to their interests or which had become meaningless.

They were especially interested in the removal of the articles they had earlier accepted on the limitation of Austria's right to rearm. The Western powers maintained that the Austrian neutrality they were going to recognize required the necessary military means to prevent violations as well as to enable the country to withstand an attack from its Communist neighbors, at least for a short time.

The Austrians had long feared that the United States would, under some pretext, delay the signature of the State Treaty because it would break the link between Germany and Italy and prevent direct communications between the two countries in case of war. My conversations with Ambassador Thompson proved, however, that these fears were groundless. He was convinced that, in the event of war, the Soviet Union would be the first to violate Austrian neutrality. In such a case the United States would be entitled to intervene in defense of the country and to maintain the link at the Brenner Pass. On the other hand, should no violation take place, the advantage of Austrian neutrality for the West would more than outweigh the disadvantage.

What the Americans mainly feared was pacifist tendencies in Austria after the end of the occupation which might prevent rearmament even if permitted by the State Treaty. The resulting military vacuum could tempt neighboring Communist states to try a surprise attack as in Korea. In this way a *fait accompli* could be created before the Western powers had had time to intervene. What particularly worried the United States was that the Social Democrats might oppose any change in the military limitations of the original text of the State Treaty. At the request of my American colleague, Llewellyn Thompson, I advised Kreisky confidentially of this concern and stressed that in my personal opinion a positive attitude of the Social Democrats toward rearmament would dispel the worst American fears and thus indirectly facilitate realization of the State Treaty. Kreisky understood immediately how important it was not to let any doubt arise that the Social Democrats were determined to defend Austria. He shared the Swedish opinion that neutrality presupposes an army and without one must remain a fiction. A few days before the meeting of the ambassadors' conference, he advised me that the Social Democratic leaders had decided in favor of an armed neutrality and would support any efforts to eliminate or reduce restrictions on Austrian rearmament. Nor would the Party oppose the introduction of military conscription. On Kreisky's request I advised Thompson of this decision. The day before the opening of the foreign ministers' conference, the Social Democrats confirmed their decision by publication of a resolution defining and confirming the positive attitude of the party toward defense.

The ambassadors' conference began on May 2 and progressed from the beginning without serious friction. I remember that the quiet and peaceful course of the conference caused great surprise among the initiated. The reason is, however, not difficult to find. Having decided on a new "general line" in foreign policy and a great propaganda offensive to support the new course, the Soviet rulers needed an agreement as soon as possible, an example they could cite as worth imitating. Since Austria had already declared for neutrality, the Soviet Union must show its generosity in order to demonstrate the advantages of this policy. The Soviet government had to a certain extent, as was soon to be confirmed to me by one of the Soviet diplomats I used to meet, thus bound its hands and was forced to make greater concessions than it had intended on questions it now considered of secondary importance.

During the first days of the conference, however, the Soviet delegation objected strenuously to many of the changes proposed by the Western powers. When the latter did not yield, new orders immediately arrived from Moscow: Although opposition to many Western demands was necessary, it could not be allowed to delay the signing of the State Treaty. After every such instruction the concessions almost came tumbling in. It was noticeably difficult for the leading Soviet diplomats who took part in the negotiations to put up with this new kind of "appeasement." At a reception I attended one of them rushed up, as soon as he caught sight of me, and complained bitterly of the American Ambassador's unyielding and hard attitude during the negotiations. "Thompson has apparently understood," he said, startled and at the same time obviously alarmed, "to what extent our freedom of action is restricted by the new general line. Since we have decided on neutrality as basis of the new line, we can't allow the negotiations to fail. We are now forced to make one concession after the other in order to save the declaration of neutrality on which we agreed in Moscow and which, of course, takes precedence over such secondary questions as the disarmament clauses in the treaty. Thompson takes ruthless advantage of his knowledge. If you wish to help the Austrians," he added, "you must as a good friend of the American Ambassador try to explain to him that he can't expect us to continue to make all the concessions. He must at least give in on one or two points. Otherwise, we might lose our patience." His judgment of Thompson's understanding of Soviet foreign policy was doubtlessly correct. I was closely informed about the course of the negotiations through my friends and could appreciate the superior ability with which he played his cards.

The Soviet delegation gradually accepted the elimination of most of the limitations on Austrian land and air forces, on the number and size of airfields, and on the right of Austria to produce or purchase war materials.

The resistance of the Soviet delegation to the relinquishment of the clauses on the limitation of the Austrian rearmament had, however, been tough and stubborn. This attitude is easy to understand. A limitation of Austrian rearmament had doubtlessly from the Soviet point of view been preferable to the armed neutrality which was to be the final result of the negotiations.

A serious difference occurred only in the case of Austrian oil production. The draft treaty gave the Soviet Union concessions equal to sixty per cent of the 1947 production of the oil fields as well as some refineries and installations and the right to drill for oil in certain other locations. In the Moscow Memorandum the Soviet government had agreed to relinquish its oil rights in return for delivery of one million tons of crude oil per year for ten years. One of the most important questions on the agenda was whether this concession should be part of the State Treaty or embodied in a separate bilateral agreement between the Soviet Union and Austria. The Western powers advocated the first solution fearing that the Soviet Union might abrogate a bilateral agreement and reoccupy the oil fields on the pretext that Austria had not fulfilled its obligations.

The Soviet government stubbornly maintained its point of view until Dulles on the advice of Ambassador Thompson declared that he could not take part in the foreign ministers' conference before the realization of the essential wishes of the Western powers. The Soviet delegation then agreed to a compromise proposed by the United States. Although abrogated in substance by the Moscow Memorandum, the original clause in the draft should remain formally in force in the final text of the State Treaty, thereby allowing the other signatory powers to intervene in defense of Austrian interests in the event that the Soviet Union should violate the bilateral agreement. The acceptance of this compromise by Moscow was facilitated by a concession of the Western powers. They agreed at the same time to an express prohibition in the State Treaty on the return of important German property in Western zones to its former owners.

The text of the Austrian declaration of neutrality was not discussed. More or less the same happened to the guaranties of independence and territorial inviolability which had already been accepted in principle, by the Soviet side at the meeting in Moscow. When the Western powers introduced the last matter, Soviet representatives at first attempted to avoid taking a position. Upon being questioned whether the proposed guaranties represented a *sine qua non* for signing the State Treaty, the Soviet delegation emphasized that it had never made any special conditions for this. Since the Western powers, as already mentioned, had no interest in the question, it was never seriously taken up again.

After the ambassadors had thus concluded their work in a surprisingly short time, the foreign ministers met on May 13, 1955. Molotov, who was unanimously elected chairman, showed, as was to be expected, particular interest in the Austrian declaration of neutrality. He read out the pertinent clauses in the Moscow Memorandum and declared that he assumed the three other powers shared the opinion expressed therein. The United States had no objections, Dulles stressed, if Austria should follow the neutral course suggested in the memorandum. The British Foreign Secretary and the French Foreign Minister agreed but added that they wished to see the actual text of the declaration of neutrality before final approval. Molotov said he believed he could conclude from these statements, that all the occupation powers would agree to an Austrian declaration that it would observe neutrality of the same type as Switzerland. The Austrian Foreign Minister then confirmed that his government intended to submit to the Austrian Parliament a declaration of neutrality which followed the guidelines of the Moscow Memorandum. The government was also willing to submit the text of the declaration to the four great powers immediately after formulation of the final draft. Molotov further stated that the Soviet Union was prepared immediately to recognize and respect the perpetual neutrality of Austria. The three Western foreign ministers expressed their fundamental agreement but explained that they would postpone formal approval until the declaration of neutrality was placed before the Austrian Parliament.

The importance which the Soviet government attached to neutrality was reflected in the speech with which Molotov closed the conference. He termed the signing of the State

Treaty an event of great historical significance. A neutral nation had now found its place by the side of Switzerland among the free nations of Central Europe. Immediately after the final meeting, which lasted little more than an hour, the treaty was signed. After seventeen years of occupation, first by Nazi Germany and then jointly by the Western powers and the Soviet Union, Austria had finally regained its sovereignty. Huge crowds had gathered in front of the Belvedere Palace where the signing took place. Their joy and cheers were indescribable when Foreign Minister Figl, along with the foreign ministers of the four great powers, appeared on a balcony gaily waving the signed treaty.

The Austrian cabinet approved the State Treaty by June 7, 1955, and the president ratified it the following day. On July 19 the government submitted the promised draft of the basic law on neutrality to Parliament. In introducing its proposal, the government pointed out that a neutral state is bound to defend its territory with all the means at its command. Too, a neutral state may not assume any obligations which might involve it in war, for example, enter any military alliances or allow foreign bases on its territory. And during hostilities between other countries, the neutral must observe the rules of neutrality recognized by international law. In its other policies, however, the neutral is not bound by any other limitations than those which arise from its neutral status. Austria could thus take part in normal international activities and, among other things, join the United Nations. At the same time, the government stressed emphatically that neutrality in no way limited the freedom and rights of the citizens. Neutrality obligated only the state, not the individual. Consequently, it did not affect intellectual and political freedom and least of all freedom of the press and freedom of speech. In other words, political neutrality did not require ideological neutrality. In closing, the government recalled that the draft was being presented after the signing of the State Treaty; Austria was thus assuming the obligations connected with neutrality of its own free will.

The Austrian Parliament passed the new constitutional law with one insignificant change on October 26, and it became effective on November 5. The four occupation powers delivered identical notes to the Austrian government on December 6. They declared that they recognized the perpetual neutrality of Austria in the form as set forth. Although the notes contained no express assurance that the neutrality would be respected, the Austrian government did not consider such an assurance necessary, since it could be assumed that a state which recognized the neutrality of another pledged itself thereby to respect. In the course of the following months Austrian neutrality was recognized by about sixty countries altogether.

All occupation troops had left even before the time limit in the State Treaty, the last Soviet soldier on September 19. Their departure had obviously been speeded up as much as possible in line with the Soviet peace and neutrality offensive.

16

The Soviet Union and Neutrality

The negotiations which started with the Moscow Conference in April 1955 had, in the course of only a month, led to the signing of a treaty which had been the object of fruitless and apparently hopeless negotiations between the four great powers for more than eight years. Why had the difficulties which previously seemed insurmountable now, suddenly, been solved as if they were play? A retrospective review of the course of the negotiations shows that it was almost exclusively the concessions of the Soviet Union which made the speedy conclusion possible.

Why were these concessions made only now and not one or two years earlier? From the Soviet point of view the single, meaningful compensation Austria granted was a pledge to perpetual neutrality after the Swiss model. As early as the fall of 1953 Nehru had, however, at Raab's request, through his ambassador in Moscow given Molotov to understand that Austria was willing to pledge itself to a policy of neutrality if such a decision would facilitate the conclusion of the State Treaty. The answer was negative. The adoption of a policy of neutrality by Austria, Molotov declared condescendingly, could not be considered sufficient compensation for the consent of the Soviet Union to the conclusion of the State Treaty.

Why did the rulers in the Kremlin attach such importance to an Austrian declaration of neutrality in April 1955 whereas the same suggestion in the fall of 1953 was rejected almost scornfully? The explanation for this is that in the short lapse of time after the Indian inquiry an unexpected revaluation of the concept of neutrality had taken place. The status of neutrality, which had previously been viewed with great distrust or at least with complete indifference in Moscow, had now from the political point of view suddenly acquired a new and completely different meaning.

The cause of this sudden change has already been indicated. In an earlier chapter I mentioned that, with the fall of Malenkov and the takeover of power by Bulganin and Khrushchev, a new general line in the field of foreign policy was adopted for the activity of the Communist world movement. This fundamental change, although not officially sanctioned until the meeting of the Twentieth Party Congress the following year, lead immediately to the assignment of a new and more important role to neutrality. At the same time, the negotiations about the State Treaty entered upon the second phase.

Before analyzing the impact of the new course and its consequences with regard to the negotiations about Austria, let me first briefly, with a few examples, illustrate how neutrality was valued in the last years of Stalin's life. The contrast to 1955 is striking and instructive. The attitude of the Soviet Union to neutrality has, however, often changed in the course of the years and has, as should always be kept in mind, continually been adapted to changes of the general line as well as to short-termed tactical considerations. Thus, the attitude toward neutrality has never been fixed once and for all. In the last years of Stalin's life, there was little room for a benevolent attitude toward neutrality. Every state whose foreign policy was not basically in agreement with the interests of the Soviet Union was considered an enemy, even though this idea was not always openly expressed.

Stalin's negative attitude toward neutrality found particularly harsh expression in the comments of the Soviet press on the policies of the two traditionally neutral states, Switzerland and Sweden. Thus, the Cominform journal (*For a Lasting Peace, for a People's Democracy*) which was personally supervised and controlled by Stalin, characterized Swiss neutrality as follows in its German-language edition of August 24, 1951: "Neutrality in the sense of the present Swiss government means trotting blindly along in the footsteps of the American warmongers to kindle war hysteria in the country, to induce Switzerland to join the aggressive North Atlantic bloc and to persecute fiercely the partisans of peace." Swedish neutrality was subjected to an equally sharp attack in the international Communist weekly *Neue Zeit* in a lead article on March 29, 1950. Even the heading "Sweden's Policy of 'Neutrality' " was significantly set in quotation marks to stress that the newspaper considered it more fictitious than a policy of neutrality in a real sense.

True, *Neue Zeit* appreciated that Sweden had not formally joined the Atlantic Pact. The newspaper sought, however, to convince its readers that the basic reason was the rejection of "American imperialism" by the populace rather than a sincere desire for neutrality on the part of the Swedish government. Although the latter officially proclaimed its positive attitude toward neutrality—the article continued—influential persons in Swedish government circles planned military cooperation with the "aggressive Atlantic Pact." In spite of all assurances to the contrary, leading circles in Sweden entertained a strong inclination toward "Anglo-American imperaialism."

The Swedish policy of neutrality was, in any case, the author of the article added, basically false since it made no clear differentiation between aggressors and victims. As a result of its close cooperation with the Anglo-American bloc, the Swedish government could not carry on a real policy of peace. Instead it contributed more or less openly to preparations for a new world war. In spite of constant repetitions of the word "neutrality" in his public speeches, the Swedish foreign minister, Östen Undén, was carrying on a policy that would scarcely appear very different if Sweden had already signed the Atlantic Pact. Consequently, under the guise of neutrality, the Swedish Social Democratic government sought to hide its real policy which corresponded closely to the demands of the American imperialists: the transformation of Sweden into a base for a future American attack on the Soviet Union.

As shown by this short summary of the press, Stalin's attitude in the early fifties meant the denial of the traditional concept of neutrality. He recognized only the neutrality which made a basic differentiation between "aggressor and victim" and sided with the victim. As a Communist state could never be an aggressor, only victim of aggression, this meant that a neutral state should side with countries belonging to the Eastern bloc. For Stalin, consequently, there was no real neutrality, only an either-or.

From Stalin's death to the beginning of March 1955 when the negotiations about the Austrian State Treaty reached their decisive phase, the attitude of the Soviet Union toward neutrality experienced a profound change. To illustrate the revaluation to which the neutrality had been subjected during this short lapse of time, a few selections from authoritative Soviet statements may be of interest. In an article about "The Neutrality of Austria and Its Meaning," published on May 21, 1955, thus, right after the signing of the State Treaty, the Soviet weekly *New Time* explained the advantages which Switzerland had derived from neutrality. Swiss neutrality, which the newspaper now, in contrast to earlier, extolled as exemplary, had, in spite of changing political conditions during several hundred years, proved its vitality. It had enabled the country to remain outside three wars of aggression unleashed by the German militarism in the course of seventy-five years. The newspaper hoped that Austria's voluntary decision to choose, of its own free will, a policy of neutrality would serve as an example for other states or, as the author expressed himself, would be "the impetus to a similar development in other countries."

Sweden, too, was praised for its neutrality which some years earlier had been characterized as disguised adherence to the Atlantic Pact. Sweden, the *New Time* declared in 1956, had struggled bravely for its right to remain neutral and refused to join the Atlantic Pact. Such a step would have endangered the position of Sweden as an independent state.

As the revaluation of the concept of neutrality as illustrated by these extracts from the Soviet press constituted an important element of the new course in the field of foreign policy, we must now examine what the new course meant, what mission neutrality had to fulfill within its scope, and, finally, how the new course influenced the attitude of the Soviet Union toward the State Treaty.

17

The New Course of Foreign Policy of the U.S.S.R. and Neutrality

The collective leadership which took over responsibility for Soviet foreign policy after Stalin's death, and, thus, also for the activity in this field of the entire Communist movement, was without doubt convinced of the necessity to abandon the "hard line" practiced by the dictator in his last years and anxious to apply, as soon as possible, a greater flexibility in the conduct of foreign affairs. Through an ostentatious propaganda for relaxation of tensions between the two camps it had, as we have seen in earlier chapters, tried hard to create a more normal atmosphere in relations with the Western powers without weakening the actual position of strength of the Soviet Union. In this way it hoped to convince the West that Soviet foreign policy was slowly but steadily changing in the traditional sense of the word, and that Moscow, consequently, might be prepared to join in a common effort to remove the real sources of conflict between the two camps. Once this belief had been deeply rooted and continuously strengthened by a series of concessions of secondary importance, the rulers of the Kremlin expected a greater comprehension on the part of the Western powers for their own fundamental demands. The *Leitmotiv* of the propaganda being the relaxation of tensions, no political question, it was said, was so difficult and complicated that it could not be solved by negotiations between countries in good faith.

In reality the Malenkov-Molotov course brought no modification either of the general attitude of the Soviet Union toward the Western powers or in basic tactics. Apart from a change from the former aggressive line to a peace offensive accompanied by propaganda for relaxation of tensions, the tactics followed the guidelines sketched by Stalin in his pamphlet of October 1952. Soviet foreign policy should mainly use the "internal contradictions" in the capitalist camp to divide these states. Every opportunity to stir up and increase the antagonisms between Great Britain, France, and the United States should be taken advantage of and utilized to the utmost.

It was, therefore, hardly surprising that when it came to negotiations between the Western powers and the Soviet Union it soon turned out that the latter had never intended to settle actual differences through mutual concessions. The Western powers were always supposed to contribute alone to the relaxation of tensions by unilateral concessions. The failure of the Berlin Conference in 1954 offered conclusive evidence of the new tactic and to a large extent contributed to shatter the illusions in many European capitals.

A new foreign policy program had apparently not been drawn up until Khrushchev had established his influence in this field in the ruling circles. In Communist terms this meant that a new strategic line for the expansion of the Communist world movement had been prepared which apparently should be valid for a long historic stage and which was based on principles which differed in many respects from Stalin's views. Its execution required some modifications not only of tactics but also of some of the doctrines considered incontestable in his lifetime. These modifications—although decided upon and put into practice much earlier—did not receive their official sanction until the Twentieth Party Congress met in 1956.

One of the most important changes concerned the prerequisites for the future expansion of the Communist movement. The incorporation of a number of new nominally independent states in Eastern Europe in the Soviet sphere of influence after World War II, all of which had been forced to adopt the same social order and the same economic system as in the Soviet Union, had, together with the victory of communism in China, according to Communist terminology, led to the division of the world into two opposing camps, the "socialist" under the leadership of the Soviet Union and the "capitalist" under the leadership of the United States.

In the last years of his life, Stalin had obviously been convinced that—aside from a few cases in which the situation had been particularly favorable as in Korea and in Southeast Asia—further expansion of the Communist movement was only conceivable as the result of new tensions and new wars between "capitalist" states. In the revolutionary situations arising in the wake of such encounters, the Soviet Union would utilize its military power to expand communism or, just as after World War II, simply by the pressure of its overwhelming strength and infiltration of the administration and the police gradually prepare the way for the inclusion in the "socialist camp" of countries defeated or weakened by the war.

Prior to and shortly after Stalin's death, however, an important political development had gradually taken place which in the eyes of the new collective leadership ushered in a new era in the expansion of the Communist movement. The creation of the "socialist camp," the growth of Soviet military might and political prestige, as well as the disintegration of the colonial system in Asia and Africa had, as Khrushchev and his followers in the Politburo saw it, changed the relative balance of world forces in favor of the Soviet Union and, at the same time, awakened new hopes that the final victory of communism was not after all so distant as had been assumed in the last years of Stalin's life. Instead of being rather a question of theoretical nature, as earlier, the expansion of the Communist world movement began to take on the character of a practical political problem whose realization might be within the reach of the present or the next generations. Moreover, this result might be achieved even if the antagonistic contradictions within the capitalist world should not for a long time or perhaps never again lead to war between the states belonging to this grouping. But if Khrushchev was firmly convinced that the balance of power in the world had shifted, that the furthering of the Communist movement, consequently, had become of greater urgency, he was, nevertheless, as is clear from a number of his statements, conscious of the catastrophe which a thermonuclear war would bring about, not only for capitalism but also for the "socialist camp." The exploitation of the present favorable condition for the world revolution must, therefore, if possible, be achieved by other means than an aggressive war. Despite all protestations of the military superiority of the Soviet Union, Khrushchev, therefore, had to change the methods by which the spread of communism had earlier been envisaged and, consequently, the tactics on which the activities of the Soviet Union in the field of foreign affairs had been based. The Communist takeover in this or the next generation should in every single country as well as internationally be so prepared and organized that the danger of a serious military involvement of the Soviet Union in a thermonuclear war would be prevented as far as possible even if this risk could not be totally eliminated. Since these decisions had to be explained and justified in ideological terms, they required a revision of some of the most important doctrines which in the last years of Stalin's life formed the basis of the requirements for the victory of the world revolution. These changes, in turn, reflected, as we soon will see, exactly the tactics which the rulers in the Kremlin intended to follow.

The first and most important doctrine which was revised in the following years was the thesis of the fatalistic "inevitability of war." This doctrine was, as Khrushchev later explained at the Twentieth Party Congress, which confirmed the decisions of the Party Presidium on these questions, undoubtedly correct during Lenin's lifetime. If the situation at the present time had changed, the main reason was that the "world camp of socialism" had become a mighty force which had not only the moral but also the material means to prevent the outbreak of a war before the complete victory of "socialism."

The proclamation of this thesis, however, by no means meant that the danger of war had been entirely excluded. As capitalism had not lost its aggressiveness, wars were always possible. The revision only meant that the Soviet Union did not, as in Stalin's lifetime, consider war the single or the most decisive factor for the realization of its long-term program: "the final victory of socialism on an international scale." (Khrushchev explained this in a speech of January 27, 1959.) If war, instead of being a "dismal certainty," had now become "a hopeful uncertainty," this amounted to saying that the present rulers in the Kremlin were hopeful although far from sure that there were other means than war to secure a victory on an international scale.

Consequently, the proclamation of the thesis that war was no longer inevitable had no influence on the attitude of the Soviet government toward the problem of armament. As a war between the two camps was not entirely excluded, military preparedness could not be neglected now any more than before. On the contrary, it must rather be strengthened, since war in the long run could only be prevented by a more and more pronounced shifting of the military balance in favor of the "socialist camp." Logically, the new doctrine not only required equality, but even a considerable Soviet military superiority over the United States. From the point of Soviet propaganda it was, therefore, of great importance to proclaim that a certain superiority already existed no matter whether this was true or not. In any case, every Soviet disarmament proposal had to be drafted so that it secured military superiority of the "socialist camp."

But if the rulers in the Kremlin had more or less renounced war as a means for the expansion of the "socialist camp" and lost most of their faith in wars between the capitalist states, one is entitled to ask by what means the capitalist system would be destroyed and the way prepared for a Communist victory on an international scale.

Khrushchev's answer was: through "peaceful coexistence" between the two power blocs.

This thesis, a familiar Communist concept but now one being linked primarily with the danger of a nuclear war, is, thus, a necessary complement to the abandonment of the doctrine of the inevitability of war; it has, consequently, become an integral and important part of the revised ideology which now forms the basis of the foreign policy of the Soviet Union. "Peaceful coexistence" has, however, as already mentioned, an entirely different meaning than the wording appears to suggest. This concept does least of all—as is often assumed—mean the abandonment of the world revolution and its replacement by friendly collaboration between "capitalist" and "socialist" camps. "True friendship and fraternal cooperation," as Khrushchev explained, is only possible between "socialist" states. "Peaceful coexistence," in contrast, is solely conceivable between the "capitalist" and "socialist" states; in other words, between states which in Communist terminology are dominated by "antagonistic contradictions." The program approved by the Twenty-second Party Congress has very significantly defined peaceful coexistence as "a special form of class war." Its main task is, on one hand, to protect the Soviet Union from aggression and consolidate its security, and, on the other, to further the expansion of Communist movements in the world by the use of all means short of a world war. Consequently, "peaceful coexistence" does not signify a truce between the two "camps." The struggle for Communist supremacy must go on but preferably with peaceful means.

Least of all this doctrine means the beginning of a disintegration of the economic and social system now existing in the Soviet Union and an evolution towards Western democracy. Western military and political power, its unity and solidarity, must be weakened, while the strength of the Soviet Union and of the "socialist camp," in general, is further built up.

The next question which arises is how, in the case before us, should the Western powers be weakened? The immediate objectives the Soviet Union hoped to achieve were, if we confine ourselves to those which directly or indirectly influenced its attitude to the Austrian State Treaty, essentially the following. (1) The consolidation of the status quo in Europe; that is to say, the legalization of the Soviet expansion after the end of World War II. (2) After the failure to prevent the rearmament of the Federal German Republic, the gradual disintegration of N.A.T.O., the neutralization of this Republic, and the limitations of its armaments. (3) An accelerated disintegration of the colonial system in Asia and Africa during which the new independent states should be prevented from joining political or economic organizations created by the United States and, generally, from being submitted to the political influence of the capitalist great powers. First of all, the Soviet Union had to concentrate its main efforts on weakening N.A.T.O. It had to encourage the withdrawal of member states as well as prevent nonmembers like Austria from joining. As regards withdrawals, it mainly envisaged Denmark, Norway, and perhaps Italy.

The final disintegration of the colonial system in its turn should be hastened by the support of Communist-inspired national liberation movements which, if victorious, would carry through, step by step, the "peaceful transition" to socialism according to the pattern followed in the East European states.

The next question was how to prevent the already independent countries in Asia and Africa from joining the Western powers and particularly from being submitted to the political influence of the United States? In the 1920s, Stalin had in a similar situation in China neglected the comparatively weak Communist Party and supported the bourgeois-nationalist Kuomintang which he hoped to gradually infiltrate with Communists and finally control. It turned out, however, that he had backed the wrong horse. It was Chiang Kai-shek who used the Communists; after gaining North China with their help, he turned on them, almost destroyed their organization, and drove them underground. After this experience Stalin could hardly trust bourgeois-nationalist circles in underdeveloped countries. He was convinced that nationalist leaders, even if they professed socialist sympathies, lacked the courage and ability to oppose the "imperialist powers" effectively. Socialist revolutions could only be brought about in these countries by Communists or by a coalition which they controlled from the beginning.

Khrushchev saw the situation in the 1950s quite differently. He changed back to Stalin's original tactics and sought to utilize the strong antagonism of bourgeois-nationalist circles toward the former colonial powers as his main "peaceful means" to increase Soviet political influence and to promote the long-term expansion of communism. The decisive criterion for support of newly independent countries should, therefore, not be the leading circles' readiness to further Communist-inspired social upheavals but rather their determination and ability to support the Soviet Union in its struggle against the "imperialist powers."

This, as already mentioned, naturally did not mean that Khrushchev viewed the transition of the underdeveloped countries to a "socialist" economic and social order with indifference. It only meant that he considered the struggle against the Western powers and, above all, the United States as a more pressing task at the present moment. Not least because of the economic backwardness of the erstwhile colonies, their transition to a "socialist" order of society must be temporarily postponed and left to a slow development by stages in the future. The first of these stages had already been entered upon with the expulsion of the "capitalist" powers from the colonies and the restoration of their national independence. The second stage, prevention of cooperation with the West, now followed.

During the preparations for this next stage, neutrality came into the picture. The rule that the struggle against the "capitalist" camp had to be carried on primarily with "peaceful means" applied not only to the disintegration of the Western political-military organizations but also and maybe still more to the former colonies. After having regained their independence they had in the second stage to be united in an "anti-imperialist" front against the United States. Both these aims would, it was hoped, be facilitated by popularizing the concept of neutrality. Neutrality would be one—but, of course, not the only—"peaceful means" which after the abandonment of the doctrine of the "inevitability of war" should not only contribute to the disintegration of N.A.T.O. and similar organizations but also prevent the former colonial states from political cooperation with the United States.

The reason was that the Soviet Union had realized that many countries which had recovered their independence could not, even if they refused to adhere to organizations under the auspices of the United States, be expected to join the Eastern bloc immediately or in the near future. It was hoped that this goal would more easily be achieved with the use of neutrality during a transitional stage. With dazzling prospects of increased security as well as other political and economic advantages which the policy of neutrality could offer them, Khrushchev hoped to bring together in one camp the European countries, terrorized with fear of being drawn into an atomic war, and the underdeveloped countries of Asia and Africa to whom the improvement of their standard of living through industrialization seemed to be the most urgent problem. The program most likely to unite countries of such different origins and with such different purposes was: freedom from associations with political blocs, i.e. neutrality.

Such a sweeping change of tactics and especially the fusion of the former colonial states with the highly civilized European countries required, however, an ideological argument. Stalin's thesis of the division of the world into two opposing "camps," the "socialist" under the leadership of the Soviet Union and the "capitalist" under the leadership of the United States, was, therefore, modified. To these two, a third —the peace camp—was added. This would include not only the former colonial states but all countries which, without regard to their geographical location, their social order, or basic attitude toward communism, for some reason wished to avoid a political or military association with one of the great power blocs. After creating a "peace camp," the rulers of the Kremlin, as Khrushchev emphasized, naturally considered it of the utmost importance to promote the growth and expansion of this camp at the expense of the "capitalist" camp. This was the origin of the revaluation of the policy of neutrality which, as previously mentioned, took place between 1954 and 1955.

Every country which left the "aggressive Atlantic bloc," or after the proclamation of its independence decided not to join this grouping or any other organization of the same category had in the eyes of Moscow so to speak, automatically achieved membership in the "peace camp." As Soviet propaganda constantly stressed, these countries had not only increased their security but could also count upon more important concessions and generally be sure of greater consideration for their wishes than others on the part of the Soviet Union. The necessity to prove conclusively that the policy of neutrality brought real political advantages was one of the main reasons why the Soviet Union, as soon as it could no longer use the withdrawal from Austria as a suitable means to prevent the rearmament of the Federal Republic of Germany, accepted a declaration of neutrality as satisfactory compensation for its consent to the conclusion of the State Treaty and the evacuation of Austria.

As the neutrality of Austria should serve as a model for other states which although in a similar situation had not yet decided upon their future policy, it was of particular importance that the Austrian declaration should come about as the result of a voluntary decision of the government. The preferential treatment held out as a reward for the association with the "peace camp," of which Austria during the coming negotiations received its due share, should convince other countries of the importance the now democratically minded Soviet Union attached to a voluntary choice.

In the underdeveloped countries, however, neutrality was, as already mentioned, designed to play another and from the Soviet point of view more important role than in Europe. It should not only prevent these countries from forming alliances with the Western powers but also fulfill another task hardly compatible with neutrality in its traditional sense. Neutrality should, in the former colonial countries, not only mean "freedom from alliances" but also include a moral obligation to oppose actively "imperialism" as Soviet propaganda interpreted this term. The Soviet Union was, therefore, very interested in blurring the difference between neutrality in the traditional sense and the pronounced anti-Western attitude which it wished to instill in the underdeveloped states of Asia and Africa. Consequently, these two kinds of neutrality should be identified with each other. They should both qualify as "neutrality" in the traditional and honorable sense, to use Dulles' expression at the Berlin Conference.

This was the basic reason why Molotov, to the astonishment of the Austrian delegation, placed such extraordinary value on the word "neutrality" during the negotiations in Moscow in April 1955 and demanded that just this word and no other term be used in the declaration which was to be submitted by the Austrian government to the Parliament for approval.

Even though Raab did not grasp the real reason of the Soviet preference of the word "neutrality" he was undoubtedly right in believing that the conclusion of the State Treaty might be jeopardized unless the Soviet demand was accepted.

18

The Conflict Between
Molotov and Khrushchev

The new course in foreign policy was not accepted without opposition. Violent and bitter struggles in the Party Presidium preceded its approval. Considerable differences of a decisive nature which affected the fundamental principles of the Party's long-range foreign policy in the new epoch of its historical development had, according to a statement of Mikoyan at the Twenty-second Party Congress, asserted themselves during the discussions. They had apparently been especially severe between Molotov and Khrushchev. No wonder, this being so, that preparations for the new general line had, according to further remarks of Mikoyan, required no less than two years to be finished. Consequently, they had been worked out and discussed in the Party Presidium from 1954 to 1956. From the scarce information which has become available, it can be surmised that Khrushchev succeeded in asserting his influence in the field of foreign policy by the end of 1954 thereby assuring the victory of the new general line and the conclusion of the State Treaty. As evidence it can be adduced that as early as October of the same year, he, along with Bulganin and Mikoyan, led a delegation to Peking for important negotiations with the leadership of the Chinese party; they finally resulted not only in considerable Soviet credits but also in an agreement on the return of the naval base of Port Arthur to China. Significantly, Molotov, who had previously taken part in all the important negotiations of the Soviet Union, remained at home. Other comments from reliable sources also point to increasing influence of Khrushchev on foreign policy at the end of 1954. A foreign ambassador in Moscow with strong Communist sympathies and close connections with the Soviet leaders reported that in conversations between leading members of the Party Presidium and ambassadors of the Western powers at the middle of December 1954, Khrushchev had been the primary spokesman on the Soviet side. Molotov remained silent and seemed remarkably uninterested. Malenkov, on the other hand, followed the discussions attentively but avoided taking a position before Khrushchev had developed the Soviet viewpoint. It was, however, left to him to attack the Western powers, if necessary.

It can, consequently, be assumed that Molotov was mainly responsible for the policy followed by the Soviet Union at the Berlin Conference in January and February 1954. On the other hand, Khrushchev's ideas had prevailed when, during the negotiations in Moscow in April 1955, the Soviet Union made the evacuation of the country conditional upon an Austrian declaration of neutrality.

This question was discussed at a meeting of the Central Committee in July 1955 which was characterized by Khrushchev himself as one of the most important in recent years. The deliberations, which have become partially known, are of great interest because of the light they throw not only on the new course but also on the causes of the conflict between Khrushchev and Molotov.

Khrushchev made a long speech in defense of the new course and explained at the same time the reasons for the decision to evacuate Austria. He especially stressed that the foreign policy of the Soviet Union had to be more elastic than ever. Since the Party Presidium had already decided on such a policy, it followed that it also had to make some compromises. Compromises always meant a loss of something in order to gain something else. In rather unimportant questions the Soviet Union must be prepared for concessions. Calculated losses within the framework of a compromise were worthwhile, if the losses were temporary and the profits permanent in character. It was clear, however, that each compromise had a limit. The situation should, therefore, be carefully analyzed in each case. Compromises should not be allowed in situations or areas where they would weaken the unity of the Communist countries. From what he said it could further be concluded that it was equally important that the stability of established Communist regimes should not be jeopardized by a compromise.

The decision of the Soviet Union to sign the Austrian State Treaty was, on the other hand, Khrushchev explained, a typical example of a wise compromise. Austria did not have a Communist government. It was an occupied country which had not yet been incorporated politically or economically in the "socialist camp." True, the Soviet Union had, through this compromise, suffered the loss of some military bases. On the other hand, it had won an excellent starting ground to show its good will to the whole world. At the same time, the military potential of the Western powers had not been increased by the conclusion of the State Treaty.

In a later speech Khrushchev violently attacked Molotov who had apparently seriously doubted the possibility of carrying out the world revolution without war or at least without serious conflicts with the capitalist powers. Molotov, who as far as can be judged had calculated on increased tension of long duration between the two great power blocs, was for this reason resolutely opposed to the abandonment of any territory already militarily occupied by the Soviet Union. Consequently, he had also bitterly fought against the evacuation of Austria.

As will be clear from a closer examination of the differences between the two party leaders, neither of them was willing to evacuate a country in which the establishment of a Communist social order and economic system had already begun and still less if it had been completed. Neither Molotov nor Khrushchev had considered the possibility of a withdrawal from Germany, since the Soviet zone had already been politically and economically integrated in the East bloc and the process of sovietization had made considerable progress. Their opinions only differed in regard to occupied territories in which sovietization had not yet begun.

As Molotov did not exclude the possibility of a war with the Western powers, he considered it inadmissible to evacuate a territory occupied by Soviet troops irrespective of whether it had been sovietized or not. In a speech defending his position, Molotov declared, with reference to compromises, that he seriously doubted that the settlement on the Austrian problem had been wise. He added that the evacuation of military bases in such a tense political situation as the present could set a very dangerous precedent for the settlement of other similar and more important problems. With this somewhat vague remark Molotov apparently alluded to the demand of the Western powers for a reunification of Germany through free elections which, if accepted, would lead to the loss of a far more important military base area than the East zone of Austria, namely East Germany.

In contrast to Molotov, Khrushchev saw no objection to a withdrawal of Soviet troops from a non-sovietized country provided, of course, that such a concession was part of a compromise which in the long run could facilitate an expansion of the "socialist camp."

During the meeting, Khrushchev also examined the political situation in Western Europe and in summing up his conclusions confirmed the views expressed in the preceding chapter. The situation in Europe at this time—that is to say in the summer of 1955—had, the Soviet leader stressed, become stabilized by and large. For many reasons—mainly international—the Communist parties in the Western countries were not able to carry out a revolution. Any attempt in this direction in any Western country would end in the complete destruction of the Communist Party in that country. By far the most catastrophic result would be the loss of cadres which might be used more effectively at some more propitious time.

While the Soviet Union would, for the time being, be content with the maintenance of the status quo and the consolidation of its previous gains in Western Europe, the decline of its political influence in this part of the world had, however, at the same time to be prevented. It was, therefore, of particular importance to maintain a permanent military readiness without engaging in a direct conflict.

The many weak points of the capitalist world were not in Europe but on its periphery, that is to say, in the former colonies. These backward countries—by which he probably, first of all, meant India and Egypt and the other Arab states—were, he stressed, the most ripe to be won over from the capitalist system. True, they were certainly not yet so far advanced that they could be said to be on the verge of a social revolution. On the other hand, they were undoubtedly ready for a revolution of the "anti-imperialistic" type. Although these states were not yet prepared to liquidate the capitalist system, they were quite willing to "isolate themselves" from the capitalist bloc. In other words, it was possible, Khrushchev meant, to prevent them from joining the "capitalist camp."

Thus, the real conflict between Molotov and Khrushchev was not of substance but turned upon the tactics of the Communist movement in the field of foreign policy. Khrushchev, however, came off victorious thereby rendering the new course as well as the conclusion of the State Treaty possible.

19

The Soviet Offensive
of Peace and Neutrality

One thing which greatly contributed to the speed with which
the two Viennese conferences had been concluded was undoubtedly the peace and neutrality offensive which the Soviet Union had, it is true, already introduced but which was
to be intensified in 1955 and the following years. As Soviet
readiness to make concessions during the two conferences was
to a great extent influenced by the scheduled intensification
of this action to which the rulers in Moscow attached great
expectations, it may be necessary to mention briefly some of
the most characteristic traits of this offensive.

First, let me recall that the Bandung Conference, so
strongly supported and advertised not only by the Soviet
Union but by the entire Communist world movement, met
in April 1955, thus, at about the same time the negotiations
on the Austrian State Treaty reached their decisive phase
with the Austrian delegation's visit in Moscow. One of the
main tasks of the Bandung Conference had been to explain
the principles of the "coexistence policy" in general terms
which would be easily understood by the masses in the underdeveloped countries. As neutrality formed an integral
part of the coexistence policy, the successful conclusion of the
negotiations in Moscow was intended as tangible evidence of
the advantages a small, nonaligned country could derive
from a policy of neutrality.

Asia, however, was by no means the only field in which the
offensive of peace and neutrality developed. At the same
time, the Soviet Union spared no efforts to prevent the Middle Eastern states from joining the Bagdad Pact between

Turkey and Iraq, to persuade them to give up the idea of political cooperation with the United States and instead decide
on a policy of neutrality. When finally the first Geneva Conference met at the end of July 1955 in order to deal, among
other things, with the question of the reunification of Germany, Soviet Premier Bulganin, who pursued quite different
objectives with the conference, used this opportunity to push
the neutrality policy.

In his introductory speech at the opening of the conference, he alleged that for some time a movement in favor of a
policy of neutrality and nonparticipation in military blocs
had steadily been gaining ground. Should any country, he
suggested, desiring to pursue a policy of neutrality, raise the
question of having its security and territorial integrity guaranteed, the great powers should, in order to encourage this
tendency, accede to such wishes. As far as the Soviet Union
was concerned, it was, as the example of Austria showed, prepared to take part in such guaranties.

In the last days of the Hungarian Revolution, a little more
than a year later, Premier Imre Nagy delivered a declaration
of neutrality and gave notice of the decision of his government to leave the military bloc represented by the Warsaw
Pact. The military intervention of the Soviet Union which
followed proved that the purpose of the policy of neutrality
was to promote only the dissolution of the military organizations of the Western powers. Bulganin's encouragement was
not meant for Communist states. The change of the "people's
democracies" to a policy of neutrality and their withdrawal
from the Warsaw Pact would have meant a loss to the "socialist camp." The "peace camp" could not be expanded at
the cost of this camp.

In an enumeration of other important milestones on the
path of the Soviet offensive to further the expansion of the
"peace camp" through a policy of neutrality, the visit of Soviet Foreign Minister Shepilov to Cairo in the summer of
1955 should first of all be mentioned. This visit was one of
the first serious political approaches to the middle-class, nationalist party which had taken over power in Egypt under
Nasser's leadership and led to the declaration by Egypt that

it intended to observe a "positive neutrality." In practice this came to mean the elimination of Western influence, increased trade with Soviet bloc states, and important armament purchases from them. The peace offensive was continued with the same intensity in the second half of 1955. In November and December Bulganin and Khrushchev visited India, Burma, and Afghanistan and promised economic and technical aid, pointing out the political and economic advantages which a policy of neutrality would in the long run bring the underdeveloped countries.

The same point of view was emphasized in a statement published by the countries of the Warsaw Pact after their meeting in January 1956. The statement laid down neutrality as the common goal of those countries in Europe, as well as in Asia and Africa, which had decided upon an independent foreign policy without ties with either of the power blocs.

When the Twentieth Party Congress met in February 1956 in Moscow, the new course, as already mentioned, finally received its official sanction. Khrushchev confirmed that one of the most urgent missions of Soviet foreign policy was to support countries which refused to join military blocs quite irrespective of their social order and economic system. At the same time, he emphasized the great interest of the Soviet Union in extending and strengthening its friendly relations with countries which were already pursuing a policy of neutrality.

This short summary, although necessarily incomplete, has —I hope—contributed to clarifying the important role the Austrian policy of neutrality was intended to play in the long-term Soviet strategic planning for the expansion of the Communist movement.

The decision of the Soviet Union to relinquish its opposition to the conclusion of the State Treaty as well as the concessions granted to Austria during the ambassadors' conference in Vienna should not only serve as encouragement for countries unwilling to be tied to political and military groups but also contribute to a better understanding of the policy of relaxation proclaimed after Stalin's death. It should help to convince suspicious political circles in the "capitalist countries" of the sincerity of the Soviet purpose and thereby entice them into believing that the Western powers could easily afford to relax their guard. In this way the Soviet Union hoped to create new opportunities for a slow but sure expansion of the Communist movement. Togliatti, the leader of the Italian Communist Party, expressed the same idea in a speech before the Central Committee of his Party at the end of November 1955 in which he stressed that the main purpose of the policy of relaxation was to do away with the domination of Europe by the capitalist powers and free a number of states, among them Italy, from the "influence of Western imperialism."

Against this setting it is easy to understand that the Soviet Union could not allow the two conferences which met in Vienna for the conclusion of the Austrian State Treaty to fail. Least of all could a failure be permitted because of differences of opinion on questions no longer considered to be of essential significance to the Soviet Union. As the peace and neutrality offensive had to be intensified, the Presidium attached much more importance to the time factor than to the maintenance of the previously agreed limitations on Austrian rearmament. The Soviet government could not waste time in senseless discussion of questions which, because of the changed situation, had now lost their relevance.

20

Austrian and Swiss Neutrality

I have often been asked why the Soviet Union chose Swiss neutrality as a model for Austria. It is impossible to answer this question with certainty on the basis of the information at our disposal at present. I must, therefore, confine myself to personal reminiscences and suppositions. First of all, it must be remembered that the idea, when it was finally brought up for discussion with the Soviet Union, originated with Bruno Kreisky. When, on March 17, 1955, he read aloud the Swiss declaration of neutrality agreed to at the Congress of Vienna, the Soviet diplomats present certainly got the impression that the Austrian government—or at least its Social Democratic members—for one reason or another had a predilection for the policy of neutrality carried on by Switzerland.

As soon as the rulers in the Kremlin had agreed to the conclusion of the State Treaty, they were undoubtedly anxious to have the policy of neutrality accepted by Austria without further delay. Since they, at the same time, were convinced that the Western powers looked upon an Austrian declaration of neutrality with certain misgivings, they feared that these powers might raise some difficulties once the negotiations in Vienna had started. The Kremlin might, therefore, have expected to get Austrian support for their point of view more easily if they had already, during the bilateral negotiations in Moscow, accepted the kind of neutrality Austria itself preferred as far as could be determined from reports from the Soviet Embassy in Vienna.

But even if this assumption is confirmed, it does not sufficiently explain the reasons for the Soviet Union's positive attitude to Swiss neutrality. When I, at Kreisky's dinner, attentively followed the conversation between him and K., I was

struck by the particular interest K. displayed when he heard
—possibly for the first time—that Switzerland had felt
obliged to adopt a policy of *perpetual* neutrality. Thus, if
asked again why the Soviet Union had a marked predilection
for neutrality of the Swiss pattern, I should answer that the
main reason was its irrevocable character.

From Moscow's point of view, two conditions were of particular importance. First of all, the word "neutrality" must
be used. Secondly, Austria should, of its own free will, pledge
itself to perpetual neutrality. If this happened, the Soviet
Union had no reason to fear that Austria, in case of the rise
of another political constellation in Europe, would shirk its
duties as a neutral state or attempt to regain its complete
freedom of action.

The great importance which the Soviet Union attributed
to the trustworthiness of Austrian neutrality is proved by the
fact that Molotov, during the negotiations in Moscow, expressed his particular satisfaction at the presence of the leaders of both coalition parties. This being so, the Soviet Union
could, as Molotov pointed out, negotiate not only with the
Austrian government but also with both coalition parties.
This was of particular importance, he continued, as these
parties together represented the overwhelming majority of
the Austrian people. What Molotov meant by these words
was that the Soviet Union could have greater confidence in
the durability of the Austrian neutrality if it were approved
not only by the government but also by the two parties which
for a long time to come would exercise a decisive influence
on Austrian foreign and domestic affairs.

How far Austria was to follow in each case the example of
Switzerland in its interpretation of the policy of neutrality
was irrelevant from the point of view of the Soviet Union at
the time of the signature of the State Treaty. This was clear
because the Soviet Union immediately declared itself ready
to support Austria's application for membership in the
United Nations, although Switzerland does not consider such
membership compatible with its neutrality.

The impression that the Soviet Union did not expect Austria always to follow the Swiss example was confirmed by a

conversation with the three previously mentioned Soviet diplomats at a luncheon I gave at Kreisky's request shortly after the signature of the State Treaty. We asked the three diplomats whether the Soviet Union considered that Austria had pledged itself to follow the Swiss example in every particular case. In other words: Would the Soviet Union be of the opinion, Kreisky asked, that Austria had broken its pledge if its government, in case the Swiss and the Swedish interpretation should differ, followed the Swedish instead of the Swiss example? The three Russians answered smilingly that it made no difference whether Austria in such circumstances adopted the Swiss or the Swedish interpretation. From the Soviet viewpoint both were equally satisfactory.

This impression is also confirmed by an examination of the legal obligations which Austria assumed in this respect. Should these obligations be interpreted only in the light of the constitutional law by which the policy of neutrality was legally established—but which does not refer to Swiss neutrality—or should the Moscow Memorandum be regarded as equally binding for Austria? The latter opinion seems scarcely tenable.

First: The Moscow Memorandum—at least as regards the Austrian offers which, in contrast to those of the Soviet Union, did not pledge the government but only four of its members as individuals—can only be considered an informal record made for the purpose of recollection and of confirmation of the promises which the four members of the Austrian government had taken upon themselves to carry out.

Second: It must be recalled that the Soviet Union, like the other former occupying powers, in its note of December 6, 1955 had expressly "recognized the neutrality of Austria as it was defined in the neutrality law." By this recognition the Soviet Union has conclusively proved that it regarded the approval of the neutrality law by the Austrian Parliament as fulfillment of the obligations assumed by the four members of the Austrian government in the Moscow Memorandum. Consequently, this document is no longer valid and can no longer be used for an interpretation of the Austrian neutrality. In this respect it has been superseded by the new constitutional law.

If the Moscow Memorandum, on the other hand, can only be considered binding insofar as it has been incorporated in the constitutional law, this also applies to the stipulations according to which Austrian neutrality shall conform to the Swiss model. Since the perpetual neutrality of Austria has been recognized as defined in the Austrian constitutional law and this law does not mention the Swiss model, it is clear that the Soviet Union by its recognition has confirmed that the obligation assumed in the Memorandum has been fulfilled although no direct reference to the Swiss neutrality is made in the law.

The explanation is not hard to find. Since the neutrality law, in conformity with the Swiss declaration of 1815 is based upon the fundamental principle of perpetual neutrality, the Soviet Union had already, through the approval of the neutrality law by the Austrian Parliament, achieved its goal. A special reference to the Swiss neutrality was no longer necessary. Whether or to what extent Austria should in each case adapt its own policy to fit the Swiss model is consequently not a legal but rather a practical political problem.

If Austrian neutrality is thus based on a national law submitted by the government to Parliament and passed by this institution, Austria is, however, not free to give up its neutrality should it choose to do so. As stated in the constitutional law, the status of neutrality is irrevocable. By the notification of the enactment and coming into force of the law as well as by the government application for recognition of its perpetual neutrality, Austria has pledged itself, at least with regard to those countries which have received and acknowledged receipt of the notification, to maintain forever its neutral status. In this way, the Soviet demand that the declaration of neutrality should be made in an internationally binding form has been met.

An analysis of the Austrian neutrality would not be complete without recalling that the government has consistently maintained that it alone has the power to interpret its neutrality on the basis of the principles of international law and also to decide in each particular case if it has been violated by a foreign power. This question came to the fore during Khrushchev's visit in Austria in the summer of 1960. In two speeches in Salzburg and Klagenfurt he developed views on Austrian neutrality which were contrary to those of the Austrian government. After having expressed his appreciation of the policy hitherto pursued, he declared that if Austrian neutrality were violated, the Soviet Union "would not stand aside." In such a case, his government would take the measures which, with regard to the political situation, could be considered proper for the maintenance of Austrian neutrality. This statement, which was repeated in its essentials at a press conference in Vienna a few days later, was generally considered as an attempt by the Soviet Union to appear as the protector of Austrian neutrality. Furthermore, the Soviet Premier added in his speech in Klagenfurt that no country might stand aside "in the battle for peace." All states, even neutrals, should take a position, obviously in the Soviet sense.

The Austrian government could not allow such statements to go unchallenged. In a declaration about the rights and duties of neutral states published directly after the departure of the Soviet Premier, it was stressed that Khrushchev's statements stood in conflict with the viewpoint of the Austrian government, which was as follows: With the coming into force of the neutrality law, Austria had assumed the obligations and acquired the rights derived by international law from the status of perpetual neutrality. As a consequence of its obligations, Austria could neither enter into military alliances nor allow foreign states to establish military bases on its territory. Furthermore, Austria had pledged itself to maintain and defend its neutrality with all the means at its disposal. As a consequence of its unlimited sovereignty and the rights derived from the status of neutrality, the Austrian government was, on the other hand, entitled to decide alone when and how its neutrality was threatened or violated by another country. In such cases, the government alone had to determine in what way the threat or violation was to be dealt with.

Since the Soviet Union made no attempt to refute the point of view expressed by the Austrian government, the discussion was ended. This government can, therefore, maintain that its claim has been admitted by silent consent. It has, consequently, not deprived itself of its right to pursue an entirely independent policy of neutrality.

21

Summary and Conclusions

From the end of 1949 to the beginning of 1954 the negotiations over the State Treaty had more or less been at a standstill. Through constantly new demands that had little or nothing to do with the re-establishment of Austria as an independent state, the Soviet Union sought to delay an agreement by any means. True, at the Berlin Conference in the beginning of 1954, the Soviet Union had been prepared to sign a State Treaty but at the same time refused to evacuate Austria before the conclusion of a peace treaty with Germany. In other words, the restoration of full Austrian independence should be postponed indefinitely.

After the unsuccessful Berlin Conference, the situation—as nobody could deny—appeared darker than ever before. But little more than a year later Soviet policy had undergone a complete *volte face*. The rulers in the Kremlin who had long tried to delay the conclusion of a State Treaty and, above all, had opposed the withdrawal of their occupation troops showed an unexpected interest in bringing about an agreement as early as possible. Many explanations have been put forward, all of which can be characterized as an oversimplification of the problem. They more or less originated in wishful thinking.

Many believed that the Soviet Union, confronted with the failure of its previous policy, had decided to alter its basic attitude toward the Western powers and was now anxious to seek a real accommodation with them. For example, the former British Foreign Secretary and Prime Minister, Anthony Eden, in his memoirs has attributed the settlement of the Austrian question to the pressure which the Western powers had brought to bear on the Russians at the Berlin Confer-

ence. This pressure, he alleged, "had in the end borne fruit."
"By this time," he stressed, "the Russians were anxious to
present a reasonable countenance to the world. Its expression
could not seem sincere while Austria was occupied by foreign
troops and the Western offer to accept the Soviet terms were
ignored."

Even if there is some truth in the point Eden has made,
many questions of decisive nature still remain unanswered.
Why had the pressure not borne fruit earlier? Evidently the
"new look" that Soviet foreign policy had assumed shortly
after Stalin's death did not seem sincere to many Western
statesmen as long as Austria was occupied. But if this was
true and the Soviets realized that a solution of the Austrian
problem was necessary for the success of the peace and relaxation offensive, why didn't they act upon this knowledge earlier? The former American Secretary of State, John Foster
Dulles, expressed an opinion similar to Eden's. He believed
—according to what he told Chancellor Adenauer—that Soviet foreign policy had changed, although not the regime itself. The main reason, as he saw it, was that the Soviet Union
had been confronted with many complicated problems—ex-
terior as well as interior—which it had been unable to solve.
The rulers in the Kremlin, he meant, were now interested in
a general relaxation of the pressure to which they had been
subjected by the Western powers. They needed peace and
quiet for some time in order to reduce the burden of their armaments and to deal with China, with the shortcomings of
their agricultural production, and many other complicated
problems. This had, according to Dulles, been the main reason for the final Soviet consent to the State Treaty and the
evacuation of Austria (Adenauer's memoirs). As is clear
from what Adenauer has told, Dulles, like Eden, considered,
in other words, that the complete *volte face* of the Soviet foreign policy was, in Eden's words, a "long-term effect of Western unity, firmness and reasonableness." If the pressure for
an Austrian settlement had in the end borne fruit, similar
pressure might now, they hoped, have the same result with
respect to Germany. This wishful thinking explains why they
took the initiative of calling the two conferences in Geneva

between heads of governments and foreign ministers in the summer and fall of 1955. True, the Western powers did not expect immediate results from the conferences. The two meetings in Geneva should rather be considered as the beginning of a sequence of conferences by which the unification of Germany through free elections should finally be achieved. The prerequisite was that the relaxation of tensions for the next few years continued to be of such interest to the new rulers in the Kremlin that they would be prepared to pay a price. The negative outcome of the two conferences in Geneva proved, however, that the Western powers had misjudged the situation. There were other reasons for the change of attitude of the Soviet Union towards the evacuation of Austria. True, the rulers of the Kremlin undoubtedly desired a relaxation of tensions. But, as often happens, Dulles had confused goals with means. The relaxation was not a goal for the achievement of which the Soviets were willing to pay a price. From their point of view it was only a means by which they, in their turn, hoped to undermine the resistance of the Western powers to their own demands and thereby pave the way for the attainment of their main objectives in Europe: (a) the consolidation of the Soviet territorial gains after World War II; (b) American withdrawal from Europe, thus fatally destroying the Western political and military alliance; (c) the prevention of a strong united Germany, integrated with the West, a result which, in its turn, was a necessary prerequisite for the integration of West Germany in the Eastern bloc some time in the future.

In this setting, Soviet foreign policy in the Austrian question, from the Berlin Conference to the conclusion of the State Treaty, can be divided into two distinct phases during which Moscow pursued two entirely different goals. During the first phase, which extended from the Berlin Conference to the end of March 1955, the main aim was to prevent the rearmament of West Germany.

Soviet expansion after the war, which had led to the introduction by forceful means of a Communist social order and economic system in the East European states and their final integration in a new "Soviet Commonwealth," had frightened the Western powers and strengthened and fortified their unity. The North Atlantic Pact had been signed; the rearmament of the non-Communist part of Europe accelerated. Finally a West German state had been established which claimed to represent all Germany. As it soon became clear that the defense of the N.A.T.O. states was almost hopeless without German cooperation, negotiations had been initiated on ways and means to render the rearmament of the Federal Republic of Germany possible.

This development exerted a decisive influence on the attitude of the Soviet Union toward the Austrian State Treaty. In view of the threat which German rearmament represented to the future expansion of the Communist movement in Europe, in strengthening the Western alliance, the Soviet Union was constrained to focus its entire attention on preventing the political, military, and economic integration of the Federal Republic in the Western bloc. In this situation the Kremlin decided to link German rearmament with the evacuation of Austria which, as admitted by Bulganin to the Austrian delegation in Moscow in April 1955, had been put on the shelf for about five years and reserved for bargaining purposes. The first opportunity to use the evacuation of Austria as a pawn in the game of preventing German rearmament arose at the Berlin Conference in the beginning of 1954. Shortly after Stalin's death the new "collective leadership" which took over power had staged a new offensive of peace and relaxation of tensions, mainly to support their propaganda against the rearmament of West Germany. The continued occupation of Austria was hardly compatible with the purpose of this propaganda which was to create the impression of a fundamental change of the Soviet foreign policy, thus rendering the rearmament of the Federal Republic unnecessary. Molotov tried to solve this dilemma by declaring in Berlin that the Soviet Union was prepared to sign the State Treaty. After it had come into effect, however, the four occupation powers should still maintain troops in their zones until a peace treaty had been concluded with Germany. The evacuation of Austria should consequently be postponed until the Soviet conditions for such a treaty had been accepted; in other words, until the Western powers had agreed to "free" elections in the Communist sense and to other terms which would have paved the way for the gradual sovietization of the whole country. This meant in reality that the occupation of Austria would continue indefinitely.

The intransigent attitude of the Soviet Union, however, was not only explained by its interest in maintaining the occupation of Austria for future bargaining purposes. Another circumstance which carried great weight in Moscow was that Molotov, who at that time still exercised considerable influence in foreign policy matters, was in principle as well as for practical political reasons reluctant to give up any territory occupied by Soviet troops.

The Soviets maintained the same attitude to all intents and purposes during 1954. The rejection of the treaty on the European Defense Community by the French National Assembly on August 30 was hailed in Moscow as proof of the success of the offensive of peace and relaxation. In the summer of the same year, the Soviet Union had renewed its proposal at the Berlin Conference to conclude a general treaty on collective security in Europe. As this treaty, in the opinion of the Kremlin, should replace the agreement on the European Defense Community and render unnecessary the rearmament of West Germany as well as the maintenance of N.A.T.O., the Soviet Union could, without deviation from its previous policy, declare that the adherence of the Western powers and the Federal Republic to the proposed security pact could, as well as the conclusion of a peace treaty with Germany, facilitate its consent to the evacuation of Austria. This concession was, consequently, more apparent than real. The restoration of full Austrian independence and the evacuation of the country was still contingent upon the abandonment of West German rearmament.

The first indication of a change in Soviet policy toward Austria did not come until the beginning of February 1955. At the end of the previous year the French National Assembly had approved the Paris agreements on the rearmament of West Germany which had replaced the treaty on the European Defense Community, rejected by the assembly on August 30, 1954. As the ratification by those countries which had not already ratified was certain, the coming into force of the new accords depended to all intents and purposes on a positive vote in the French Senate (Council of the Republic).

It was, consequently, of fundamental importance to the Soviets to prevent such a vote. To this end they counted on the support of a great part of public opinion in France where opposition to the rearmament of West Germany was still strong. The most effective means of preventing a positive vote in the senate was considered to be the calling of a four-power conference to deliberate simultaneously on the German and Austrian questions. It hardly mattered whether the conference should yield a positive result or not. Merely calling the conference, it was hoped, would influence public opinion in France by strengthening belief in the possibilities of ending the "cold war" by a settlement of the differences between the two great power blocs. In such a case, the rearmament of the Federal Republic would no longer be necessary or could at least be postponed for the time being.

In spite of strong pressure from public opinion in several countries, particularly in France, the Western powers, however, refused to participate in any conference on the German question before the ratification of the Paris agreements. As week after week passed without any sign of a change of attitude in Washington and London, the nervousness in Moscow increased. The Soviets became threatening, and Molotov declared that future negotiations on the German as well as Austrian question would be completely pointless once the Paris agreements had been ratified by all countries concerned. To emphasize its threatening attitude the Soviet Union used an insignificant transfer of American military personnel to the French zone to accuse the United States of a flagrant violation of the control agreement. Towards the end of 1954 the Allied Council, whose chairman during this month was the Russian Ambassador, was called to an extraordinary meeting, during which the ambassador hinted at the possibility of a division of Austria along the demarcation line.

As the rulers in the Kremlin undoubtedly had hoped, it was feared in Vienna that the Soviet Union would use the alleged violation of the control agreement as a pretext either to cancel it or to give notice of its withdrawal from the council. In both cases the Soviet Union could consider itself released from the obligations of the agreement and begin preparations for the sovietization of its zone of occupation. But even if the Kremlin undoubtedly had harbored such designs, it was something entirely different it had in mind at this time. By hinting at the possibility of a separation of the Eastern zone from the rest of the country after the earlier pattern in Germany, the Soviets hoped to cause a panic and make the Austrian government more amenable to the new proposals which were now being prepared and would be submitted to the Western powers and Austria a little more than a month later.

Although the propaganda for relaxation of tensions had been successful in preventing the ratification of the treaty on the European Defense Community, the approval of the Paris agreements in many countries showed that it had now failed to achieve its purpose. Something must be wrong. The policy carried out by the Soviet Union in order to make the propaganda of relaxation of tensions credible had mainly consisted in "liberalizing" measures without real political significance or in the abandonment of demands which under prevailing conditions could never have been forced through. The majority of the Presidium now realized that in order to convince the West that the basic aims of their foreign policy had changed, it was necessary to offer at least one concession of substance which, without weakening the position of strength of the Soviet Union, would, nevertheless, be generally considered of real political importance.

The evacuation of Austria and the conclusion of the State Treaty was an obvious choice, the more so as such a concession could at the same time be made contingent upon the abandonment or at least the limitation of the rearmament of the Federal Republic of Germany. This meant that some territory occupied by Soviet troops would have to be given up. But Khrushchev and the majority of the Presidium considered this entirely justified if the propaganda for relaxation of tensions could thereby be made more effective and the rearmament of the Federal Republic prevented at the same time.

Although defeated, Molotov was chosen to frame and explain the new proposals. This he did with great tactical dexterity in a foreign-policy address before the Supreme Soviet on February 8, 1955. His most sensational disclosure was that the Soviet Union would be willing to consider the evacuation of Austria before the conclusion of a peace treaty with Germany. As, however, the rearmament of the Federal Republic would increase the danger of an *"Anschluss"* of Austria to Germany, he added, the conclusion of the State Treaty and the evacuation of the country must be made contingent upon an agreement on effective guaranties against such an outcome. Although Molotov in his speech as well as later refused to specify the nature of the guaranties he had in mind, it was clear that the only guaranty the Soviet Union considered effective was the abandonment or at least the limitation of the rearmament of the Federal Republic of Germany. Consequently, even if the Soviet conditions had been substantially modified and the demand for a peace treaty abandoned, the evacuation of Austria was still linked to a partial solution of the German question. Another, and as soon became evident, still more important condition put forward by Molotov was that the four-power conference the Soviets had earlier demanded should be called as soon as possible in order to deliberate on the guaranties against *"Anschluss"* in connection with the German question.

In dangling before the eyes of the Austrian government the prospect of considerable but not yet specified concessions, the Soviets hoped to induce it to put pressure on the Western powers in order to persuade them to give up their opposition to a four-power conference. The Austrian government, however, rejected the repeated suggestions from Moscow to this end. Owing to the determined opposition of the three Western powers, the four-power conference had not yet met when the debate on the ratification of the Paris agreements began in the French Senate on March 23.

Confronted with its new failure to prevent the rearmament of the Federal Republic, the Soviet Union now decided to alter fundamentally its tactics in the Austrian question. Two alternatives seem to have been seriously considered. One was to divide the country after the German pattern. The other had its origin in the deliberations of the Presidium on new guidelines to facilitate the long-term strategic goals of the world Communist movement, which—initiated shortly after Stalin's death—had been going on for more than two years. Once the devastating effects of an atomic war not only for the capitalist but also for the "socialist" camp had been fully realized, the rulers in the Kremlin found themselves constrained—in any case as long as the United States maintained its military superiority or at least equality with the Soviet Union—to carry out their attempts to weaken and finally break up the "capitalist camp" mainly by "peaceful means." One of the means decided upon was the furthering of the policy of neutrality. This led necessarily to a reconsideration of this concept. As late as the end of 1953 Molotov had contemptuously rejected an Austrian offer of neutrality which the Soviets at that time considered insufficient compensation for the evacuation of the country. Now, on the contrary, the policy of neutrality had a new and more important task to fulfill from the Soviet point of view. It should, on one hand, contribute to undermining N.A.T.O. and similar political and military organizations, and, on the other, prevent the recently independent, former colonial states in Africa and Asia from joining political and economic organizations under the auspices of the United States.

In this way a third camp—"the peace camp"—should slowly emerge which in the view of the Soviet Union should include not only the former colonies but all countries which, without regard to their geographical location, their social order, or basic attitude towards communism, wished, for some reason or other, to avoid a political or military entanglement with either of the two great power blocs.

Every country which, by its policy of neutrality, had, so to speak, automatically achieved membership in the "peace camp" had, according to Soviet propaganda, at the same time not only increased its own security but could also count on greater consideration of its wishes on the part of the Soviet Union. It was, however, necessary to prove conclusively not only in words but also in deeds that the policy of neutrality was likely to bring real political advantages to the countries by which it had been adopted. This was the main reason why the Soviet Union when realizing at the end of March 1955 that it could no longer use the evacuation of Austria to prevent or delay the rearmament of West Germany finally abandoned the idea of dividing the country after the German pattern. Instead it chose to accept a declaration of perpetual neutrality on the part of Austria as a satisfactory compensation for conclusion of the State Treaty.

The choice of this alternative which ushered in the second phase had, however, not been dictated by these considerations alone. The rearmament of West Germany had, as appeared from my conversations with K., considerably increased the fear in Moscow that Austria, once it had recovered its full independence, would soon be brought under the political and economic influence of its powerful neighbor. Once the Federal Republic had again become a great power, it was feared that Austria would, just as in the years preceding World War II, consider itself a "second German state" and never make any foreign policy decisions contrary to German interests. If Austrian industry, in addition, should be infiltrated by German capital, the country would, although not legally, to all intents and purposes become a part of the Federal Republic.

This, K. explained to me, was what the Soviets really meant when they talked about the danger of *"Anschluss."* And, considering the great sympathies for Germany within many groups of the population, this danger, he added, was not all imagination but very real. Molotov and his followers had apparently maintained that the "danger of *Anschluss,"* in the meaning now defined, could only be warded off by a continued occupation of the Soviet zone. Khrushchev, on the other hand, held that the strengthening of the Federal Republic by a close political and economic collaboration with Austria could, as the Swiss example proved, just as well be effectively prevented by an Austrian declaration of perpetual neutrality. From the Soviet point of view "neutrality," consequently, was a political means by which not only the weakening and final disintegration of N.A.T.O. and other similar organizations should be hastened, but also, it was hoped, Austria should be prevented from a closer political and economic association with the Federal Republic whose influence within the Western bloc, it was feared, would grow more and more as years passed.

Such is the background which explains the determination of the Soviet Union in the sixties to prevent Austrian membership in or association with the Common Market. As this organization is considered in Moscow not only an economic but also a political union, Austrian membership or association would be regarded as a devious way of evading the obligations the country has assumed by its declaration of neutrality. Molotov had, it could be alleged, been right after all. It had, as he maintained, been beyond the power of neutrality to prevent Austria from joining a political organization dominated by the Federal Republic of Germany.

At the time of the signature of the State Treaty there was a widespread opinion in the West that the main reason the Soviets had finally accepted the State Treaty was to create a model for a subsequent solution of the problem of German reunification. The government of the Federal Republic, in other words, had missed a unique chance when, after the conclusion of the Austrian State Treaty, it did not immediately initiate bilateral negotiations with the Soviet Union and offer a neutral status in compensation for the reunification of the country on the basis of free elections. The two cases, Austria and Germany, can, however, never be equated. First of all, there is a difference in relative importance of the two countries. Secondly, neutrality, as already mentioned, was for the Soviets not a goal in itself but only a means by which a close political and economic association between the Federal Republic and Austria should be prevented. As the goal, consequently, was to forestall the strengthening of West Germany, it is absurd to believe that the Soviets would have been prepared to contribute to a still greater extent to this end by allowing the unification of Germany by free elections in the traditional sense. Because of the pronounced Western sympathies of the overwhelming majority of the German population in the East and in the West, Moscow would have considered even a neutral reunified Germany with its considerable economic and military potential as a latent danger in the future.

In addition, unification would have meant the abandonment of a country which had already been sovietized and integrated in the "socialist camp." If Moscow had accepted an Austrian declaration of neutrality as a compensation for the evacuation of the country and the conclusion of the State Treaty, the main reason was that such a declaration, it was hoped, would, in the long run, further the expansion of the world Communist movement.

In contrast, the reunification of Germany on the basis of free elections would have meant not only the strengthening of a capitalist power but also a decisive setback for the expansion of the Communist movement. It is, therefore, hardly surprising that Khrushchev several times declared that a reunification of Germany was only possible after the establishment of a Communist social order and economic system. Even the neutralization of Germany would not—Khrushchev told the French Prime Minister, Guy Mollet, at the end of May 1956 (Adenauer's memoirs) —be sufficient compensation for the reunification of the country on the basis of free elections. The Soviet Union, he said, preferred 18 million Germans on its side to 70 million against it, even if a reunified Germany were neutralized. But if a neutral Austria was never intended as a model for a reunified Germany, it should instead serve as a model for a divided Germany or, in other words, for the neutralization and isolation of the Federal Republic.

Although the purpose was to destroy gradually the unity of the Western bloc by popularizing the idea of neutrality there is, however, nothing to show that the Soviets—as has been alleged—had a special interest in grouping a number of states in a "neutral belt" right through Europe from the north to the south, from Norway to Greece. As far as I could understand from my conversations with Soviet diplomats, Moscow would have been quite satisfied with the adoption of neutrality by any state belonging to N.A.T.O. without regard to its geographical location.

Before concluding this chapter one more question should be touched upon. Certain journalists and literary "intellectuals" in the West have, at the time of the signature of the Austrian State Treaty as well as later, assured us that the Soviet regime is slowly evolving in a more humane direction, is turning into something resembling a parliamentary government, and will eventually hardly be distinguishable from the Western democracies. Is this view justified? The Soviet leaders themselves are, I think, the best qualified to answer this question. Let us now see what opinion they have expressed.

Shepilov, the former foreign minister, rejected the idea of a fundamental change as early as February 1957: "The strategists in the bourgeois countries," he said, "who like to regard their own wishful thinking as reality, figure that the Soviet Union is in the process of a kind of 'evolution' and that it is about to cast away 'some essential principles of the dictatorship of the proletariat.' We are now supposed to be changing from the red that we once were, not, it is true, to white but rather to pink. These speculations and theories about an 'evolution' of the Soviet system in the direction of a bourgeois regime represent nothing but idle inventions and fantasies."

In a speech to the Twenty-third Party Congress in 1966, N. Podgorny more or less confirmed what Shepilov had said. Speaking about the potentialities inherent in the socialist system he added: "This puts into an absurd light the assertions that have been appearing abroad concerning some sort of 'capitalist transformations' taking place in the Soviet economy, some sort of 'liberalization' of socialist society, which is allegedly developing toward a rapprochement with the 'democracy' of the so-called free world."

These assertions which Podgorny characterized as "slanderous fabrications" were, however, he reminded his audience, not new. When the construction of a socialist economy had first begun, he said, there had been shrill claims that by forming industrial trusts and by introducing piecework, etc., the

Soviet government was embarking on the path of "conniving with the bourgeoisie."

Although not mentioned by Podgorny, the same is true of Soviet foreign policy. As long as an examination of the strategic goals of the Soviet Union proves that they remain unaltered, this policy remains unchanged. In Europe the primary goals are still the withdrawal of the United States from Europe, the destruction of N.A.T.O., and the prevention of any other similar organization of the Western powers. The attainment of these goals has been attempted by different tactical means—at the time of the signature of the Austrian State Treaty by popularizing the concept of neutrality—at present by the conclusion of a European Security Pact. This, in turn, is a necessary prerequisite for the future Soviet domination of Europe which is and has always been the long-turn strategic goal Moscow has set for itself.

Notes on Sources

Page 84: For Roosevelt's remark about the withdrawal of the American troops from Europe, see *The Foreign Relations of the United States: The Conferences at Malta and Yalta*, p. 617. The Soviets had apparently to a great extent built their post-war policy in Europe on Roosevelt's remark which they considered almost a promise. The men in the Kremlin have evidently not yet overcome their anger at this "broken promise." In his speech at the Twenty-third Party Congress in 1966, the foreign minister, A. A. Gromyko referred to Roosevelt's remark in the following words:

"Kein anderer als Präsident Roosevelt erklärte auf dem Krim-Konferenz, dass amerikanische Truppen nicht viel länger als zwei Jahre nach Kriegsschluss in Europa verbleiben würden. Diese Erklärung wurde am 5. Februar 1945 auf dem zweiten Sitzung der Konferenz im Palast von Liwadia abgegeben.

"Es is zehnmal zwei Jahre vergangen, doch die U.S.A. Armee steht immer noch in Europa und beansprucht allem Anschein nach dort einen ständigen Status."

Page 99: According to A. Schärf, *Österreichs Erneuerung* (Wien, 1955), p. 80, the Communist Party counted on twenty-five per cent of the votes at the general election. This percentage is apparently nowadays in Communist circles considered a prerequisite for a successful infiltration of the government and the administration in a capitalist country, in other words, for using the "parliamentarian way" for the transfer of power to the party. When Kreisky in the fifties once asked an East German journalist who had wished to see him, on what conditions the Soviet government could be expected to consent to "free elections in the Western sense in

Germany," the answer was that this might be possible if in the future Moscow could be pretty sure that the German Communist Party would obtain a minimum of twenty-five per cent of the votes cast in an all-German parliamentary election.

Page 102: About the plans of forming a coalition government with the Communist Party in Austria, see Gruber: *Zwischen Befreiung und Freiheit* (Wien, 1953), Chapter X. See also Schärf: *Österreichs Erneuerung*, Chapter 20.

Page 107: The source for Bulganin's disclosure is President A. Schärf's secret journal, see note below.

Pages 115–119: This chapter is mainly based on British and Soviet official documents: (1) *Documents Relating to Meeting of Foreign Ministers of France, United Kingdom, the Soviet Union and the United States of America, Berlin January 25–February 18, 1954* (Her Majesty's Stationery Office, London). (2) *Die Berliner Aussenministerkonferenz der Vier Mächte, Dokumente* (Wien, 1954).

Page 115: For the Soviet conception of free elections, see, among others, Molotov's speeches at the Berlin Conference, particularly his speech of February 4; also speeches by Walter Ulbricht in 1955 and 1957.

Page 116: The account on this page is based on information received by the author shortly after the return of the Austrian delegation from Berlin.

Page 118: Among the representatives of this view is David J. Dallin who on page 256 of his book, *Soviet Foreign Policy after Stalin* (New York, 1961), says: "The principle of Austrian neutrality had been accepted at the Berlin Conference."

Page 119: Quoting a so-called D-paper of July 1957, Dallin said in *Soviet Foreign Policy after Stalin*, p. 252: "Molotov's actual goal was a Soviet mutual security treaty with Austria

on the pattern of the mutual security arrangements concluded between the Soviet Union and its small neighbours in
1939." This statement is obviously based on a misunderstanding. Kreisky, who was a member of the Austrian delegation at the Berlin Conference, has told the author that as far
as he knows no such suggestion or hint was made during the
conference by Molotov either to the Austrians or to the Western powers. Quite another thing is that the "solution" officially proposed by Molotov (that is: conclusion of the State
Treaty with continued occupation of the country) would
have created a situation in Austria similar to the one which
arose in the Baltic states after the signing of the mutual assistance treaties with the Soviet Union in the fall of 1939.

Some time toward the end of 1954 the author asked K. how
the Soviet Union had imagined the occupation of Austria
after the conclusion of the State Treaty as proposed by Molotov in Berlin? Should the whole country, as before, still be
occupied by troops of the four powers or should each of the
four powers only occupy certain *"Stützpunkte"* in their
former zones in the same way the Soviet Union had done in
the Baltic states. K. answered that his government had not
yet made a decision on these two alternatives. Both could, as
far as he understood, be the subject of negotiations.

On page 256 in the same book, Dallin again writes on this
question in connection with the negotiations between Austria and the Soviet Union at the Moscow Conference, April
1955. "There were again, as in Berlin, Soviet hints and feelers about a mutual assistance pact to supplement Austrian
neutrality." "If Germany should again attempt an *Anschluss,*
Soviet troops might be available to save Austrian independence." This is also a misunderstanding. In President Adolf
Schärf's "Journal" on the Moscow Conference, in the author's possession, there is no mention of such a suggestion or
hint. If the Soviet Union had had such a design, K. would
probably, before the departure of the Austrian delegation,
have attempted to sound out Kreisky or the author or both
of us about the possibility of an Austrian acceptance of a
mutual assistance pact. On the other hand, when Dallin
writes about the availability of Soviet troops if Germany

should again attempt an *Anschluss,* he has evidently been confused by the repeated hints before and during the Moscow Conference that the Soviet Union would like to reserve its right to reoccupy its former zone if a danger of an *Anschluss* again should arise. On this particular point K. tried, as mentioned in the present book, several times to sound out Kreisky as well as the author.

Pages 120–130: This chapter is based on official documents as well as on conversations between the author, State Secretary B. Kreisky, and Ambassador L. Thompson.

Pages 131–154: The notes of the Soviet Union referred to in this chapter have been published by E. Jäckel: *Die Deutsche Frage 1952–1956: Notenwechsel und Konferenzdokumente* (Frankfurt am Main, 1957).

Page 132: See the report by John Foster Dulles in the *Department of State Bulletin,* Vol. 30, nr. 767, March 8, 1954 and Royal Institute of International Affairs, *Survey of International Affairs,* 1954 (London: Oxford University Press, 1957), p. 157. See also Jäckel, *Die Deutsche Frage.*

Pages 133–134: The Soviet reaction to the rejection of the treaty on the European Defense Community is judged on the basis of a secret report from Moscow which the author had the opportunity to read.

Page 134: Malenkov's speech was published in German translation by Dietz Verlag, East Berlin, 1954. As to the success of the Soviet propaganda in socialist circles in Western Germany, see Konrad Adenauer, *Erinnerungen 1953–1955,* pp. 394–408. The Austrian socialists, however, did not indulge in the same illusions as their political friends in Western Germany.

Page 139: The text of the statement of January 15, 1955 available to the author was published in German in *Ostprobleme,* Cologne 1955.

Page 155: Text of Molotov's speech of February 8, 1955 in No. 6, *Für Dauerhaften Frieden, für Volksdemokratie*, Bucharest, February 11, 1955. The Soviet notes to the Austrian government mentioned in this chapter refer to the texts available in the Austrian Foreign Office. See also Adenauer, pp. 394 and 410–420.

Pages 161–172: The account of Kreisky's dinner party is based on notes the author made on the following morning. According to Kreisky none of the Austrians present at the party had made notes.

Page 182: As to the mood prevailing in the Austrian delegation, the narrative is based on the secret journal of President A. Schärf, see below.

Page 185: The narrative is based on the secret journal the Vice-Chancellor Adolf Schärf, later President of the Austrian Republic, made every day during the Moscow Conference. The journal was read and checked by Kreisky who supplemented it with some reminiscences of his own. About two weeks after the return of the Austrian delegation to Vienna, Schärf gave a copy of the journal to the author as a personal gift. The author was authorized to use the material in the journal for his own reports to the Swedish Foreign Office provided he promised to keep, for the time being, the text to himself. When, after the retirement of the author from active diplomatic service, this book was being written, he asked and got permission to use the material for the book on condition that the text was not to be published.

Page 192: During the ambassadors' conference, State Secretary Kreisky and Ambassador Thompson informed the author every day of what had happened at the conference. This chapter is based on the notes the author made.